# A Woman's Voice

# Sarah Foner,
# Hebrew Author of the Haskalah

Translations by Morris Rosenthal

Layout and cover design by Joe Buchwald Gelles


Rosenthal, Morris E.
ISBN 0-9666251-2-9




Library of Congress Cataloging-in-Publication Data

Foner, Sarah, 1854-1936.
   [Works. English. 2001]
   A woman's voice : Sarah Foner, Hebrew author of the Haskalah /
translations by Morris Rosenthal.
      p. cm.
   Includes bibliographical references.
   ISBN 0-9666251-2-9 (hardcover)
   1. Foner, Sarah, 1854-1936--Translations into English. 2. Foner,
Sarah, 1854-1936--Childhood and youth.   I. Rosenthal, Morris E.,
1963-   . II. Title.
   PJ5052.F6 A26 2001
   892.4'35--dc21
                                    2001002595


Dailey International Publishers
19 Brookside Circle
Wilbraham, MA 01095

*In memory of*

*Samuel N. Foner, Ph.D.*

*A favorite uncle and enthusiastic supporter of the translation of his grandmother's books to English.*

# ⤳ Acknowledgements

Hanah Ehrenreich, Tracie Shea, and Franklyn Dailey for their proofreading and manuscript suggestions.

Professor Joel Kaminsky of Smith College for his instruction in Biblical Hebrew, the importance of historical context in interpretation, and the use of the standard reference materials.

Professor Shmuel Bolozky of the University of Massachusetts, who introduced me to Hebrew Poetry and the structure of the Hebrew verb, simultaneously.

Rabbi Moshe Sachs, Ph.D., of Jerusalem, for the lion's share of my Hebrew education. Rabbi Sachs has been an inexhaustible well of knowledge on all matters Judaic, along with opening his home to me for months at a time, and providing much needed nutritional and intellectual balance to my life.

# ⤴ Table of Contents

# ↪ Introduction

The Haskalah, or Jewish Enlightenment, spread into Eastern Europe from Germany over the course of the nineteenth century. As the Haskalah spread, it seemed to many as little more than a rationale for assimilation and conversion to Christianity, but eventually it provided the basis for a new Jewish national identity. A key component of this identity was the revival of Hebrew in the secular press, where it was used in scientific books, journals and newspapers. The introduction of fictional works in Hebrew came relatively late in the Haskalah, with the first Hebrew novel, Mapu's *Love of Zion*, appearing in 1852. Writing in Hebrew demanded tremendous commitment from authors, who were consciously pouring their efforts into works whose potential readership was far more limited than it would be for similar works in Yiddish. The vast majority of Hebrew readers in the 1800's were male, and the only compositions by women to appear with regularity in the Hebrew papers were Aguna requests. These terse descriptions of missing husbands, along with the plea that they either be sent back home to their deserted and destitute wives and children or forced to grant a divorce, were usually written by proxies.

Sarah Menkin Foner (1854-1936), wrote about the issues that were important to her in the language she cared most about; Hebrew. Her romance novel, *Love of the Righteous*, was published in Vilna in 1880 during the author's twenty-sixth year of life, and was the first such book by a woman in Hebrew. The main themes in the novel concerned the institution of arranged marriages and the vulnerable position of Jewish women in Eastern European society. She dressed the plot in the style of the early nineteenth century romances by the French author, Eugene Sue, whose *Paris Mysteries* was the first popular novel to be translated into Hebrew. Foner was still living in her father's household when she wrote *Love of the Righteous*, but soon after the first volume was published, she married Yehoshua Mezach, a Hebrew writer some twenty years her senior. The brief marriage ended in disaster, and Foner was left with a child and with little further appetite to wax poetic on the subject of romantic love. After another period of living at home in difficult economic circumstances, she married the Hebrew playwright Mayer Foner, a man her own age, but one who did not share her respect for traditional Jewish observance. They traveled about the Pale of Settlement working as itinerant teachers before settling in Lodz.

Male authors, despite their protestations to the to the contrary, did not welcome with open arms the competition of a woman. At the same time, many men wrote under female names in both the Hebrew and Yiddish press, in order to cash in on the perceived need for a feminine sensitivity in the literature. These early stages of Hebrew literature were over-served by the presence of literary criticism, due to a dearth of new works to review and a surplus of willing critics. Foner uses the introduction to her short story, *The Children's Path*, to inveigh against the lack of civility amongst the Hebrew writers of the time, and the calumnies they cast upon one another. Foner herself would suffer through personal and professional slights throughout her active writing career, which extended from 1880 to 1919. Her novella, *The Treachery of Traitors*, was published in Warsaw in 1891, first in Hebrew and later in Yiddish. This historical fiction set in the time of the Second Temple served as a dual vehicle for Foner. First, by hearkening back to a period of Jewish military and political independence, she could add her voice to the budding Zionist movement. Second, she was able to weave into the story several female characters who prove stronger than any of the men. The liberties she takes with history, as recorded in the *Josephon*, are telling; such as having the would-be usurper torture and kill his own wife, in place of his brothers-in-law.

While living in Lodz, Foner founded the Daughters of Zion Society, for the education of Jewish girls in Hebrew and Jewish history. In 1903 she published a memoir of growing up in 1860's Latvia, *From Memories of My Childhood Days*. It contained strong Zionist content and harsh criticism of religious intolerance. Foner was especially critical of the Jews inability to peacefully coexist with one another, even while living under the constant threat of violence from the Russians and the Poles. She attended an early Zionist conference before leaving the European continent and her second husband permanently behind for England and America. Foner published a short Biblical fiction in Yiddish titled, *The Women's Revolt*, while in England, the back page of which carries an advertisement for her three most recent Hebrew works. During the Haskalah period, Hebrew authors, unlike their Yiddish counterparts, were largely paid "in kind." The publisher would supply authors with an agreed upon number of their own books in place of advances and royalties, which they would sell if they could. The last story of Foner's to appear in print was published in an American journal, *Shaharut*, in 1919, a charming story of how the author came to learn Hebrew as a little girl. Foner spent the final years of her life in the home of her son in Pittsburgh, PA.

# ➾ Translator's Notes

All of Foner's major Hebrew works were written before modern Hebrew was reintroduced as a living language in Israel and most of her grammar and vocabulary are of Biblical origin. Many of the authors of the Haskalah salted their works with quotes from scripture. In fact, the vast majority of male authors learned their Hebrew in Yeshiva, an advanced religious school from which women were excluded. Foner was extraordinarily well versed in scripture, often using words that appear in the Bible only once or whose meaning is ambiguous without choosing a commentator to follow. Her use of the Biblical vocabulary is sometimes exaggerated, such as the identification of pastries prepared at Purim using a Biblical word for cake found only in II Samuel along with a "three sided" descriptor, rather than identifying them as Hamantashin. A full set of the translator's language attributions are presented with the short story, *The Children's Path*, by way of example. The majority of the translator's language attributions were removed from the novel for readability. A draft version with complete footnotes can be found at www.fonerbooks.com. Foner's language and style evolved throughout her writing career, but some brief statistics on quotes and language use from her first novel may prove illuminating. The list below gives the number of occurrences followed by source book.

| | | | |
|---|---|---|---|
| 48 - Psalms | 9 - Habakkuk | 4 - I Kings | 1 - Micah |
| 44 - Isaiah | 7 - II Samuel | 3 - Leviticus | 1 - I Chronicles |
| 37 - Job | 7 - Exodus | 2 - Obadiah | 1 - II Chronicles |
| 29 - Proverbs | 5 - Ecclesiastes | 2 - Esther | 1 - Daniel |
| 25 - Ezekiel | 5 - Song of Songs | 2 - Judges | 1 - Joshua |
| 25 - Jeremiah | 4 - Deuteronomy | 2 - Zechariah | 1 - Lamentations |
| 15 - Genesis | 4 - Amos | 1 - Nehemiah | |
| 12 - I Samuel | 4 - Hosea | 1 - Numbers | |

Foner sometimes uses the device of breaking a biblical quote into two parts and having the parts said by the same, or different characters, in close proximity. Original footnotes from Foner's books are identified as such. All other footnotes are added by the translator in an attempt to clarify the text, call attention to meanings of Hebrew proper names, point out particularly interesting language usage, or to indicate longer biblical quotations. The translator has frequently taken the liberty of inserting proper names for pronouns without noting the change, but has otherwise attempted to remain as faithful to the original text as modern English allows. Proper names and place names are written phonetically without reference to any standard system. The chronological order of translations in this book does not follow the publication order, rather the memoir material is presented first. This way the reader may learn something about the environment in which Foner grew up through her own words before reading her fictional works.

— *Morris Rosenthal*

# 1.

*From*

## Memories of My Childhood Days
*or*
## A Look at the City of Dvinsk

by Sarah Faige Foner of the House of Menkin

*Printed in Warsaw, 1903*

*In the memory of my parents,*
*Joseph and Shaina Menkin,*
*who were a branch from the trunk of the Vilna Gaon.*

# ⤳ Foreword

Honorable Readers

Behold, I shall present the readers a picture of many colors and great value. These true events I saw with my own eyes or I heard from the mouths of reliable and reputable people who happened to live in the city of Dunaburg, now known as Dvinsk, between the 62nd and 71st years of the last century. Many years have passed since that time and I have lived in many great cities, but none of them can compare with her in matters touching my heart. Therefore, I have taken upon myself to present her before the readers, with no cosmetic makeover, but with things as they were, both the light and the dark. I will not build anyone up nor flatter them. As this period was rich in stories and events, I will hold it up for display in order that the generations which come after us may know the character of the people of the last century, in their evil-doing and their goodness.

*The Author*

# ⁀ Chapter One

The city of Dvinsk, as it was in that time, was truly a large and lovely place containing all things. In her were found Torah, fear of the heavens, charity, kindness and wisdom, but neither were burning ignorance and superstition lacking amongst the masses. The Haskalah was then a prized and special creation whose birth we witnessed, but in the eyes of the majority it was a monster to be destroyed in its early stages of development. The government compelled every father with more than one son to give a son up to study in Gymnasium.[1] I'll speak about this later when I give an account in full detail.

Neither were lies, cheating, violence, robbery, theft and other equivalent things lacking, but speaking of them won't add to the prestige of the city or of the children of Israel.

The city of Dvinsk in those days seemed to me to contain every wonder. It was built to a proper order and rule, the city walls were equal in length and breadth and the windows of every house weren't even in number, but three, five, and so on. If a house plan didn't include windows in numbers like these, then they made a red outline on the outside, as if a window were there. The homes were nearly all stone, except the Rabbi's house and a couple others, which were built of wood, according to my memory of the time. These houses stand yet before my eyes; Freidlander's, Malkiel's, Zalkind Zacharia's, the son of Rabbi Leib z"l[2] who was also known as Reb Leible the Lazy, Gordon Yerichom Zalman's, Ruben Yitzchak's, Israel Horowitz's,

---

1. High school, or other western style modern school.
2. Lit. Zicharon L'vracha — Of Blessed Memory.

Gloskin Valvel's, and the run-down house belonging to Kloyna which stood half finished because the owner was sent to the land of exile (Siberia). Also the homes of Liebenson Bartzik, Fagin Yitzchak, Gittel Lieberman, Meir Katzbaum and Neisen Bach. Between two of the stone houses stood a small, lowly, wood structure, on the verge of collapsing any moment. The owner of this house was an impoverished widow who eked out a living with a small stone hand mill with which she ground grain, and her name was Faige Hapavilankarn. She had a daughter married to the son of Yankel Vavil Pashnick, who most people called Pashtock. If somebody asked after Pashnick from morning to night he wouldn't get a response, only to Pashtock; and he served in Freidlander's business. She also had a son and his name was Bashka, a youth of fourteen, but I'll talk about them in the course of my story, in sequence.

When I came to Dvinsk, the city was buzzing with two topics: the Rayphali and Meir Roshkas, so let me explain the meaning of these two names. The city of Dvinsk that I have described was really known as Niyar Palin, but the old city known as the Old Suburb was found close by, and the name really fit. The houses were of wood, small and lowly and trembling to the point of falling down, rotting from great age and black like coal, with grass sprouting between the planks and on the roofs. The streets were gloomy and disordered, and manure, mud and filth would immerse one to the knees. This old city was close to the great fortress that had been built as an armory, and was an amazing sight for those who saw its architecture. From one side of the fortress to the old city extended a road or pasture called Rayphali. The neighborhood of Rayphali preoccupied the whole city, children and adults alike. In every house, in every shop, on every street, if two people stood or sat and talked, they spoke knowingly about the residents of Rayphali. If a man were robbed or plundered of some item, money or goods, then he who was robbed or plundered had to go to the Rayphali where he would be quickly answered. There were found kind and goodly counselors who would rescue the unfortunate from his distress once they witnessed it for themselves. But not for free, God forbid, but for money, "ransom," as it was known in the vernacular. All the doings of the Rayphali are not in the power of any person to describe or write, but I shall tell a little, and from this little the reader will be able to understand and imagine who the Rayphali were. One time a woman was walking along carrying a loaf of bread and some butter in her hands. She saw that her shoelace was untied so she set the bread and butter on the ground next to her feet and tied her shoe. When she lifted her eyes, the bread and butter were gone, and she hadn't seen or sensed a thing. Another time, a woman stood to bless the candles on Friday evening at twilight, and candlesticks were silver candlesticks. After the blessing, she placed her hand over her eyes to recite the prayer known to women, and after she finished the prayer and opened her eyes, there were no candlesticks and no candles.

One man married off his daughter and gave the couple two thousand silver coins, while the groom had a thousand of his own. They opened a dry goods store, which stood in the midst of other shops. One bright morning the young man rose and went to his store to find it barren of all goods, only the empty shelves remained in their places. The man began to yell bitterly, waving his hands and running here and there like one insane. But the goods were gone, with no sign to give away their hiding place. His relatives and neighbors from the surrounding shops comforted him, told him not to despair in his search. Better he should take action and go to the Old Suburb where he would find the good folk of the Rayphali who would inform him what to do. He ran there, and along his course he met people who asked him why he was running in such a hurry. When he told them about the disaster that had befallen him, they shook their heads and whistled through pursed lips. The whistling gathered many more people, and they spoke amongst themselves and asked each other, "How, and in what way, can we help this unfortunate whose goods were his sole support and who has no other business aside from his store?" Then, one of the bystanders called out, "I have some advice for you. Tomorrow you will come here in the early morning and I'll be waiting for you and will show you the house of the Reb Yankelah. You will petition before him and maybe he will be able to save you. But beware lest you be late in the hour of your arrival, because many are those who are early at his door, and only the early will succeed." Full of despair and hope, the man went home and told his friends all of these things. They cheered him up and said, "It's a certainty that your goods will be returned to you, only we don't know how much money the ransom will be."

The next day the young man rose in the morning and ran anxiously to the Old Suburb, and there he met the man who had promised to come the previous day. "Come," he said, "and I will guide you to the dwelling of Reb Yankelah." Along the way, the man told him of the greatness of Reb Yankelah, of his kindness and open handedness. A great Torah scholar lived in his house to teach his sons Torah, and was always a guest for the meal at Reb Yankelah's table. The scholar was also paid a salary, and in his free moments he taught Reb Yankelah the laws of astrology. Presently they arrived at an old house supported by two wood columns. The house stood in the midst of the Rayphali suburb, which was also considered part of the old city. The man showed him the entrance to the house and he repeatedly cautioned him that he should call him "Reb Yankelah" and that he should do everything he was told. As the young man entered the house, he was received by a woman in her middle age with a fine demeanor and a scarf covering her hair, whose appearance and bearing testified to her being the mistress of the house. When the young man asked her for Reb Yankelah, she answered him, "It's my husband you seek? Then you have a long wait, because he only stood to begin his prayers a half an hour ago, and he won't be finishing in a hurry. If you want, leave now and return in two hours, or you can sit here and wait for him." She showed him a place to sit and returned to her work next to the stove, preparing breakfast for her husband. Many other people came, but when his wife told them that her husband had only been praying a half an hour, they left. But the young man remained in the house and waited, even though he felt as if he were sitting on burning coals. He saw a tall figure moving about in the next room, full-fleshed with a great belly. The man wore a long garment of black silk with a long silk belt that wrapped twice round the hips and still trailed on the ground, peeking out from under the huge, expensive tallit which covered his head and his great stature. As he paced about the room, the edge of the tallit fluttered up, and the silk garments were visible. On his head and his left arm he bore an oversized tefillin, and he was punctilious like a Rabbi, praying from the Siddur *The Way of Life*. In every sentence and word, when it's incumbent on a religious man to be whole-hearted and spirited, he complied strictly, like at "Open your hand and provide . . . ," in the saying of the "Shema." He did so whole-heartedly, chanting in the proper melody. In the final analysis, he prayed according to the law like a great man. The young man was happy when he heard that he was praying the "Shemona Esreh" because he thought in a short while he would complete his prayers. But he was mistaken, because at "Ashrei" and "Come Zion" he removed the fancy tefillin of Rashi and put on the teffilin of our sages. After he concluded his prayers, he began to say "The Gates of the Day," Psalms, and after all of this he also said "Hoke Yisroel." It grew black all around for the young man because he was close to fainting. However, "To every pleasure I have seen an end" said our poet-king, and so did the young man see an end to the prayers of Reb Yankelah. He came into the room and gave his greetings. Though the young man desired to rise in his presence, Reb Yankelah didn't let him and said, "Sit, because I'm about to begin my meal and you'll eat breakfast with me, since without a doubt you haven't eaten yet." His wife brought over a basin with a two-handled cup full of water and he examined his fingernails, then he took the cup in his right hand and poured on his left hand, washing his hands according to the law. He sat at the table crowded with rich food to eat and called the young man over, then began to converse with the youth.

"And what do you want? Please tell me, my son, who are you and what is the matter?"

"I'm such-and-such the son of such-and-such. When I closed my store the day before yesterday, it contained goods valued at around three thousand silver coins. Yesterday morning when I arrived at the shop, I found it empty of all goods. Just the tables, benches and chairs remained as a remembrance, nothing more. I pray sir, put a price on my disaster. It's only three months since our marriage and we are left naked and uncovered with nowhere to turn. Who will hurry to my rescue?"

"Could it be? Is it believable?" asked Reb Yankelah like a man stunned, and he nodded and whistled, "All of it they took?" he asked in addition. "Oy, Vey. This is a great offense. But what do you desire from me?" he asked the youth, knowing he was heaping burning coals on his head. "What can I do? Did you truly think that I can save you? Why?"

"Reb Yankelah," the youth cried tearfully, "I don't know anything about it, but many people who saw my soul's distress counseled me to go to you and petition you. Also one man called you by your name and showed me to your dwelling, so I took to heart to come to you and ask, maybe?"

"Enough! Say no more. I am with you in your sorrows, and everything that can possibly be done on your behalf I will do. But before I can begin to seek after and investigate this matter, you must weigh out four hundred silver coins on my palm, to stick a bone in the throats of the Shularim."[3] The young man wanted to oppose the price, but Reb Yankelah didn't let him speak, saying, "This is the last offer, the choice is yours."

The youth didn't say another word but ran to his relatives and told them, so they said to him, "Go quickly, and bring the money that they demand, and it's reliable and certain that by tomorrow your goods will be returned to you, not an item short." Thus it happened. The next morning, when he went to his store he found all of his goods resting on the shelves in the proper order and rule, as if an experienced shopkeeper had arranged them knowledgeably and tastefully. But he didn't know and hadn't witnessed who had laid the goods out in their places because Reb Yankelah had cautioned him not to venture from the door of his house all night or to spy on the place, on his life. From these few instances, I imagine that our hon-

---

3. *[Original footnote]* So the people called every offender when they wanted to revile and shame him, and so were called the Jewish youths who began to study in Gymnasium, and with this reproach a person could boil the marrow of the blasphemer.

orable readers will understand a little who the Rayphali were. Meir Roshkas was an honorable man who wanted to put an end to the ravages of the Rayphali. He cultivated their friendship for a long time until he knew all their comings and goings, and knew them all by name or even by their voices when he couldn't see them. Afterwards he traveled to Petersburg and was granted such authority that the police in Dvinsk must hearken his voice in all that he commanded them. Several years he worked strenuously, until he'd removed the Rayphali from every alley, one by one. One time he requested from the police one hundred Cossacks or more, and everything he sought they gave him immediately. His words were heard and enacted as the words of a governor's command. At first, he carried out his actions in secret; afterwards he did them publicly, but as a result he couldn't leave his house without bodyguards, and many police were posted by his door to guard him from fear both night and day. Every prison and every cell in Dvinsk, in the fortress and the city, were full with the denizens of Rayphali. As long as there were a couple men left of the Rayphali, or even women, Meir Roshkas couldn't be sure of his life. Finally, all that remained of the Rayphali were the old, the weak, the blind and the crippled. Most of them had been sent to Siberia, but despite this he still wasn't sure of his life, and he said, "As long as the places of the Rayphali stand, even the ruined houses, my life isn't a life." One time, he was walking down the street, returning home with two police bodyguards. Just as he came to the door of his house, he recognized that one of his guards was not a policeman but a Rayphali disguised in a police uniform. Nobody had noticed! The man's intention was to kill him as he sat confidently in his home. So, Roshkas pretended that he hadn't caught on and he returned to the police station. There he requested ten more men and instructed that they go secretly through the streets in order that nobody should notice, then close to his house they should fall suddenly on the bodyguards and arrest them quickly. The people in the street thought that Meir Roshkas and the police had gone crazy because they arrested other police, but when the men were brought to the station and stripped of their uniforms, Meir Roshkas identified them by name, and they were Rayphali. They had earlier invited the real policemen to a pub and gotten them drunk, then tied them up with rope in the cellar. They had taken their service accoutrements and their uniforms, put them on, and gone and taken their places. Then they waited for the coming of the hated man, their sworn enemy, but he was above all of the Rayphali, in both wisdom and cunning. Even so, he said, "As long as the Rayphali neighborhood exists, even if it is desolate and ruined, I will fear that from under the ground they will come out to take the revenge of their fathers on me." One time, Meir Roshkas passed by a window, and saw that many silver utensils were resting on a table next to the open window of a kitchen, and the cook wasn't there. The silver lay there, and nobody put out a hand to take it. He called the mistress of the house and said to her, "And what are they saying now? Is it possible that you are all thinking that since Meir Roshkas is here, the days of security and relaxed vigil have arrived, so that you can leave things in an open window and nobody will touch them? Let me warn you all, don't continue to act this way, because this is how you will build up a new Rayphali, who are now almost lost from memory." He lived in constant fear and nervousness and apparently he returned to Petersburg. I don't know anything more about him. As to the Rayphali neighborhood itself and how the old suburb came to an end, that I will relate in the course of my story.

## ⌐ Chapter Two

The house of Friedlander raised itself over the city like a shining star in the mighty heavens, not just because of its external beauty, but because of its inhabitants, its Jewishness, and the good activities within the house. There were four brothers, Reb Meir, Reb Michal, Reb Leibel, and Matil, the youngest. Matil lived in Petersburg, the capital, to conduct his business, and the three elder brothers lived in the city of Dvinsk, all in one house with their families. They had a beautiful shul within the house and the three of them conducted themselves as one family. In their business, their expenses and income were all together, and in the shul they all worshipped together. Their wives and children came every Shabbat and holiday and worshipped in the shul. All of them prayed and all of them understood, because they studied Hebrew from learned teachers. The smallest girls that didn't yet know how to read a book, three or four years old, sat in their places with siddurim in their hands. Throughout the services even the little ones sat like modest women and didn't desire to speak idle words. The women and their daughters were very modest, God-fearing, and for purity of conduct there weren't the like of them, but surpassing them all was Sifra, the wife of Reb Meir and the daughter of Reb Joel Fromkin. She was a God-fearing woman who distributed gifts to the impoverished and didn't send anyone away empty handed. When Reb Meir married off his eldest son, Reb Moshe Mordechai, he made a great feast for the poor. From all the surrounding villages and from the city of Dvinsk itself masses of the poor and destitute streamed to enjoy the feast that Friedlander put on for them. For a whole week before the feast, the Shamishes declared every evening in every house of prayer that Friedlander was making a feast for the poor, in order to awaken their appetites, and the feast went on two days in a row. These days were a holiday and a vacation for all of the helpers and managers of Freidlander's house, and everybody dressed in Shabbat clothes and served the poor, including the brothers and family members. All of them welcomed guests joyfully. Aside from the feast, they distributed money with a generous hand, and they sat with the poor at the tables during the meals. Musicians played constantly to cheer the hearts of the poor and the wanderers. This was the law of the house, a house of generosity, of which just a fraction has been displayed to the honorable readers.

# ᵕ Chapter Three

This was the time of the great revolt in which the Polish rebelled against mighty Russia. It grew and strengthened to a violent crescendo, and the Polish dispensed their wrath on many of our people.

Behold, this is the fate of a people without a country, a people without a support and buttress. A wandering people that neither seeks and nor finds a rest for the soles of its feet. If a Jew will find a place according to his spirit to pitch his tent, behold how quickly he will realize that it's not solid ground but sand and dust. Therefore any passing wind could uproot and overturn him on his face, along with all his children and cattle, and it wouldn't be known what became of him. Here were the Polish people whose fate and condition was worsened by their own actions, who had enough to worry about themselves. For all that, not a day went by that they didn't carry out some scandalous slaughter of our people. In the big cities, it wasn't such a disaster because the people were always on guard, but in the small cities in Latvia and the towns where our people lived they had massacres. Always dispersed and exposed, when a stormy wind begins in any land, a Jewish woman is sickened and trembling in her knowledge that she will always be the scapegoat. So were the Polish people like little children, in that if one youngster struck his neighbor who couldn't retaliate, in his anger the neighbor would hit a different child who was sinless and guiltless. They were angry at the Russians and took their revenge on the Jews who hadn't done them a wrong; only they thought we rejoiced in their rout. Our people who suffered the most were in the cities of Kopishak and Vabalnik, and the many towns surrounding these cities. One time, they burst into a town not far from Kopishak where a Jewish family lived, and cried to them "Give us food and if not we will hang you from the tree that stands before your window." The Jew answered them, "On my life and soul, besides flour I haven't got a thing."

"You see?" one shouted, "The ugly Jew is faithful to the Russians and wishes us ill, otherwise why won't he give us bread? Come, let's hang him first, and afterwards his wife and children." His wife began to quake from fear and told him, "Go to the next town and borrow or buy bread from them and bring it here." And as he went, they warned him, "Take heed to hurry back, and if not we'll know that you devise evil against us and then we'll hang your wife and children together." When the Jew returned with loaves of bread and handed them over, they said, "If she hadn't advised you to give us bread, you wouldn't have wanted to give it to us. Therefore, you are loyal to the Russians." They all unified around the idea that they should hang him. "Yes, yes," they all cried, of one mind for a hanging. In the next moment, they hung him on the tree before his window, where he hung twitching until his soul flew up to the Master of Souls to complain before Him about his bitter fate.

The next day, the Russian army arrived with a thunderous noise and they cried, "Where is the traitorous Jew who bought bread from the other towns to give to the rebels, as we were informed by the shepherds?" So the unfortunate woman showed them the dead man and they released her, only they asked her to show them which way the rebels had gone and she showed them. They pursued the rebels and caught them, because they had hidden in the forest in pits and thickets, and they put an end to all of them. Three days later more Polish came to the woman's house where she was alone except for her little boy. The older sons had gone to Vabalnik to rent an apartment for the family so they could leave the town. On their arrival the Poles fell on her murderously and said, "You showed the Russians where our brothers were and they were killed, so have a dose of your own medicine," and they killed her also.

I could relate to you tens and hundreds of incidents like these which occurred at that time, because many members of my family lived and still live today in these places, and from them I heard. But this isn't the body of my story, and its only by-the-way that I recorded a little from the memories of the days of my childhood.

At the same time that this confusion and consternation precipitated itself, there also rose confusion and consternation in the camp of Israel in the city of Dvinsk. This on account of a feud and falling out that at first was limited, because in little matters they were able to smother the fires of contention, but later went far off course. Such was the case with the feud and schism that divided the hearts of the people, each man from his brother.

The old feud revealed itself these many years after the days of the Vilna Gaon z"l and the Lebovitcher Rebbe. The adults kept the hatred hidden, but between the children there was feuding and quarreling always. If two children met, seven or eight years old, it would begin with words of scorn and revile. The Hassid's son would insult and curse the Gaon, and the son of the Mitnaged[4] would scorn the Rebbe. And if people gathered for some celebration or some assembly, or if they sat in a Succah, Mitnagdim and Hassidim together, then the Hassidim would begin to talk about the prominent Mitnagdim. At first they would mock them, and if the Mitnaged responded with some barbed words from the quiver, then their wrath would be kindled and it sometimes came to blows. One time, many Hassidim were sitting in at a party in the banquet hall of Uncle Aaron Yehoshim (such was called the owner of the facility) and there also sat there one Mitnaged. He was a rich merchant and well versed in Torah, Reb Pavel Friedman was his name, or Pavel Ziesalm from the city of Zager.[5] They rose to laugh, as was their habit always, and to ridicule and scorn the Mitnaged Rabbis and Gaonim, and they wouldn't be quiet. In the end they enraged him, as they knew he was thoroughly a Mitnaged. He couldn't bear it any more, and opened his mouth and told them a story from the Torah, but with many sharp points, on which there isn't enough room here to repeat. They clamored to beat him to death, and if he hadn't hastened to flee by the way of the window he sat next to, they would have murdered him.

And it happened one day that one of the inhabitants of the "Dancing" Street entered his son into the impossible,[6] and he was a Hassid who served in Freidlander's business. He invited Rabbi Pavel Rappaport z"l and honored him as Sandak,[7] and Reb Michal Friedlander wasn't remiss, and he also came to this mitzvah[8] meal. The Friedlanders never rejected such a request, even from their employees, and Mitnagdim from the best of the city were also invited to the meal. The mohel was Zalman, the butcher, or as he was

---

4. Lit. "opponents," the opponents of the Hassidic movement. Mitnagdim is the plural.
5. The town Sarah Faige was born and spent the first seven years of her life.
6. They made a Brit for him, a ritual circumcision.
7. The man who holds the baby during the Brit.
8. A positive commandment.

called by the majority of the people, Zalman The Crude. Zalman, the butcher, was this sort of man — when he stood in the courtyard and the women and girls with their fowl gathered around him, he seemed to me to be the king of death. Later, when I was grown up and had read *Paris Mysteries*,[9] he looked to me like the slayer in the slaughter house who butchered and butchered without having his fill, and so he was. He stood in a weird anger and butchered. Once, when a girl approached him and said in Yiddish, "Reb Zalman, Reb Zalman. Butcher mine quickly because I haven't any time," he threw the slaughtered chicken that was in his hand forcefully into her face. Sometimes girls fell fainting from great sensitivity and were taken home injured. If a Hassidic man was angry against his neighbor or some Mitnaged, he would incite Zalman the butcher against him, and then the only option for the man was to flee the city. This was Zalman the butcher, and he was invited to circumcise the son. So, the father was a Hassid, the Rabbi a Hassid, the mohel a Hassid, and the majority of the guests were Hassidim. Only a couple Mitnagdim who were business connections were there, and Reb Michal Friedlander headed them.

And it happened that when they sat to eat and drink the mitzvah meal, the Hassidim began to speak about the Gaonim of the land, first in whispers and afterwards in full voice. So Reb Michal Friedman called out, "Please don't, brothers. Don't profane this mitzvah which is so important to Israel. Why provoke people who sit tranquilly with you?" Then Zalman opened his mouth wide and began to speak slander, revile, and even curse all the Gaonim of the land — Reb Chaim Walzner z"l, Rabbi Zalma z"l, Rabbi Itzaleh z"l, and above all the great Gaon, the grand Rabbi of the Exile from Vilna, whom he showered with energetic curses. Friedlander called out in anger, "If you wanted to curse all of our great sages, why did you invite us? Don't you know that bitterness will follow after this?" Reb Michal cried angrily to the Hassidic Rabbi, "Rebbe, apply the

---

9. *The Mysteries of Paris* by Eugene Sue, translated to Hebrew by Kalman Schulman in 1857.

law. Aren't you obligated to discredit The Crude and to fill his mouth with gravel for his disgraceful doings? Aren't you a Rabbi, Chief Rabbi of the city, how can you be mute? Isn't their Torah also your Torah, how can you despise it? Aren't you prepared to make a ruling?"

The Rebbe answered him coldly, "Me? Am I not prepared to make a ruling? I'll do it quickly. He can speak, or he can not speak."

Reb Michal cried in anger while taking a couple steps backwards, "Brothers, separate yourselves from this bad company." The Mitnagdim who were there gathered around him, and he proclaimed, "I and my compatriots ban the butchery of The Crude. The meat that he slaughters is unclean meat, blemished meat it is, until he travels with ten men of those who hear this to the tomb of our master, the Vilna Gaon."

And they all cried, "Banned, Banned." "And you," he said turning to the Rabbi, "Also you we don't absolve, and while we are getting a Mitnaged butcher we'll also get a Mitnaged Rabbi!"

"That won't happen," the Rabbi retorted angrily.

"It will, it will," cried Friedlander, "Quickly, in the near future."

"While I live it won't," returned the Rabbi, "Only if I'm no longer alive."

"Then let it be as you say," cried Reb Friedlander angrily and went out. As he was leaving he called again to the Rabbi, "The ban is on the condition that Zalman doesn't travel to Vilna in the company of ten men to seek the pardon from the Gaon of our people. If he goes then my words are canceled." He said this and left with all the Mitnagdim. That day they called a council with the great men and scholars of the Mitnagdim, and called for a ban on the butcher The Crude. They proclaimed in every study house of the Mitnagdim that it was now forbidden to eat meat in Dvinsk. All week the Mitnagdim didn't taste the flavor of meat, but on Thursday, Reb Friedlander issued orders to bring in a couple of cattle and also a different butcher. I don't remember if the butcher they brought was from Greiba, which was a suburb on the other side of the River Dina, or from some other city. I only remember that the butcher slaughtered the cattle and we ate meat until satiated, but not to excess. And if there had been a question of the lung[10] it would have been declared traif.[11]

When Zalman the butcher saw that the Mitnagdim had devised a way to eat meat without him, he was distressed, and he sent word to Reb Friedlander to tell him that after Shabbat he would travel to Vilna with ten men. On Sunday morning, Zalman arrived at the station with ten men to travel to Vilna, but many Hassidim ran to him to reheat the conflict, and they said to him, "Zalminka, you're crazy. The spirit will enter your father.[12] You're traveling to the city of Vilna? Are you comfortable approaching the tombs of the holy men with them knowing what you said about them? Won't they make you into a mound of bones! If you want to live, return to your home." When he heard these words he became afraid and he went home and the ban remained in place.

After these events, the Mitnagdim brought a judge to the city, and his name was Reb Pina. They also brought a butcher and established their own slaughter house for meat. Thus the feud was rekindled, and as a fire will progress and spread to the four corners of the house if firemen don't labor to extinguish it, so spread the conflicts and divisions in the city. In every house, in every study hall and in every store and street, nothing was heard besides, "Mitnaged and Hassid, Hassid and Mitnaged." At first the women made mistakes since they didn't know which butcher shop was Mitnaged and which was Hassidic, and so they mixed up the products. Then there were great problems such as when a man came home from work and sat down to eat, and while eating asked his wife where she got the meat. She told him Yitzchak Fagin's butcher shop, which was the Hassidic butcher shop. He cried out loudly, "Oy, Oy, You have fed me unclean meat!" Or if a woman bought meat from the butcher shop in the house of Leible Kermis, which was the butcher shop of the Mitnagdim, a Hassid would be leaping to his feet and crying out, "Oy, Oy, You have fed me traif meat!" And every night, when my father z"l came home from

---

10. Whether or not the cow was kosher.
11. Not kosher.
12. i.e. He will turn over in his grave.

the house of study, he would tell my mother z"l that the Shamish had declared that everybody who bought meat that day from Yitzchak Fagin's butcher shop had rendered his kitchen utensils unclean. A day didn't pass that the kitchen utensils weren't made traif in many homes on both sides. So passed weeks and months with the flames of the conflict spreading from day to day, and the hatred on both sides reached a pinnacle. The Mitnagdim made preparations to request a new Rabbi, but it wasn't lightly that they took this step, because Rebbe Pavel was also a Rabbi to their taste. One time, a woman went to a butcher shop to buy some intestines, but she wasn't sure if maybe she had mixed up the butcher shops. So she asked, "Tell me please if these are "Hassidisher Kishkas" or "Mitnagedisha." The butcher grabbed her by the back of the neck and threw her out, but after he wrote in big letters on the door, "Meat for Mitnagdim here."

Around this time, a rich Hassid married off his daughter. The wife of Rabbi Pavel came to the feast with another rich Hassidic woman named Gittel Lieberman who owned a big liquor business. When the women sat at the table to eat, all of the conversation and discussion was on the division that was in the city. The wife of the Rabbi became assertive and said. "The Mitnagdim are truly crazy in their thinking that the Vilna Gaon was a great man, and that over this they are willing to kill and be killed. I know who he was." And she started to curse him, and as she was cursing she raised up her foot and showed the woman her heel and said, "My heel is more dear than . . . ." She caused Gittel Lieberman to laugh and clap her hands and say, "The Rebbitzen is entirely correct, he is that," and she added to the filth and cast darts at the Gaon and his students.

# ᔕ Chapter Four

At this time the end came to the old neighborhood and Rayphali, because the Petersburg Railway Company found it proper to lay a new track through the middle of the old city. They assembled and brought in surveyors who measured the old city length and breadth.

They surveyed and in the end demolished almost all the Old Suburb. They paid the full price for all the condemned property so the owners would be able to build new houses, and many people were greatly happy with these sales. Despite this there were also many who cried and could find no peace of mind in the transaction. But another problem even bigger than that was waiting for the congregation of Dvinsk, and it angered every heart and disturbed the rest of every person. The fortress needed renovation, and according to the construction plans they had to dig up the old graveyard, which was remarkable for its size already. In every house were heard stories of ghosts and spirits. Men and women, boys and girls, all gathered around an old woman who told them some wonderful things, because she remembered a similar incident from her childhood in a different city. Many of the dead had come to their relatives in dreams and complained about the evil people upsetting their rest, how they were now wandering the world lost and without peace, and other stories like this. We were afraid to venture out from the door of the house during the day, even more so at night. Not only the children were frightened, but the adults also.

The best men of the city, above all the brothers Friedlander and Israel Horowitz, strove greatly so we could receive an injunction from Petersburg, the capital, that they bypass and not touch the nearly full graveyard. So, on one side the rail went at a diagonal and didn't touch the cemetery, and on the other side the foundations for the castle were poured without impacting the graveyard. Despite all of this, a couple of times people came and reported that they had seen human bones. The Shamishes of the burial society were dispatched and they returned the bones to their resting places. However, it was no longer possible to bury more dead there. A decree was issued lest anyone take it lightly and continue performing burials there, and any transgressor was subject to severe punishment. Therefore the community of Israel in Dvinsk had to establish a new cemetery.

The land was purchased, but who wants to be the first in a new eternal home? So there was unease in the city. If a person got sick he was struck with anxiety from the fear that he would be the first to consecrate the new cemetery, and he would request from the Lord that he send them a very old man to be the first.

Behold their supplication came about. A ninety year old man became sick and sent for the Gabbi of the burial society and said, "Behold, I can see that my end has come to me, but I request that you hire a Kaddish sayer for me (for the man was alone, he didn't have a wife or children), and that all the days of Shiva three men will sit next to my grave, and a candle will be burning all the days of Shiva." The head of the burial society and the Gabbi promised to fulfill his wish. The man died on the sixth of Adar in the evening, and a fast was called for the whole city the next day, the seventh of Adar. The burial of the old man and the consecration of the cemetery took place together. All of the people of the city, from the greatest to the least, walked after the bier of the dead, and with the exception of the children, they fasted as if it were Yom Kippur. Boys who were studying Torah walked after his bier reciting psalms, and in the new cemetery everybody circled seven times with the coffin. All the people said "Vayihee Noam" and some other songs from psalms, and they buried the man with very great honor and kept their promise to him. They also did many other wonderful and charitable things before the consecration, such as making a couple weddings for poor grooms and brides, and more. After all this, another three or four people passed away before evening. The people of Dvinsk made proper order and rule in the cemetery. They divided it into three sections, for men only, women only, and children only. Surely they made order between the dead, but behold the disorder between the living. Aside from the feud that unfolded before me, there were other divisions due to the lack of housing. The residents of old city had believed they received a good deal for their old houses and the price of land, but where could they get housing now? Almost all of the inhabitants of the old city were segregated in a narrow area that contained all of them when they came to live in the new city. The cost of apartments was dear, the owners of housing raised their prices, and there was a great outcry in the city. So the city officials provided a strip of land very far from the center that was very cheap, practically free, and every man bought enough land to build two houses and a large garden. The price was twenty silver coins, this to be paid in two installments, but it was incumbent on the purchaser to hurry to build and finish construction in a period no longer than three months. Land was bought by the like of poor teachers, scribes of books and mezuzot and teffilin who were always part of the family of the poor; tailors, and door-to-door men, all of them bought land. The work was started, but the poor didn't have the means to build their homes. But then, the value of the land rose quickly, to the point where a poor man could sell half of the lot and get for that half five or six hundred silver coins, and then he had enough in hand to build his house with some left over. As the houses multiplied, the value of the land increased, until two years later the price for half of a lot that a person had bought for twenty silver coins was up to five or six thousand.

Here I must take a little detour from my story of that time to recall more recent days, seventeen years ago. It came about by chance that I traveled by way of Dvinsk, after I had abandoned her for many years. It was a time when the ideas of the Lovers of Zion[13] were gaining acceptance in our politics, and when the train reached the last station of the Petersburg line, I had to disembark and get on another train. I saw from a distance a great metropolis so that I almost couldn't believe my eyes. "Could this be the city of Dvinsk?" I asked myself, "Is it possible that in the course of fifteen years the whole city has been replaced, that most of the stone houses have been exchanged for wood homes?" It wasn't that my eyes were at fault. I stood astonished at the sight and couldn't comprehend it. By and by, the train came and went, and I remained standing amazed in my place. A teamster approached in his wagon and said, "Without a doubt you want to travel to the city. The way is yet very far, and the train that shuttles from the Petersburg Railway to the Riga Railway has already passed by." Then I started as though from a dream and asked, "Am I in Dvinsk?" "Yes," he answered me.

"But what is that city there?" I asked. "That can't be Dvinsk." The

---

13. The early Zionist movement.

teamster laughed at my ignorance and said, "Is it not the new city that has been built up for eighteen years now?" Then I emerged, as if from a trance, and the memories of my childhood began to rise up in my brain one by one, and light up my eyes. I sat in the wagon and asked the teamster to drive very slowly, in order that I could examine the city from every vantage point. I couldn't pry my eyes off it for a moment, and only when I'd stared at it from every side and my gaze returned to the starting point, I cried as though to myself, "My people, my people. How long will you build your city on mounds of sand, that a passing wind will overturn her on her face. Now I can see you are able to do it, and there is no preventing you from accomplishing a thing if only you desire it, but your creation will only go to strangers and other people. Look now, look at this place that was desolate and ruined when I saw it in childhood. Terror and fear would fall on a man when he saw the place from afar. The children told me that demons nested there, and on every mound lived a little demon with a big hat, and that when a man would pass by, the little demons became big in an instant and killed and strangled anyone who trespassed. The adults said these were no demons, only robbers who found for themselves a nest there. Now, after eighteen years, a lofty city is being built here, and it won't lack a thing. Even cool fresh water is found here."

"So, my people, take this to heart and redeem also our desolate land, will you not return? Didn't it happen here that poor rebels were made into upper-class house-holders? Why don't you bring about great changes there also? Isn't your welfare in your own hands? Here you dwell on foreign land, there you will dwell on the land of your fathers." How satisfying and precious this moment was for me, in my recollection that here on this once desolate land now appeared a great shining city like this, even though it wouldn't be mine now or ever. How fine will the moment be when I am privileged to see the land of my fathers, desolate and destroyed by time, resettled and speedily rebuilt. Would it be hard to give up this empty life for a precious moment like that? "And who are they that withhold from themselves this great pleasure? Isn't it ourselves!" So I spoke with tremendous feeling, but the wind blew against my face and stopped up my words into profound silence. Since then another sixteen years have passed. The Lovers of Zion, a small stream that sprang forth from the hearts of a few, has become a mighty flowing river, casting its living waters from afar to quench the tongues of those who thirst. Now, thank heavens, the Jewish community is moving and alive, and opinions have changed in favor. Now there are many who think as I did then. But we still have far to go, very far, because many yet walk with their eyes closed, not seeing potholes and stumbling blocks below their feet . . . But I will return now to my story from my childhood. The divisiveness still hadn't ceased, the fire of feud still wasn't quenched. There was little satisfaction for the people in their feud because the antipathy widened, and the women of the Hassidim also began to speak badly, along with their sons and daughters.

And it was on Shabbat "Chazon" in the second year since the troubles had begun, at the point of the reading of the Haftorah, at the moment the reader chanted these words: "So spoke the Lord, King of Hosts, Mighty One of Israel, 'Alas for you, I will ease me of my foes and wreak vengeance on mine enemies,'"[14] when voices were heard from all sides, "Fire, Fire, The whole street goes up in flames!" In another moment, the fire had caught hold and spread to almost the whole city. From every direction in every street the same broken cry was heard, "Fire, Fire." All Shabbat and Sunday the city burned and smoldered from almost every side. The firemen were unable to find a way to extinguish a fire so large and terrible. Sunday morning the fire department from Petersburg came, but they didn't succeed in putting out the fire until Monday evening. Then the people were able to go look at the destruction that had been done in the city. More than half the houses in the city had burned, even though there were many stone houses and few wooden ones. The house of the Rabbi had burned down to the foundation. This wasn't the first fire of the summer, because the Poles set fires in many cities, but I hadn't ever seen a fire like this. Many people carried the few belongings saved from

---

14. Isaiah. 1:24.

the fire and brought them to the edge of the second city. When they all gathered with their possessions and were about to sit down and rest, from the items themselves the fire broke out and devoured the majority of what remained. All the people were left naked and lacking everything, and the once beautiful city was now in total shock. The high, blackened walls and the empty places cast such a dreadful fear on me that even today, when I bring forth my memory of this vision of destruction, I'm seized with trembling.

The fire was quenched, and the city was resurrected from the ashes and began to live and rebuild from the destruction, but the flames of dissension burned without end. Scorn and condemnation against both the living and the dead were always heard from the Hassidic side more than from the Mitnaged side. The Mitnagdim proceeded on their own. They set up a Judge, slaughterers and butchers, all Mitnagdim. They requested a head Rabbi and attempted to receive permission from the Rabbinical council to get a Mitnaged Rabbi, because they were a large congregation. The Hassidim also did their own thing, cursing and belittling the living and the dead. They took a dog and hung a wooden placard around its neck on which was written, "This is Nachmon Eidel." One led the dog by a rope, and many Hassidim ran behind striking the dog with switches and yelling, "Go, Nachmon Eidel, Go, Go." Let me will describe for you who this man was. Reb Nachmon Eidel of Raglyot was the husband of Chaya Sarah Gordon, a very rich woman. He was at that time in his youth. My father z"l said about him that in all his days he hadn't seen a youngster like him, so well versed and incisive, like a great Rabbi who had sat and learned for fifty years without a break. He was so observant that none surpassed him in the old generation, let alone in this generation. As a charitable man, there wasn't his equal, everything he had he gave to the poor. He was also Gabbi for visiting the sick, and it was his responsibility to sign off on free medicine for the poor, that they could receive it without payment. A man or a woman would come to him and ask him to sign for some prescription, and he would ask them how many children they had and how much they earned. When he heard how tight things were with them, he would take money from his own pocket and give it to the woman to buy chicken, or wine, or meat. So he acted always. He also knew how to read the biles and tell anyone his illness. Now he is a great rabbi living in a big city, and he has already had his rabbinical ordination for thirty-five years. This is who Reb Nachmon Eidel from Raglyot was. But I will not speak about the living now, I shall only speak about events that have been.

Gittel Lieberman had a son, Moshe was his name, a man in the prime of his life, and very wealthy. He and his mother owned a big liquor business. And it happened that one evening he went into one of his stores wanting to get a drink of water. He poured himself a large measure of 95% alcohol, tipped it up to his mouth, and in a moment he fell to the earth dead. This happened two weeks after the fire in which all of the stores and warehouses of Gittel were burned and she had great losses. The man in whose house the feud had started lost his son a few weeks later, and he went to live in another house, saying the wrath of the Lord was on this place, and the building would remain as a reminder of sin.

# ᕰ Chapter Five

It happened on the Thursday before Shabbat "Slichot" in the second year after the beginning of the schism that wailing was heard in the city because Rabbi Pavel fell ill. Friday morning it was heard in the city that it was very grave because his sickness was a black tumor (have mercy on us). The surgeon cut out the pollution, but the operation didn't go well and with nightfall and the exit of Shabbat "Slichot" his soul returned to God. Here was the end of the all the divisiveness, and God protect other cities from schisms like this. A great loss was suffered by Dvinsk in the passing of this Rabbi, he had great learning and worldly wisdom, and in his connection to and mixing with the common people he was unique. It was told about him that in the days of his youth he had been a big merchant, but in the end he lost his business and became a Rabbi, and many tradesman sought his advice.

On the Sunday of "Slichot" the Rabbi was brought to his grave, and all the people gathered to mourn and weep over him. Almost all the Jews of the city went out to accompany him, Hassidim and Mitnagdim alike, including Michal Friedlander. The processional with the coffin and the dead Rabbi passed by the house of "The Brit," where the schism had started, because along this street all the dead of the city were brought. In the houses of the Jews who had gone outside came non-Jews, and the moment the coffin was borne past, a woman poured vomit out the window directly onto the coffin and shroud of the Rabbi and soiled it. So there was a great outburst and crying and wailing amongst the people, and they had to delay the funeral until they could prepare new garments for the Rabbi z"l. At the cemetery, as the coffin stood on the earth and the Hassidim approached to request pardon from him, Reb Michal Friedlander said to Saul Hirsch Horowitz, "Let the two of us go and we will also seek pardon from the Rabbi," and the two of them went. When they got to the Rabbi's coffin and wanted to touch it, a bunch of Hassidim fell on them yelling loudly, "Murders! You killed our great Rebbe, and now you've come to revenge yourselves on him and sully his honor even after his death! Hit them! Strike our enemies! You will not live and breath!" Saul Hirsch made himself scarce, climbed over the wall and fled, because on the other side of the wall he had a rented factory. But Friedlander didn't flinch, and they threatened to kill him. Yankel Vavil Pashnick approached and cleaved through the mob until he came to Friedlander (he was a Hassid but he served in Freidlander's business) and he spoke out, "Strike me if you wish, but of Reb Michal I won't let you touch a hair." He saw in the distance one of Freidlander's men and called to him, "Run quickly to the fortress and get help." The man ran and took a horse from Freidlander's team which was waiting for him behind the wall, but before he went he stood his ground a moment and yelled loudly, "If you want to live, don't set your hearts to lay a hand on him, because all of your lives will be forfeit." They beat Yankel Vavil and injured him but he got in their way, so the Hassidim pushed them and pressed them against the wall. Afterwards they called, "Hold a moment, don't hit him, just force him to concede to us that he won't bring a Mitnaged Rabbi to the city." Friedlander stood there white faced as a corpse, and he couldn't get out even a soft sound. He only recovered a little when he heard many voices shouting, "Cossacks are coming." A hundred Cossacks burst into the cemetery and began to strike the people with whips and reins, and the mob began to flee and yell. Then Freidlander's wind returned to him and he called, "Please don't hit them, after all they are engaged in burying the Rabbi of the city. Here are wages for you." And he paid them with a generous hand. They waited with him a long time, until he had the strength to walk to his wagon, because the mob had pushed him so hard against the wall that he couldn't draw a breath. Once he was seated in his carriage to travel home, he didn't move from his place until the Cossacks rode back to their barracks.

After the festival of Succoth, messengers were sent from the city to every Jewish community to seek a great and suitable Rabbi for the Mitnagdim of Dvinsk. They sought and found the great genius, Reb Aaron Saul Zelig (he had three names) the Rabbi from Proznay, and he promised them he would come before Passover. The messengers returned home happy and in good heart, and blessed God that he had put before them a Rabbi of their hearts desire, and waited with pining eyes for his coming.

## ⤚ Chapter Six

The Mitnagdim waited for the Rabbi, and the Hassidim brought in the interim Judge, Reb Shlomo, brother-in-law of Reb Zacharia Zalkind, in place of a Rabbi, and they considered getting themselves a Rabbi. But for the time being there was no quiet in the city, and both sides grated on each other. Every incident and every event that happened, be it on one side or the other, they blew it out of proportion, even though this winter was almost two years since the beginning of the disagreements and the feud.

During the winter a man named Rueven arrived from the city of Dishna. He was an old man of around sixty, a great Hassid, and his son Chaim came with him. He had been a big baker in the city of Dishna, and for forty years he had baked in that city. The Rebbe had blessed him that he should succeed, and he had succeeded. But during the last summer when their had been major conflagrations in many cities, there was also a big fire in Dishna, and Rueven the baker was wiped out. A rich Hassid, Bartzik Lewinzahen, along with some other rich Hassidim, backed him with a thousand rubles and brought him to Dvinsk. They rented him a basement apartment in Vavil Gloskin's house to set up a bakery. My parents z"l also lived in that courtyard, and the whole time the craftsmen worked to fix up the bakery and a very expensive giant oven, the baker and his son were at our place, cooking with our stove and always drinking their tea in our home. One time, he said to my mother z"l, "Shaina, I don't know how to thank you or honor you for your good will. Despite the fact you're from the family of the Gaon, you do favors for Hassidim even while we are reviling him." She always answered, "Tuvia sins and Zingud is found liable for lashes."[15]

All of the work for the bakery was finished and he prepared all the equipment associated with a large bakery. He brought in many sacks of flour of different types, yeast, butter, and other things he required, because the next day he would begin his work. "But before I start," he said, "I must have a celebration for my benefactors and for all the men who pray together with me." We can say one thing in praise of all Chasidim, a good attribute they all had then whether great or small. They don't put the prince before the pauper. To a rich man's celebration came all the impoverished, and to a poor man's celebration came almost all the rich Hassidim of the city. He didn't neglect my parents z"l, because they also went to the party, or as it was called in Yiddish "Zoof Merkal." Although I was then a little girl, I went with my mother by telling her that I loved to hear their songs. Many people gathered in the big room that was prepared for the bakery,

---

15. Talmud Bavli, Pesach 113b.

both rich and poor together, and they sat around a long table that the baker made from the planks which were intended for holding the challot[16] and loaves. My mother sat in the second room with two other neighborhood women. I didn't want to sit next to my mother, so I posted myself at the threshold of the door the whole time to see what would happen in there.

Rueven the baker stood on the table a barrel containing around 20 loog, full of strong whiskey, and he set up glasses suitable for a blessing for all the celebrants there, along with finger food and doughnuts. When my mother z"l saw that there wasn't a decanter, she said to the baker, "Reb Rueven, why didn't you take a decanter from my house to pour the liquor into. It's not good to pour from the barrel straight into the glass." So he called me and requested that I bring him the big decanter. I ran to our house and took the big decanter, and went back down into the basement to give it to him. But when I returned, I found the glasses already had been filled without a decanter, because they hadn't been able to wait. Rueven stood with a copper loog measure in his hand and filled the glasses. And in another moment, the sound of ringing glasses was heard, each man's with his brother's. "L'chaim Bartzik, L'chaim Zinka, L'chaim Maska, L'chaim Ruvelah." And they drank, and a second, and a third, and then they began to yell in full throat, "L'chaim Rebbe, L'chaim Hassidenu, Death to the living Mitnagdim, from the hollow of the sling may they be cast to their cursed deaths."

Everybody dining there heard these few words, and like an electrical flow they passed between the company from the least to the greatest. They all began shouting the words that the first ones had said, with the little boys adding to the din. So they were all caught up and they started banging their fists on the table. Full glasses of drink were spilled and the liquor soaked the tablecloth, which was ours. My mother z"l said, "Behold my wages for the good I did them. Our fine tablecloth will be ruined yet."

But they hadn't said enough and they became inflamed and shout-

---

16. Fancy show bread.

ed and cursed the living Mitnagdim, and the dead Gaonim, and above all the Vilna Gaon, whom the cursed energetically. Then my mother got up from her place to see what was going on, how my father z"l felt about this bad turn of events, and she saw that he had also gotten up from his place. And he said, "It isn't within my means to fight with you since you are the majority, but I'm not going to sit here with such a light-headed group. Let the owner of the vineyard rid himself of thorns, because painfully thorny are you all," he said and exited. And when my mother saw that Rueven the baker was also inflamed from the heat of the liquor, she said to him, "Rueven, will you go along with these envious cowards and pour oil on the on the generation of generations? I said that you would keep quiet, but here you are in this bitter company. Don't you know this conduct will bring no success? Behold, I hope you will be happy if you escape here by the skin of your teeth. What did the Gaon do to you? Why aren't you afraid to demean and curse him? Pray know that the devil incites you to speak strangely and perversely to your detriment and the detriment of your wife and son." Thus she spoke, then she also left the house, pulling me after her. All night they worked themselves up and drank and got drunk and yelled until their throats were hoarse. When it grew light in the morning, they started to leave in slow steps, each man dragging after his neighbor, and they yawned and teetered in their progress like drunks. After noontime, when my mother saw that the baker and his son were up from their sleep and didn't come for a hot drink, she said, "Without a doubt they are ashamed to come drink in my house." And she sent me to invite them. When they came they both said to my mother, "What bad men and sinners we are! It is incomprehensible that you don't maintain hatred for us. We thought that you'd never allow us over the threshold of your home again." Then my mother z"l answered them, "To take revenge or hold a grudge isn't a Jewish virtue. For God is the prosecution and the judgment. Who am I to take revenge over some spills, and not give you water to drink?" They drank and ate and went to the bakery to bake. They mixed flour with yeast and made every kind in wooden troughs, with butter only, oil only, water only, and they kneaded it and made dough. And the dough rose, each kind in its trough, and they stoked the oven as was fitting. Then they made loaves and laid them on platters after which they put them in the oven. And behold! Black encased the lovely loaves that were made from fine flour, butter, saffron, and other expensive ingredients known to great bakers.

They took the loaves from the oven, and behold, they displayed the properties of ice. From a big loaf was made a little one, thin like matzo. The baker had planned to price a loaf with butter at five kopecks, and a loaf without butter at three kopecks, but nobody was willing to pay even one penny. He thought that maybe the yeast wasn't good, maybe the oven, maybe the flour, so he took different flour and different yeast and watched the oven more carefully, but the next day his loss was even greater. So it was the third day, and all the days of the week. On Friday he prepared himself to bake challot for his Hassidic friends in saying, "I will see what happens with the Shabbat challot." And my mother asked Rueven to permit her to bake her challot in his oven. He said to her in great happiness, "I will bake as you desire." Mother braided the challot and put them in the oven, and when a few minutes had passed, Rueven peeked into the oven and jumped from his place and said, "Wonder of wonders, wonder of wonders. The challot of Shaina (so my mother was called) are shining from the oven, while my challot darken like black humiliation." And his challot left him with a name like his loaves had given him, and nobody would touch them or pick them up, because they were black as coal and thin as matzo.

The next day on Shabbat, when he and his son arrived at the shtieble to pray, he told what had occurred in the matter of his challot and the challot of my mother. So they all called him stupid and laughed at him greatly. On Sunday of the second week, the baker requested of my mother to make him a platter of loaves and that she, herself, put them in the oven herself, in order that he should have proof. He was beginning to believe that the Lord was scorching the work of his hands. Although my mother was weak of strength and very delicate, and she had never tried to bake in the oven of a baker, despite this she said, "So it will be, and I will also see and have proof."

She made him a platter full of loaves in the manner that he showed her, then she took the loaves and placed them in the oven. He also took loaves that he made and put them in the oven. And he cried like his heart was torn, hot with tears, "I believe you were absolutely correct in telling me "The devil incites you to anger to your own detriment and the detriment of your wife and son." I won't achieve anything here, but I will lose the money until it is gone, and I will return empty to my city." And he took the loaves from the oven and feared what was coming, because those that my mother made were good and beautiful while his couldn't be shown to anyone. The next morning he invited a couple Hassidim and asked that also they stand and watch this wonder, and he asked my mother to come also. But my mother didn't want to do much labor and she made six loaves. He put what he had made in the oven, and afterward my mother put her six loaves in the oven, and the Hassidim stood and watched the whole time. After a while, Rueven approached and took the loaves out of the oven, and they were all black like coal, only six were exceedingly beautiful. So they all shrugged their shoulders and left. Later, he brought in an extremely experienced baker on the advice of the Hassidim, who told him maybe he didn't understand baking. And the learned baker baked there a couple of times, and it didn't work out for him any better than for Rueven. Three months he labored and toiled, and he lost all his money and returned in deep frustration to the city of Dishna.

## ⤳ Chapter Seven

A time of happiness arrived for the community, and the congregation in Dvinsk celebrated and rejoiced. Every diligent hand was put to work making arrangements and preparing a suitable welcome for that great Rabbi in Israel, Reb Saul Zelig of Proznay. A large and ample house with beautiful furnishings was prepared for him. On the day of his arrival, all of the great men in the city got up in the morning; the brothers Friedlander, the brothers Israel and Saul-Hirsh Horowitz, Reb Nachmon Eidel of Raglyot, Yehoshua Eliya

Yodenzahen, Reb Yitzchak Yehroham Dishkin, son of Rabbi Dishkin and brother-in-law of Zacharia Zalkind, Reb Leib Shalom Yafa, my father z"l, and many others. They all went out of the city to wait for his arrival, sending men before them to greet him on the way, and they all came to the place where they would await him, the leading lights of the city and almost all of the Mitnagdim. The fathers brought their little children with them, and when he arrived, they all cried, "Blessed is he who comes in the name of the Lord." Friedlander got out of his carriage and asked after the Rabbi's health, then took him in his carriage to his house, where Friedlander made a great party in his honor. The next day the Rabbi went to his own house, and everybody accompanied him with rejoicing, enthusiastically acclaiming out loud, "And he will be our Rabbi." He was the first Rabbi to the Mitnaged congregation in the city of Dvinsk from the time of its inception. They would love the Rabbi exceedingly well because of his greatness in Torah, his modest nature and a pleasant disposition that was beyond compare. He received all people and related to them in a relaxed and welcoming manner, with good words and encouragement like Hillel the elder. Who wouldn't love a Rabbi like this? So the joy multiplied throughout the city tremendously, but the Hassidim said, "The Mitnagdim are like a barren woman who doesn't give birth until seventy, and when she delivers this son of her old age, she thinks he is without equal. But when another woman has six boys better and healthier than her only child, then she doesn't gaze raptly at him so much." But the Mitnagdim answered, "Verily did Sarah bear a son at ninety years of age, who took the place of Ishmael, whose mother bore him in her youth." And so were heard arguments from both sides.

So the Hassidim became jealous of the Mitnagdim, and they brought in a new Rabbi, Reb Leib from Hamla. This action brought about new developments on both sides, and the news aroused even the sleeping from their places. Here was the thing: the Proznay was a big Gaon, so he allowed almost all questions,[17] while the Hamlay rejected almost all questions, until it was a topic of conversation

---

17. Questions of kashrut.

amongst everyone. With the Proznay, all the questions were kosher, and with the Hamlay, all the questions were traif. The butchers began to complain because the majority of their oxen were declared traif and they said, "The butchers of the Mitnagdim are waxing very rich while we become more impoverished from day to day." If a Hassidic wife had a chicken or a fat swan and she had to ask if it were kosher, she would think, "And what will happen if I ask the Hamlay? Without a doubt he will declare it traif. And if I ask the Proznay, then it will probably be kosher. And what can happen to me if I go to the Proznay?" So she would go and ask him, he would declare it kosher, and she would be happy. And at meal time she would explain her wisdom to her husband, and he would jump up from his place and say, "You have fed me traif." And the woman would be bewildered and wouldn't know why he was so shocked and she would ask in wonder, "What's this? Do Hassidim have a different Torah? Isn't he also a Rabbi, so why can't we ask him a question? That their Kiddusha[18] is different, this I understand. But if they have a different Torah, that I hadn't known." So the feud began afresh and this caused the Rabbi from Proznay much sorrow.

It happened on the first night of Passover that one woman amongst the Hassidic wives cooked a stew from a fattened goose, and she found in the stew an ear of oats. She ran to the Hamlay who was dressed in his best garments for the holiday to go and say the evening prayers, and when she came and showed him the question he said, "The meat is chometz, as is the stock and the pots you cooked in." The woman was stunned, and she said, "Woe unto me, what will be. I don't have anything to cook or to eat for the whole of the holiday, except a little ox meat I was going to put in the cabbage. How can I put that before six people, myself, my husband, the maid, and my three children?" And she went to the Proznay saying, "Maybe he will declare it kosher." And so it was, and she rejoiced in great happiness. When the family sat down to the Seder and the time for the meal arrived, she told her husband about the fatted goose. He got up from

18. Level of holiness.

his place and wouldn't eat, and he went to the Hamlay and told him about the matter of the question that he had rejected and the Proznay had accepted. So the Hamlay called the Shamish and sent him to ask in his name, where the Proznay had found precedent in the law to permit the swan.

The Proznay answered him, "We pump from the same spring, but in the place where you find forbiddance, I find acceptance. If you desire to know it precisely, come to me and I will make it known to you."

There are those who say he didn't go, and those who say he went that night to the Rabbi from Proznay who made him understand, and from that time the feud was laid to rest in the city. But the people were still divided into two; the Mitnagdim by themselves and the Hassidim by themselves.

## ⁀ Chapter Eight

At this time there was a great famine in the surrounding towns, and almost every day many people came from the towns and villages to recuperate their health. In Dvinsk there was bread, though the cost rose greatly, but in the little towns they couldn't obtain it any price. If they did get bread there, it was mixed with leaves from the courtyards that were dried, ground, and blended with the flour. In Dvinsk, they blended corn flour with bran. The price of this bread went up to ten cents per pound, when two years earlier the price of good bread had been two cents, and white bread (Sitnazir in their language) was three cents. I remember a couple other things on the subject of the famine that are fitting to talk about. One time my mother sent me to buy two pounds of white bread and she gave me a ruble of paper money and told me, "First exchange the ruble for small coins." The price for changing a ruble was between eight to ten cents. So she told me "First exchange the ruble and afterwards to buy the bread, but beware that you aren't cheated, because they openly swindle everybody that they are able to cheat." I went to change the money. Alongside the stores stood a row of money-changers with tables and iron boxes. The money was kept in the boxes. I went up to a money-changer and she changed the ruble for me. She counted out the money in her hand, and nothing was lacking, but when it was in my hand, there were twenty cents missing. I returned it to her and she counted it out in my hand again, and so we did two or three times until at last it seemed to me that I hadn't been cheated. But when I turned about to go I only had seventy cents in the place of ninety cents, because she had secreted two silver coins of ten cents each between her thumb and hand. Afterwards people told me that this was always the procedure with money-changers. I went to buy two pounds of white bread but there wasn't anymore, so I bought two pounds of corn bread for ten cents. I brought my mother the change which remained from the ruble, summing sixty cents and she sighed and said, "Two pounds of corn bread cost me forty cents." My little brother ate a small piece of the bread and sickened with a serious illness in his intestines. The doctor, Nathanson, tasted the bread and cried, "What's this? One could die from this bread! Aside from there being more bran than flour, there are also leaves from the field in the bread, and the leaves burn the heart and the guts like fire!"

Even as the famine was growing in the city and the price of flour and crops was climbing higher and higher, Reb Israel Horowitz was in business to supply the fortress and the armies in the principality. He had a great quantity of corn flour since he had bought the business before the famine, and it was in three warehouses, one of his own and two he leased from other men. When he delivered the flour to the royal granary at the fortress, the commander of the fortress examined the flour along with captains from the army and doctors, and they found that it was no good. They decided unanimously that the flour wouldn't do and they returned it to him. They gave him three months to bring good flour, and if he didn't supply the flour within this time limit, he would lose his military franchise, and they would take the three warehouses from him. There was happiness and rejoicing amongst the Hassidim in Dvinsk as they told one another that they would now see the collapse of one of their most hated opponents. How could he possible supply different flour during a time when the price of flour was going up every day, and what could he do with the great quantity of flour that had been returned to him, because the flour really was very bad. But Horowitz didn't think so. He took all the flour from the granaries and brought it to a place he prepared for the purpose, and he hired many people to work. The people he hired were all poor Jews that had been idled and without work throughout the famine, and the job of these people was to pick the small stones from the flour, to bring it to be milled at a second mill, and to fill sacks. A few days went by and announcements were heard in every house of study that everybody who wished to buy corn flour cheaply should go to the square next to the river Dina. There was a big building prepared for this by Reb Israel Horowitz and there one could obtain corn flour for seventy cents a pood,[19] when to this point the price had been two rubles per pood. At first only the poorest of the poor bought, the middle class refused to buy, in their thinking, "If it wasn't good enough for the army, it's not good enough for us." Afterwards they tasted the bread and they saw that it was better than the bread sold in the bakers market, because it was pure corn flour, free of adulterations, save for a musty odor that was noticeable at the first encounter. However, the diner didn't have any bad feelings after eating it. So there was happiness and rejoicing because not only the poor bought, but also the middle class home-owners bought the flour. In every house, every street, and in every house of study they praised the name Reb Israel Horowitz. Everybody blessed him, everybody prayed to the Lord for his well being, and they said, "A second Joseph has risen up to keep alive many people in the days of this awful famine." Not only in Dvinsk, but also from surrounding towns and villages they came to break their fast, thanks to Reb Horowitz. But the small merchants and bakers cursed him, and they said to themselves that he'd snatched from their hands the stone house they would have built with money from despoiling the poor. Two months passed and the price of grain was cut in half. Even more than the price of grain had been raised by the big merchants in Germany, the

---

19. 16 Kg or 35 lbs.

price had been raised even higher by the small grain merchants and bakers who await price run-ups and famine as if a joyous occasion. And so Reb Israel Horowitz saved thousands of people from death by starvation. Many people took their wages in bread, and for a whole year he sustained most of the city and the surrounding towns with bread. His prestige grew, and neither did he lose any money, because he sold all of the flour. By and by the price of grain came down. When the deadline arrived and he had to bring the full amount of flour to the army granaries, he obtained grain at a fair price and didn't lose a thing, because he kept the franchise. And he made himself a name in the country, a good name amongst his people, an eternal name that won't perish.

## ⇜ Chapter Nine

At this time the administrators of the schools received an edict from the minister of education to compel every father who had several sons to send at least one of them to study in the gymnasium. So the principal of the gymnasium in Dvinsk went out, along with the mayor, Eaglesram and a writer from the city council. They with them the late Reb Tzvi-Hirsh Rabinowitz, who was a great Maskil[20] and lover of the Haskalah. The four of them went about recruiting souls for the Haskalah. A couple of people who had already had a scent of the air of freedom, those who came from other cities where the Haskalah had already begun to blossom, were amenable. But the majority, above all the Hassidim, withheld their children from this and hid their sons from them. If a man had three sons, he would say that he only had one and that he was needed in his business. So they went about wearing their legs out with walking, with little to show for it. They came to the great house of Reb Yerichom Zalman Gordon, and they found his sons, about five of them, sitting and

---

20. Enlightened or educated man — from the same root as Haskalah.

learning with a Melamed.[21] They asked the boys if they could understand some other language, and when they answered in the negative, the principal told the father that according to the order of the Minister of Education he must give at least one son to go to the gymnasium. The father couldn't refuse them, so he signed that during the next three months he would prepare one of his sons with the required basics, that were then very minimal, and then send him to gymnasium. They believed the great Gordon had made a huge sacrifice by agreeing in writing to send one of his sons to the gymnasium, because after a signature there's no going back, honorable readers, and God forbid that you should be suspicious of the validity. But for men like him in this period to send their sons to Azazel[22] to be made into a Shkuler[23] or Shkovart, as everyone would call a youth like this, would be a great injustice to his family and honor. The Lord always provides to His faithful extra insight in order that they may know and understand from beginning to end. So Gordon sent word and invited the woman Faige Hapavilankarn, who I mentioned at the beginning of my story, and he said to her, "Listen to me please, Faige, and don't jump at me. If only your husband lived and your son walked the straight path, then far be it from me that this idea should come into my heart. But everybody knows, as you yourself know, that your son Bashka is an outcast and abandoned youth, and there isn't a house in the whole street that doesn't have a window broken by your son's hand. He has no desire to learn Torah, and what will be his end? Therefore, give him into my care, I will dress him, I will feed him, I will satisfy his thirst and take all financial responsibility onto myself. I will also be as a father to him and he to me as a son, and he will be called by my name. Only he will have to learn in gymnasium, and you will see how much better your son is from now on."

"But I ask you, Reb Yerichom Gordon, won't they force him to convert?" Faige asked with tears streaming from her eyes.

---

21. A religious teacher of children.
22. The demon or place in the wilderness where the scapegoat is sent on Yom Kippur.
23. Student, one who goes to a government school.

"God forbid, God forbid, this isn't the case. It's only that they want him to learn in gymnasium. I can't send a son there, because aside from sons I have three daughters. If I had a son attending gymnasium, no other respectable family would want to marry into mine. Did you know that my daughter-in-law, Reva, the wife of my son Yitzchak, is from the family of Romma with the best connections in Sklau. How could I show my face before my in-laws?"

And Faige continued to cry and she said, "I have been greatly chastised by the Lord because my husband was taken from me. I have been left an unfortunate widow supporting myself with a hand-powered mill, and my strength isn't up to it. He is a wild son, he runs in the streets, and he doesn't want to work the hand mill even once. It isn't possible for me to provide for him, and I am very unhappy on this account. I will accede to your request only if he wants it so." And she went out of Gordon's house with a troubled and breaking heart because the Lord had continued to chastise her until she was forced to give up her son as a sin offering in place of a rich man's son to study in gymnasium. On arriving home, she told her son in broken words why the rich man had called her, thinking that he too would cry like her. But on hearing what Gordon wanted, the youth jumped and leapt like a goat from great joy. He didn't delay a moment, but ran to Gordon, and with open joy said to him, "My mother told me what you want to do with me, and here I am your true and simple servant in all that you command, only send me to school." And from that day, Bashka was Gordon's.

Three months of preparation passed, and for Bashka Gordon, the exam time arrived. He studied the preparatory lessons with all his strength, not that so much learning was required in those days. When he stood for the examination, he emerged crowned with the name of a good and attentive student, and they sat him in the first form. Bashka put on a shirt in the place of traditional clothing, and went out for the first time in a gymnasium student's uniform, with gold buttons that sparkled from afar. He gloried in and was proud of these, and in his spare time he walked from street to street to show everybody. He was in truth a handsome youth, smart also, but he was a fatherless orphan and had been unable to accept direction. If some-body chastised him with words he answered them with stones. In his wildness his hand had been against everyone, and everyone's hand against him. His mother had called him a "wild man" and the people in the street all called him, "Faige's city he-goat." But now he received new names, "Shkovart" and "Shkuler." His mother complained con-stantly to her acquaintances that she was devastated by the death of her husband, because if only he had lived her only son wouldn't be going to gymnasium. After two years passed she was comforted by the knowledge that her son went to school because it became a joy for her rather than a disaster. He studied with tremendous diligence and the school teachers all loved him, and when he finished the third form he received as presents sixty silver coins and a valuable book. The few Maskilim there were in those days became close to him. Doctor Nathanson spoke well of him in the house of another Maskil, and the man hired him in his free hours to teach his two sons to pre-pare them for gymnasium. So he was paid a real salary and support-ed his mother with this money. More yet, when he met his old friends in the streets and they called him derisive names, he didn't pounce on them and hit them as previously had been his rule, but with sweet and positive words told them about his happiness. In the course of three years he brought forty street kids like himself to the gymnasi-um, and Doctor Nathanson, Tzvi-Hirsh Rabinowitz, and the phar-macist Wyshvanski saw to their expenses and clothing. Bashka stud-ied with great diligence and good conduct, saying, "I don't want to dishonor the name of Gordon." Every year he advanced higher and higher, and when he finished learning in the gymnasium they sent him to the capital city, where according to many people he rose to the high rank of "State Counselor." He later did many good turns for the children of the rich man who had adopted him as a son. So from the sons of poor rebellious people were made respectable, high-placed men. The rich people and the observant Jews had thought that if they didn't send their children they could halt the Haskalah in it's path, but who can halt a flood that in the course of time will overflow all its banks? There was a big war, an internal war, between fathers and sons, mothers and daughters, and children of the observant fled their parents and scattered in every direction. This one cried, and that one cried, yet in every place they came to were found benefactors who supported them with advice and money.

# ⤜ Chapter Ten

Honorable readers! Here I must stray again from my story and let my thoughts float free after being imprisoned, as I compelled myself to write only about things I have seen or heard and not allowed myself to follow my muse. But my ambitions return, and therefore I will express my heart-felt thoughts and the understanding reader will judge them. Is it not known to all of us that it is the fault of the ultra-religious and the prideful rich that our nation has been brought down and feelings blackened against us. Our holy Torah has also been diminished because the majority of our people make light of the importance of our Torah and nation together, to the point where one who hates us and wants to scorn us to our faces just calls us "Jew" or "Hebrew." This condemnation and contempt is like a hot iron on living flesh, and a few, or maybe many during this time, left entirely from amongst us and are gone. If not for anti-Semitism coming twenty-four years ago to Berlin, the concept of the Lovers of Zion wouldn't be here now, and the Zionist movement wouldn't have come about five years ago, a great movement scattering light throughout the world like the revolutions of the sun. Who knows what would have finally come of all the hopes and aspirations of Israel. It didn't happen like all the ultra-religious supposed, that Israel would die in the melting pot of the Haskalah, God forbid. But when the Haskalah began to develop, it was precisely the rich and the religious who should have sent their sons to school, because at that time, they weren't forced to write on Shabbat, nor were they even required to go to school on Shabbat. On Sunday they could go to their schoolmates, their non-Jewish friends, and learn from them the Saturday lesson, and by Monday everybody would know the lessons, whether they were Jews or non-Jews. If they had sent the older youths who had been raised in the lap of Torah and Mitzvot and had mastered it all, and had they afterwards absorbed the Haskalah, then the Haskalah would have been to Judaism like a necklace on a neck. They would have risen and succeeded, bringing Judaism along with them. Moreover, our people didn't take to heart where it would end. At that time it would have been easy for them to found gymnasiums and universities for themselves, so that every father today wouldn't be compelled by fear and anxiety to sign that he gives his son of his own will into the hands of teachers, to desecrate the Sabbath and much more. And what did they do back then? Who were the majority of those going to gymnasium at the beginning? Street kids without morals and Derech Eretz,[24] or Yeshiva students who threw off the yoke of Yeshiva, service and the Torah, all together. And they were angry and vengeful against the rich and the home-owners who hadn't given them enough bread to satisfy themselves, even though they had labored for them. The house-wife looked out for herself, the maid looked out for herself, and the principal of the Yeshiva was at the head of them all. He was, according to many, like a bear in ambush, in their fear that he mark them out and strike. When these people took the Haskalah into their hands, it was seen by them as a lash to revenge themselves on those who had despised them and pursued them in the name of the power of the Torah. That is to say, wasn't it thought a mitzvah by us if we took a man who ate without ritually washing his hands and gave him as a sacrificial offering to the army, in the place of a rich man's son, or the son of an ultra-religious, and so-on and so-on? First these new Maskilim cast aside the Torah and commandments, next they became prideful in their knowledge and they caused heartaches for the religious, since God no longer had hands to hurt them or chastise them as before. That was their first revenge, and their second was that they attracted the young generation, children of upright parents who had lived by Torah and work. And the wind blowing in the world at that time stood by their right, because the young also want-

---

24. Proper Jewish behavior, the way of the land.

ed to inhale the air of freedom and liberation. But their parents hands turned them away and barred them from doing anything. The sons realized they had found new protectors who would see to their futures, so they left their parents all together and set out on a path paved for them by their new benefactors. They didn't stray right or left, and ten years later a new generation was born, a generation embracing near apostasy, entirely atheist, as we all know. At the beginnings of the birth of anti-Semitism there was an article from Helisivotgrad, I don't remember if it was in Ha-Melitz or Ha-Maggid, in which was written: "What is the Shulchan Aruch[25] to us? Isn't it already destroyed by mildew? We, ourselves, will make a new Shulchan Aruch. This we all know, that we shall not steal or murder, and aside from this there is nothing. And what did the Holy One, Blessed Be He, do in folding up all those ideas with the ideas of the majority of peoples in one package, and pulling it from the casket and scattering it amongst all the peoples in the world to its length and breadth? They were taught to make a Shulchan Aruch for themselves and call it by the name anti-Semitism, and by the laws of this Shulchan Aruch inflame themselves and strike our brothers leg upon thigh. In Germany came the first blow, in Kiev the second, in Bialystock the third, and on and on, and they judged us without the Shulchan Aruch. So see and accept proof that it is no good for everyone to make a Shulchan Aruch for himself. Who is guilty for our disaster and all the disasters that befall us if not the ultra-Orthodox, who don't understand from beginning to end, and think that the ideas of men are worthless. The Haskalah has done us a great good, because before the Haskalah we were as dust underfoot, our pride and spirit together. We were contemptible and despised and we ceased to be men not only in their eyes but also in our eyes. We were a target half scorned at the leisure of the Polish. Once, at a great feast in the house of a prince, they took two Jews and gave them medicine to make them vomit in the greatest measure and tied their beards together, this to that. They stood them in the middle of a room around which

---

25. Lit. "The Arranged Table." The definitive codification of Jewish law from the middle ages.

sat all of the guests, and everyone can understand the situation of these wretches. Truly this is an eternal hatred for an eternal people, a hatred that will not weaken as long as we dwell on foreign land. The discrimination will not cease. But the difference is this: Before the birth of the Haskalah they hated us in thinking that we were unsuccessful people, we were as savages in their eyes. Afterwards, they hated us for our abilities and our much higher diligence. If the hatred will not cease, isn't it better that they hate us for our diligence and ability, and not for our brutishness and lack of humanity? So on every front the Haskalah has brought us improvement, and most of all, she brought us the Zionist movement."

Now honorable readers, it's for you to judge the matter. Is not the Zionist movement the second kingdom come in our lifetimes to improve our conditions? Yet another benefit is that she has come to repair that which perverted the Haskalah through the sin of not understanding how to receive it. That which was lacking for us in the Haskalah will be completed for us in the Zionist movement. In conclusion, she has come to make us whole and to return to us what the first Haskalah took from us, this being; Love of Torah, Love of our Land, our nation and brotherhood. Instead of everyone sitting within his own circle by himself we will sit like brothers together. The true religious will be remembered with goodwill and blessings as those who came to the aid of the Lord in their heroism. If the Lord is with us, we all extend a helping hand, each man to his neighbor, and we won't go about any more in anger and rudeness like our fathers did. Although there are found Zionists who are yet far from our Torah, it's not terrible, because won't they return to us? Their spirit will return to their land with them, and bring on them a blessing.

And when all the religious are absorbed, they and their children into this great movement, then the Lord will return us from captivity, and we will go up to the land of Israel and flower as before. But if you also do like the deeds of the generation of the Haskalah, isn't it just yourselves you are holding back and not your children, the young people who aspire to the movement and to life? They will be taken into the great movement that will soon fill the ancient void, and if you withhold this happiness from them, who knows what your children and your children's children will say later?

# ⌇ Chapter Eleven

The house of Kloyna was then in the middle of construction, and it was his second house, but he would not complete it. They said about him that he was the first head of the Jews of Dvinsk. In the days of the kidnappers he did as all the profiteers did.[26] Kloyna was the Gabbi, the new administrator, head of the congregation and the mohel. In his house were stored all the records of the community, of the dead and the living. In summary, he was head and first amongst the community of the Israel in Dvinsk. They said about him that he had a good qualities and bad. For example, if a Jew had died in Dvinsk he was buried immediately, and if a father had to make a Brit for his son, it was the custom to prepare all day and wait for guests, sometimes drawing the thing out until evening. But when Kloyna rose to power, he reversed the system. When he came to a man's house to circumcise his son, he wouldn't delay even a moment, although many times they said to him, "Reb Kloyna, the Baal[27] Brit has gone out but will return in a moment, and it's proper to wait for him." He wouldn't even wait for the father. And if somebody died he would say, "What's the big fuss? Wait a little, wait. To bury a Jewish man you rush and to make a Jew you delay!" Despite this, he buried many Jews, and not just after their deaths but also while they were still alive, as did all those profiteers in that time. This burial for the children, the other for the adults.

---

26. *[Original footnote]* And this was the fate of the children: They were sent to a far province, there they were given to a farmer or a discharged soldier to raise and to force them to give up their religion. They remained there until they were eighteen, then they were brought to the army where they served twenty-five years. Accordingly, most of these unfortunates never returned to their parents or their people, because most of the parents died from anguish. The kidnappers and their employers were all Jews, and they didn't remember the covenant of brothers in order to profit from injustice. Theirs was the profit of Jacob's sons.

27. The father.

I heard from the lips of a mother of a kidnapped boy who told me, "Fifteen years have passed since the criminal night and every time I tell about it my blood boils inside me and I see it as if it were happening now. My husband had died, and I had two sons, one married and the other six years old. Erev Simchat Torah was the night. I lived in a small humble house and my son slept in my bosom. I was thinking that the next day I would go with him to the village of the Wyskam settlement where there is a farmer who knew my husband, peace be on him, and he will hide my son as he did last year. It didn't come into my heart that the evening of the festival of Simchat Torah, in which they drink and get drunk, they will do a thing like this. I was asleep, and the door was closed with a wooden bolt, but they broke it, and before I could figure out what was happening, the boy was in the hands of the kidnappers. They didn't heed my broken screams to the highest heavens and they left. Yes, they were drinking and were drunk, these men, on the profits of the harvest they made of us. When I went that morning to Kloyna, he was sitting at a table arrayed with rich foods. My heart was filled with grave wounds, and I fell at his feet and cried and implored him to return my son, the soft little boy, and I would bless him with many blessings. But he answered me, "I have nothing to do with whether it is your son or the son of another woman who is taken, but if he is in our hands we can't return him to you." I saw that he had set his heart like a stone and even poured salt on my wounds by saying, "Don't be afraid, this little one will grow to be big. If he will not grow up in your house, then in the house of somebody else." When I heard these words I poured out my wrath on him, and in my anger I gave him all of the curses written in the Torah, then I left. It's true that I saw there was revenge on this murderer, but did this heal me? Behold I am sixty years old today and much time has passed, but my wounded heart hasn't healed and never will."

Another poor woman had a son, a lad of sixteen years, who was her sole support. When the son was taken to the army, the mother went to cry and plead before Kloyna on behalf of her son, as he was sitting and drinking tea in the morning. When she saw that he wasn't paying attention to her words, she cried loudly, "Cursed you will be, murderer. Your wife will be a widow and your children orphans like my son. The money you took for my son will change to a curse in your guts, because it's my blood and the blood of my son you are drinking." Even then he didn't answer her a word, only drank the tea and said, "Ah, How good. How sweet this tea is!"

A couple of years passed, then the wrath went out on Kloyna. His exact crime, I don't know, only that he was judged and sent to Siberia. He was sent away about the time we arrived in Dvinsk. I never saw him, just his stone house that stood in the middle of construction because he started to build it but couldn't finish it. Then, a thing occurred which was like a healing medicine to the whole city of Dvinsk, and they talked about this wonder for a long time, all of the people of the city from the least to the greatest.

A soldier from the city of Vitabesk wrote a letter to his mother. The letter was carried through many homes and shops, and every time they read the letter, people in the crowd drank a round on it, and here are the words of the letter!

*Dear Mother. Yes there is a God judging in the land! Did you know that Kloyna is now in the city of Vitabesk, and he is doing here the same things he did in Dvinsk? There he was making changes all over the city, and also here in Vitabesk he is making changes all over the city, with a broom.[28] But listen, my mother, do you not remember eight years ago when I got the first letter from you, full of your mourning and loss, and amongst your words you told me that you yelled at Kloyna, "Murder! Isn't it the blood of my dear son you drink and not tea!" and he answered you something like this, "Ah, How good, How sweet!" as if it was sweet to wound us and drink our blood. Now I have seen our enemy more than I could imagine or hope. A couple of weeks ago I was sent, myself and my comrades in arms, to guard prisoners who were being sent from the prison to clean the streets of Vitabesk. When I looked at the prisoners, I picked out Reb Kloyna even though it was*

---

28. *[Original footnote]* Yiddish for this line from the letter.

*hard to recognize him. He was pulling a barrow and a broom to clean the streets and gather the manure, and to haul it outside the city after-wards and dump it there. At first, I was overcome by the urge to take revenge on him, not for my blood because I am a man now, but your blood, dear mother, your blood which has poured like water onto the ground. But then I scolded myself and said, "Evil fool, from him will you take revenge? From him? The little you can see of his condition now and what can be expected for him in the future, is that a small revenge? No! No! To repay good in the place of evil, that is true revenge." At that moment I took a cigarette from my pocket, and when I saw that my comrades weren't observing I gave it to him, and he gazed at me with great thanks. And when the time came for them to haul the manure out, I said that he should pull the smallest load because he was the weakest of them all. Truthfully, he isn't the Kloyna he once was, his wide fat belly now hangs like a sack and his full handsome face is gaunt and blackened. All week he worked in the streets and when it was my turn to change duty with another soldier, I requested my commander that he send me back in somebody else's place. I am liked by all the offi-cers due to my usefulness and diligence, so he didn't turn me away empty. I remained as a guard, and I did everything in my power that I could to do good by him. I even gave him food and money, according to what I could obtain. On his sixth day of work, when all the other prisoners went to eat the afternoon bread, I took him into my custody and went with him to a restaurant. There I bought us both meals and cigarettes, and I also gave him money. And that day, when he finished eating, he said to me, "My son, My son. Who are you that you are so merciful on a wretch like me?"*

*"The heart knows the bitterness of the soul," I answered him, "I was also a wretch twelve years ago on account of you, Mr. Kloyna, because I am the son of the widow Devorah for whom I was the sole support." And when I caused him to recall my name and the name of my dear mother, he fell to the ground in a faint. I picked him up and request-ed our officer send him to recuperate because he was sick. I comforted him and told him that if I hadn't been destroyed by the tortures of my*

*sorrows as a far wandering youth, nor should he lose hope in the Lord that he who is smitten may also be made well. But he didn't accept the consolation and the next week he was sent elsewhere. Believe me, dear mother, that he belongs to God. If it were in my hands to save him, then I would save him with all my heart and soul, I grew so warm and tender to him. But if the Lord smites a man, who can heal him? Trust in the Lord, mother, and in a little while you will see your son, because in five months I will have completed twelve years of my service. Then I will be sent for a year of leave to see you and live with you, to make you whole and comfort you for your mourning. You will see that I am completely healthy, tall and strong, and you will see and rejoice in your heart because I've also learned the Russian language in every detail and grammatical rule. My commander has told me many times, "Hirshka! When you get to your city you can be a good teacher of the Russian language." I hope that in another three years I will be permanently discharged, because the good and just Tsar Alexander the Second has given the decree that service be for fifteen years and not twenty five, and we hope that we are included in this accounting. Live and be well, my mother, live and trust in the Lord, and Shalom to you and to all our brothers scattered to all extremes of the land and far islands.*

*Your son who longs to see you, Hirsch Kvillikam*

## ⤳ Chapter Twelve

The house of Meir "Angry Cat" stood at the center of a main street. I never got to know Meir himself, because he was already dead, but I knew his wife. She had a daughter, although not her birth daughter as she had no children, but a poor young girl, a relation, whom she took in as a small child to bring up. It was told about Mrs. "Angry Cat" that when she was young, she bought a cat to raise, and she entertained herself by putting all sorts of jewelry on it. She placed on its neck a string of expensive pearls that she wore about her own throat, which was worth three thousand silver coins, and she put on his legs all of her countless rings, every last one. A locket with a picture set in precious stones she laid amidst the pearls on the heart of the cat, then she took him on her arm to the railing to see his beauty in the light of the sun. When she reached the railing, the cat jumped and fled with the valuables, and he never returned to this day. Therefore, she was known forever after as "Angry Cat," and her husband was also known by this name, Meir "Angry Cat." During the years we lived in Dvinsk, she married off the daughter she had brought up. After two years, the two of them, the daughter and her husband, wanted to throw her out of the house, saying to her, "Aren't you a stranger here? Our Uncle Meir bequeathed us this house, what are you doing here! But, if you want to live here and not interfere in our business, fine. Live here and eat, nothing more."

The rich woman started to cry and she said, "Cursed is the day that I brought this sorrow into my house. The townsfolk laughed at me many years ago because I adorned my cat with precious jewelry worth five thousand silver coins and he fled from me, and for this they call me "Angry Cat." May the Lord grant me the ability to cause this cat of mine to also flee me also. I gave her three times five thousand silver coins, and they called me afterwards a hundred derogatory names. I don't take it to heart, only let me be freed from my disaster. My dear friend," she continued to cry, unable to stand upright, "Will you not take a lesson from me? I advise every woman that if the Lord rewards her with children, good, but otherwise not to set her heart to take strange children into her house, because they are strangers. The strangers have shortened my life with their goodness, and in the end, either they will drive me from my dainty home that was prepared for my old age, or they will take themselves away. If only she had been raised in her parent's house in poverty. Then if I had given her one thousand silver coins as a dowry on her betrothal day, she would have kissed my hands and feet and I would have been for her "Dear Aunty" beyond compare. Since she was raised in my house like a king's daughter, and I didn't withhold from her anything her heart desired and made her a rich woman, now she wants to inherit me while I'm still alive." And as she foretold, she was later forced to leave her home.

The house of Reb Zacharia Zalkind was very large and beautiful. He was greatly learned in Torah, he feared the heavens, and was a great scholar. The Hassidim tell about his father, Reb Leibel the Lazy, that when the Hassidim from Dvinsk came to the Rabbi Reb Mendle z"l in Lebovitch and asked his advice, on their telling him they were from Dvinsk, he said to them "Isn't Liebelah the Lazy in your city? So why come to me?" One time, Zalkind sat talking with my father z"l and he said in these words, "Reb Yosel," (so was called my father z"l), "Do you remember the time the two of us sat in Volozhin[29] repairing cloth boots when we were learning from the Gaon Reb Itzlick z"l." This I must elucidate, that Reb Zacharia wasn't involved with the rift concerning the Rabbis, for better or worse, and he had studied with Reb Itzlick z"l and paid great respect to all of our Gaonim. He was a very rich man, with businesses expanding throughout the land, and it was said about him that he had spoken a couple of times with Tsar Nicholas the First.

The House of Malkiel began to shine. The brothers began to show the world their greatness, and these are their names; Shmuel, Kalan, Bartzig, Itza, and Zelig. The last of these was a great idiot, he lived in the Malkiel courtyard and the successful Shmuel supported him and his daughters, one of whom was also a great fool. I remember when Zelig walked in the courtyard, it was his job to drive all the children from the yard. Then the children would all hold up their little hands and wave "Shalom" to him, then with great speed extend their middle fingers, making him mad. Afterwards the little boys and girls would return and count on their hands how many middle fingers Zelig got that day, and this was great amusement for the children.

Shmuel's wife, Chaya-Mona, was of a beautiful appearance and very wise, and everyone called her the queen of the family. Shmuel

---

29. The largest and most famous Yeshiva of Belarus.

was then a member of the local council, but the citizens of the city said that he was not the counselor but she, for every meeting and each session he had to attend, he didn't go by himself but with her. There was a shul for Hassidim in the house of Chaya-Mona's parents, Avrahamiel Efrati and his wife Sarah Faige, and they were respected people, generous, of great integrity.

❧

The memories of my childhood I have laid before you, honorable readers, without cosmetics, just events as they were. I don't know any more because in 1871 my father settled in the city of Riga, so my observations were completed. I have fulfilled the promise that I made to myself, that if the opportunity came to hand, I would write a memoir. Earlier, my pen wasn't strong enough to write memoirs, because then was a time full of pleasant visions and dreams. Everybody pays attention only to the present; the past isn't remembered and no attention is given to the future. Every writer and author writes warnings to the younger generation, "Go to the light of the present, take it in your grasp and don't let it slacken. The past is not for us and don't aspire to the future." Then the "present" arrives by itself and slaps them in the face and says, "Be done with your pleasant dreams! Realize that you don't have a present. Look behind you and see a great chain, a strong chain, that if you only grasp it will lead you to a good future, because only in the future can you expect happiness." I also value the chain of the past and therefore I hold onto it with both hands, but I value even more the future and say, "Happy is he who waits and arrives." Now I have found it proper to write down the past from the memories of my youth.

*Lodz, 3 Tamuz 1902, The Author*

# ⌒ From Memories of My Youth

One more episode I must add to the memories of my youth, and due to its great importance, I'm putting it in it's own section.

Around 1863 or 1864 news was heard in the city of Dvinsk, news that occupied the whole community, young and old. A convert from the land of Germany who had converted to Judaism there was coming to Dvinsk. Many people talked about him, and each told of his origins differently. One said that he was the son of the German king, another said he was the son of the king's teacher.

One day, my father z"l returned full of joy and told us that he saw the convert in the house of Reb Israel Horowitz that day, where he had spoken with him. My mother z"l, and even though we were little girls, also my sister and I, cupped our ears to hear the words of my father. We greedily swallowed everything he said about the convert's appearance, wisdom, good heart and gentility, and how he had learned Hebrew and Chumash[30] in Germany. How great was our desire to see him and speak with him, but how could we possibly hope for a joy like this, to see the righteous convert and speak with him? He was always at Freidlander's house or Horowitz's house, these being the greatest and richest in the city.

Then came the day that two young men dressed in splendid clothing arrived at our house. One of the young men approached our father z"l and said, "Reb Yosef. Here I have brought you an honest student and it will benefit him if you study Talmud and Bible with him for an hour or two every day." The second young man approached to greet

---

30. The Five Books of Moses.

my father, and my father hugged him in his arms and kissed him twice saying, "Come in, blessed is the Lord, sit on my right, and like a seal on my heart I shall place you always." The first young man who was a member of the Friedlander family left, and my father called to my mother saying, "Shaina, come here and let me present you to Reb Yitzchak, the righteous convert from Germany." My mother respectfully asked after his health, and we stood far back, afraid to approach him. But on the second day the man said to my father, "Sir Teacher, I must get to know all the members of your household, even the little ones, because you are all dear to me, very precious." From that day I became accustomed to him and talked with him. After his studying, he would sit with us a long while and talk with us, telling us about the customs in his land, and anything he could do to give us pleasure he didn't hold back. Every day he was more and more dear and honored in our eyes, in our seeing the goodness of his heart, his wisdom, and his modesty, because he wasn't prideful even with the smallest of the small. He studied Bible and Talmud. He started the Bible from the beginning and the Talmud with tractate Baba Metzia from the first chapter "Two are Holding." I also remember the time when he finished a chapter he was learning and understood it properly. He rose from his place and kissed my father saying, "Sir Teacher, if only you could feel now the emotions in my heart, then you could comprehend that there is no word in my vocabulary to thank you for this precious learning. A treasure of great value is hidden in the Talmud, nothing in it is worthless. Yes, yes, this valuable learning had been lacking in me. Now I feel that it fills up my soul inside." My mother sometimes said to my father, "What I really want is to hear about his history from his own mouth. But to ask him to tell it isn't proper, because maybe there is something hidden in his story, and since he is an honest man, he couldn't fabricate and answer our request while remaining tranquil in his heart. It's not urgent, we will wait until he tells us of his own volition." After a month passed, he rented an apartment in the house of Masha Mamin in the courtyard where we lived, in order to be near us always, and he was very happy. He was very beloved by us and we fulfilled with alacrity anything he asked of us. My brother Beryl Menkin, who is now a Rabbi in Cardiff (England), was then a two year old boy, and didn't leave him alone for a moment. When he saw Reb Yitzchak take out a pinch of tobacco to smoke he would say with exaggerated love, "Reb Yitzchak, do you want a wooden match?" When Reb Yitzchak nodded his head, my brother ran quickly to bring it to him. His childish happiness was a joy beyond compare when Reb Yitzchak took the wooden match from his little hand, thanked him, and patted him on the cheek. One time, Reb Yitzchak left our house, but immediately afterwards the door opened again and he returned quickly with a face as white as death. My parents were very shaken, and he was unable to speak, just pointed with his finger at the door. My mother went out and saw that there was a piece of pork tied next to the door of our house. She asked around and sought after what had occurred, and some youths told her that the Christian maiden who lived in our courtyard had done this thing. My mother asked her "Why?" She answered, "Why did this one make us abominable by becoming a Jew? I would slay him right now if only I were able." He couldn't eat bread all that day because he was depressed. He was a complete Tzaddik, none were like him. One time when my mother sent me to bring him tea in the morning, he was standing in his room praying. He wore tefillin with a big tallit over his head and back, and the siddur in his hand was wet from his tears. When I saw this I was frightened. I set the tea on his table and went quickly out of the room. When I told my father he was amazed and commanded us not to interrupt Yitzchak again during his prayers.

One day he arrived at our house earlier than he usually came and was very happy and light-hearted. His joy was apparent on his face, and my father asked him, "Reb Yitzchak, you have news today. Would that you always be so happy."

"Yes, yes, my dear friend. On account of this I came early today. Please know, my dear friend, that today makes two years since I was granted my heart's desire and my name was called in Israel, Yitzchak ben Avraham,[31] and this day was the happiest of all the days of my

---

31. Male converts to Judaism take the surname "son of Abraham," female converts "daughter of Sarah."

life. It's a wonder to me that for almost eight months I have been in your house, regarded as a beloved son in your eyes, and beyond doubt your souls have desired to hear about my history from my own mouth. Despite this you have never asked me once, and you surely knew that I wouldn't withhold from you any desire, even the most difficult thing. Strangers weary me with their questions, but you, my dears, don't make any request of me. Here I am on this happy day to tell you of my origins, from my childhood up through the present, and give praise and thanks to the Lord for bringing me to this day. Here I am studying Bible and Talmud and understanding what I learn, and I have learned very much during this period." He sat down next to my father and we all sat around him to listen to his words, and here they are:

My father was the palace administrator (Kammarharar) for King Wilhelm in Germany, but due to illness he was given leave and returned to his estate in Landsberg, not far from Berlin. His name is Erlich. My father is Lutheran and my mother is Catholic. In my childhood I was a heretic, without belief in the faith of my father, and my mother was always complaining that she didn't know what would become of me. I had no desire to go to church, and when I occasionally attended on her orders, I didn't pay any attention to the words of the priest. In my studies in school, in religion class, I asked so many questions that the teacher became short-tempered and angry, and shouted loudly, "Stupid boy, what do you want! Listen and don't ask. If you multiply your questions you won't learn a thing." But I was stubborn, "If you won't describe for me with sound logic this passage that goes against common sense, comprehension and reason, I won't learn it." So he set me on my knees in the corner and all of the students laughed at me. But I didn't mind his disciplining me. This happened many times until the priest wearied of bearing my stubborn rebelliousness. He came to my mother's house and complained in her ears that I was a complete atheist and a non-believer in everything. So my mother took me from the school, and on the advice of my sister who was married to the administrator of the Staten district, I was put in a Catholic seminary to be made into a priest, despite my anger and fury. My mother's instructions lay heavy on me because I was a prisoner of this obedient band, who were all men of God. My father didn't interfere with my education and sometimes he laughed inside when he saw the anger of my mother. When I went to my new school to hear these new, or old lessons, I started doing the same as before, surrounding them with questions and objections that they couldn't bear. At my mother's instructions they began to pressure me with words and punishments. Once when I went to my father to complain about the harshness of my teachers, he said laughing, "Why do you inform them what you are thinking in your heart?" I wanted to act according to my father's advice; to be at peace with them and not tell them my hearts thoughts, but I wasn't able, because my spirit compelled me. So I was at war, war with my mother and war with my soul's feelings, and a whole year I suffered pains in the body and pains in my soul until I couldn't bear it and fled the place never to return. I was thirteen years old then, and my father sent me to a school in Berlin. There I studied three years until I completed the course, and when I finished, my father took me into his business to supervise his accounts since he knew that I had mastered accounting. Good times arrived for me, days of freedom and days of delight. Every day I worked a couple hours at my desk, because I had to figure many accounts, like the produce of my father's fields. His houses and the village brought him an income of forty thousand silver coins per year, and all the accounts were under my control. My father was satisfied, and I loved him and honored him like an angel on high who had thrust away all of my sorrows, because when I came under my father's patronage my mother ceased quarreling with me. But despite this, she dealt badly with my father and I on account of his letting me be free-spirited. I loved the hunt, and whenever I had free time I went to hunt animals and birds. When I lay in bed at night I read books, not novels, but books full of serious matters and delights. While I was in school in Berlin I bought myself a world almanac in the German language and this I valued more than gold. In my free time I didn't put it down until I had it almost memorized, also the Bible I read and reread many times, and other books reproduced in German. I read these books every night until I fell asleep. Often I was occupied with strange thoughts, thoughts that mystified me how and in what manner they stole into my brain. But as they came, so did they go, making room for others.

A day of holiday arrived for us and I had the day off from work. My mother and younger brother came to my room and asked me to travel with them to the great cathedral in Berlin. I knew they would go to the Catholic church, and I was consumed with hatred for the priests for all the needless suffering they had caused me during the year I studied with them. I put them off with a lie and promised to go after them on my horse. They believed me, because they knew how much I loved to ride, and they set off. Once they had left the courtyard, I saddled my horse, slung my gun over my shoulder, and whistled to my faithful dog who came to my side. My horse was a beautiful stallion that swallowed the miles at a gallop. I mounted him and rode, not to the church and not to Berlin, but to the forest to hunt. I covered the forest to its length and breadth without shooting a thing because I wasn't out for a hunt. My spirit had brought me here, my spirit bore me and lifted me on imaginary wings, upward and outward without end. I hadn't eaten, except for breakfast bread, but I didn't feel hungry, thirsty or tired, nor did I sense that my horse began to move slower. I just wanted to soar to the heights and ask what is good for a man, how can he find peace for his soul and his feelings? Can it be possible that he find satisfaction in mere food, drink and fine clothes? Will these cheer the soul that seeks things more pleasant and noble? I didn't notice that my horse stood leaning against a tree as I flew and soared, and all the days of my youth passed before me: My mother's rules, my teacher's rules, my questions, their answers and punishments, and my bitterness and stubborn rebellion. I weighed it all on the scale in my mind and found that I was still far from my goal, a great distance, and God knows if I could obtain it. Yes, I thought, only God who examines our hearts will pardon me and help me, as you will hear in the course of my story. I plumbed the depths of my thoughts and didn't know my soul. Then behold! The dog began to bark loudly, and pulled strongly at the corner of my cloak until I roused from my meditative state. I opened my eyes and it was dark all around. I looked up at the thickening and blackening skies, and a great wind came up and made the trees groan. The branches shuddered and moved violently, like the arteries of my heart, and they bent down their tips from above my head to touch my ears, as if to say to me in noisy voices, "Fool! Don't you see that it's dark all around you and soon lightning and thunder will fill the forest. Get moving fast, don't stand there. Save your life!" These words, or thoughts, urged me on and put hope in my heart, and the darkness and storm in the forest brought me clarity of thought. I mounted my horse, and even though he was hungry and tired, he still went at a gallop as if I had charmed him with Arabic words. I stroked his mane and off he went, and my dog came after us. I knew that it was yet very far to my father's house, and I wouldn't arrive before the rain overtook me, so I turned my horse up the path that went to the house of the lessee. He held a large portion of my father's land by lease, he was a learned and upright Jew, who was also rich and good-hearted. But before I could reach his house, the rain poured down with lightning and awful thunderclaps sounding their voice and showing their great destructiveness. I took pleasure in this terrible vision and didn't know why. My horse rose to the task, but when I saw that I was close to the lessee's house, I dismounted and grasped his reins and led the two of us, slowly and with dignity, despite the heavy rain coming down. My dog ran ahead, apparently he ran to notify the lessee's household that I was on the way, because in another minute, the lessee and his servant were out to greet me. The servant took my soaking jacket and my horse and gave me a different jacket in exchange, and the lessee put his arm around me and hurried me into the house. There I sat down to rest and my host asked if I had trekked long in the rain. "The lightning and the rain have so engaged me," I answered, "that I didn't feel the rain. I imagined that on the day the Torah was given to Israel there wasn't lightning like this. So why this lightning now? Isn't the Torah already given?"

"Not to everyone, my honored Sir," answered the lessee with a gaze that penetrated to my heart. These wise words rocked my cherished thoughts, as if a new spirit had entered inside me, and the idea that was hidden in his words transformed me into a different man. I had plumbed the depths of my thoughts and ended up in my heart, and now I had to figure out a course of action from all of this. The mistress of the house came in and set food before me and sweetly requested me to eat. Then I remembered I hadn't eaten all day. I gazed around the room we were sitting in and behold, it was full of splendor and beauty more beyond that of regular days, and I asked energetically, "Tell me please my friend, do you also have a holiday?"

"Yes sir," the lessee answered me, "In a little while the Sabbath will arrive in beauty and glory and we Jews must greet it in rejoicing and splendor. The Sabbath is the best present that was hidden in the vault of the Lord of the World that he graciously gave us, so we must acknowledge that goodness." Every word he spoke and every syllable that came from his lips were like balm to my soul, because he spoke wisely.

This good man stood at my right to serve me and didn't lift his eyes from me. Apparently he understood my thoughts, and he said:

"My dear young man. If only you wished to honor me and to stay here and eat supper with us this evening, then I would know I have found favor in your eyes. Please don't refuse. I will send the Lady, your mother, a messenger to inform her that you are here with us this evening." "I accept the invitation with all my heart and soul," I answered him, "With joy I contemplate sitting in the company of such upright people as yourselves. But don't inform my mother of any of this, she will think that I'm in Berlin."

The room that I sat in was full of light and cheer. A silver candelabra with seven stalks sparkled on the great table which was covered with an fine tablecloth. Candles on the walls cast light from every side. The master of the house went to another room to pray, and when he returned we all sat down to the table. I sat to the right of my host, and as we sat at the table he elucidated for me the value of the Sabbath and other precious things that I should know. Every question I asked he answered me sensibly and knowledgeably, and I felt I was in a different world. The evening left a good impression on my heart and from that day on my love for and trust in this man grew, until I made him my secret advisor. Every Friday night I went to this dear Jew and celebrated their Sabbath in their family circle. I told him of every precious and secret thing I had and consulted with him, because I felt in my soul that this man was very near to me.

One day I sat at my desk to work, but I had lost a vital ledger. I started to search for it and to rummage through all of the letters and bills that were in the writing drawer, but it wasn't there. I searched the top drawers and the bottom drawers and it wasn't there. I opened one drawer that had another drawer inside, and within that drawer I found a small leather sack, wrapped up and tucked away. I opened it and discovered letters in old, faded script, and although the writing wasn't smudged, I still couldn't read it. I took the sack and hid it in my pocket, closed the bottom drawer and continued to search for the ledger. Then my father came in and said to me, "I forgot to tell you that I found this vital ledger under the desk yesterday and put it in my pocket. Now wake up and be more careful in what you're doing, because if it hadn't been found we might have been greatly damaged." I took the ledger from my father's hand and bowed my head to show that he was justified, but I wasn't able to answer him a word, as the desire burned within me to know what was in these new found letters. My workday passed, I closed up the desk, put on my overcoat, saddled my horse and galloped off to my friend and companion, to see if he could find the basis of the words in the letter. I arrived at his house and he greeted me joyfully.

"I have an urgent matter for you my friend," I said to him, so he escorted me to his special room and closed the door behind him. I related to him a summary of what had happened, and showed him what I had found. "It's Hebrew writing," he cried, and read thirstily in great astonishment. He began reading through every letter one after another, and he lost his voice from amazement, and shock was plain on his face. He read every letter from beginning to end and then said to me with a radiant face, "My dear friend, your father and your grandfather were Jews. His father gave up his religion under compulsion during the great destruction that took place in Germany. In order to save himself from death, he accepted the Lutheran faith with his wife and children, amongst whom your father was numbered, then ten years old. His genealogy is written in the letter, along with which family in Israel he is from, his name and in what city the conversion took place." He read all the letters to me from start to finish, translating to German.

When he finished reading, I cried ecstatically, "What a find I have made! Now I draw close to my goal. The Lord has helped me. To the rock from whence I was cleaved I shall return. The Lord is the God of my fathers and will also be my God, and Israel is my people. It's already a year that I've walked about carrying inside the thought of becoming a Jew, and now I will be so, whatever may come."

This man, even though he had understood my thoughts from before, still became very worked up and asked me, "My friend, maybe this is just a mirage to allay some other problem, and after a while you will regain your composure? A step so grave and exalted isn't made in one night. Haven't you read about many of the events that happened to our unfortunate people who have been found for most of their history in bitter exile; the servitude, the hardships, the robbery and murder we suffered from many cruel savages. Now it's been ten years since the ruler of this land freed and liberated us. "The Jew is also a human being," they said, "All of them, from the least to the greatest. Emancipation and equality will be given to him like all men." The cries of the masses still ring in my ears from '48: "Liberty. Fraternity. Equality. There's no difference between the Jews and the Germans! Open the ghetto gates!" Now things are good for us. Now positive and compassionate words are heard. If only it will remain so. But my dear friend, will these enlightened days be extended? Will they continue? Time will tell. This isn't the first time such a false light has appeared to us. Didn't Spain give us freedom and liberty almost beyond measure, and with what did we leave there? That is known to all. You are the son of a great and honored man, a world full of honor and prestige awaits you. Will you abandon all of this to join a wretched people and be tortured when they are tortured? Not so. Not so, my friend."

"No, No," I cried, "I will not do otherwise. My grandfather sold his faith for his life and I will return to the Lord and buy it back for me and my descendants forever. I will return again to my people. May God test me so, and more also. Please don't speak to me any more about this issue." From that day forth he thought of me as a Jew. I divested myself of many things that are allowed to all peoples but forbidden to Israel. The dear man remained my secret advisor, and every time I came to his house he taught me Torah. He translated many books for me that had not yet been translated, and he strove to obtain for me those that were translated. His primary advice was that I fulfill my obligation to the army of my own free will, because I was eighteen, and doubtless I would lose much time later in changing my condition. I served for a whole year in the cavalry and I attained the rank of a junior officer and I also received a medal for my skill (and he showed us his insignia and medal). When I fulfilled my service I returned to my father's house, and there I began to employ my skill to speed me to my goal. I wrote a letter of request to the king himself and I attached the Hebrew letters inside it. A year went past and I was summoned to the great council, and there was asked different questions. In the end, they intended to send me to a mental asylum, but many helpful people stood by me and I wasn't sent there. They called in doctors who examined me and decided unanimously that I was healthy and whole, and then they began to consider the matter seriously. After their consultations were finished, they said that if my father will agree to the thing, they will give me my wish. But if he didn't agree, I would be forbidden from it by law, sentenced to five years of hard labor, and stripped of my standing and rights. When the time arrived for my father to stand before the seat of Justice, he was very upset because he was a man of faith and peace. He had never done another man wrong or been involved in anything that was against the laws of the land, and he asked me, "What is this about?" So I answered, "Don't be frightened, father. I haven't stolen or robbed, I am only returning to the God of my ancestors and of my people. Your grandfather was a Jew and I am returning there." Two tear drops rolled down his cheeks from his eyes, but they weren't tears of hate and condemnation, but tears of despair because we would be separated forever and his love for me was a true love. He didn't say another thing, just sat at his desk as I accounted for him all the matters of his estate. I went over all the accounts and notes, and nothing was lacking. He placed a pouch on the table with about two thousand silver coins and wrote on it these few words, "You have served me faithfully for three years, here are your wages." But I didn't touch a bit of it and I went out of his house never to return. I didn't take anything with me from my father's house, except for the name Erlich. He traveled to Berlin and I traveled to Breslau. I lived in the house of the Rabbi of Breslau and waited for the verdict, if I would be imprisoned or free. Even in Berlin I had beloved friends who kept me informed of all the happenings there. I received a letter from one of my friends in which he wrote, "Your honorable father, on arriving at the courthouse, was asked by the chief justice if he agreed with your plan to convert to Judaism, and he answered 'Yes'." He did this because he loved me and didn't want to hurt me, and he knew that without his approval I would have had laid on me an awful sentence that would bring even more shame on his family than a son who converts to Judaism. So he signed his name that he agreed to the wishes of his son. I was luminous and happy, but I waited another six months before they returned my letter with permission to become a Jew. All this time I lived in the house of the Rebbe who taught me to read Hebrew and also taught me Torah. I was careful in fully performing all of the Mitzvot according to the faith of Israel, only on Sabbath before sunset I lit myself a cigarette to smoke. One time the Rabbi saw what I was doing and it wasn't right in his eyes. He said to me kindly and calmly, "I hope when you accept the full yoke of the kingdom of heaven you won't do this thing again. If you had only waited another hour you would have observed the Shabbat properly." Then I answered him, "Rebbe, don't think that I can't restrain myself from smoking, God forbid, that isn't it. Didn't our Sages of Blessed Memory record, "A non-Jew who observes the Sabbath is punished by death" because is written in the Torah, "The Sabbath is a sign between me and between the children of Israel." How could I sin in my soul and transgress the words of the Torah!"

The Rabbi cried from joy and strong emotions and blessed me and from then on I was the apple of his eye.[32] He arranged many entertainments on my behalf to amuse me until I received the written approval, to the delight of my hearts and the hearts of those who loved me. Then the rabbi and the leading lights of the city began to make preparation for my admission into the impossible. Rabbis and rich men came from many cities to share in my happiness. On the morning of that day all the invited guests came to the house of the rabbi and a Torah scroll was brought, and the rabbi read from the scroll the parsha *Lech-Lecha* "and Abraham was ninety-nine years old, etc. . . . ." When everything was prepared, the rabbi approached me and said, "My son, maybe we should bind your hands and feet, so you won't cause some accident?" So I answered, "God forbid. Is it possible I couldn't make this sacrifice to the Lord when if he sought my life I would give it to him with all of my heart?" And they did with me as I requested and I was named Yitzchak ben Avraham, and here I am today two years in the Jewish world. They ate and drank and rejoiced all day and all night long then returned to their homes, and I lay in the house of the rabbi. For two days I didn't feel any great pain, but the third day I became sick with fever, and heat spread through my body. From day to day my condition worsened and the doctor said that I was dangerously ill. All of the people of the city were stunned and didn't know what to do. The rabbi of Breslau, in whose house I was staying, remained there day and night without moving from my bed until the Lord helped me. Finally the doctor said the danger had passed, but the sickness ruled over me for more than six months before I returned to full health. Then all the Jews in the city and surroundings celebrated in great happiness. After all of this, I said that I must go to Russia and see my brethren there because I heard they were very observant and learned in Torah, and I wanted to learn Torah and know her path. There in Breslau lived a rich businessman from the city of Warsaw and he invited me to travel with

---

32. Lit. He kept me in the pupil of his eye.

him to Warsaw. The man was rich and a Hassid. I traveled with him, and I was welcomed by almost all the Hassidim in Warsaw when we arrived. There was happiness and rejoicing in the rich man's house, and every day there was a feast like a king's feast in his home. I thought that all of the Jews must be very happy, yet the image appeared to me unbidden of a poor Jewish peddler who had sometimes come to our house to buy old items. How he bowed his tall stature to all the servants and maids who made him little presents of worthless things. So, I thought, "It's true then, the Jews of Poland are rich, because I haven't seen any poor or destitute in all these days I've passed with you in feasting and celebration." One time, the rich man said to me, "Reb Yitzchak, this week we will travel to see the Rebbe of Radin, and there you will see a great man beyond compare. That same day I was invited to see the Rabbi of Warsaw, and he was very disparaging and astonished at how and why I'd chosen my dwelling with the Hassidim. I said to him, "'Piety' is the meaning of 'Hassid', and I seek the God-fearing." He answered, "As do I." Three days later we all went to see the Rebbe of Radin; I, the rich man in whose home I was staying, and many other Hassidim. We arrived, and they renewed their habitual feasting and drinking. Week after week passed, month replaced month, and I went constantly to the Rebbe's house. Every day different people and new guests arrived, but the old guests didn't leave or move from their places, and they filled the city. The houses and stables, the barn lofts and basements were all filled with different people from different cities until there was no place left. Every day I ate my noon meal at the Rebbe's table, my breakfast in another man's house and my supper in a different man's house, but on Shabbat I ate all three meals at the Rebbe's table. At first I couldn't eat without a knife and fork, but the Hassidim laughed at me and jeered me saying, "A Hassid you will be called? As long as you need a spoon, a knife and a fork to eat you aren't fit to be called a Hassid! Watch us and do like us." I went along with them and I was made a Hassid like them in the full meaning of the word. Only one thing was hard for me. When I sat at the Rebbe's table and listened to his words of Torah, I wanted very much to understand, but I didn't understand a thing. Once I complained to the rich Hassid about my lack of comprehension, since I couldn't understand any of his Torah lesson. He answered me laughingly, "Slow one, this isn't necessary. Why should you understand? Was I not born a Hassid, and have I not studied since the time I was weaned from my mother's breast? Not a year has passed that I haven't been here twice and visited with the Rebbe, and every time I have heard much Torah, and despite all of this I don't understand but a fraction of a small part. And you wish to understand? It is only the hidden Torah he explains to us. The angels, only they may understand, not us." Eight months I lived there and I didn't know what I was doing. I drank with them, I ate with them in their manner, from the hand to the mouth. I danced with them, I sang their songs, I listened to their stories. The little I had learned in Germany I knew, but nothing more. I prayed with them and they put on me another Tefillin, and when they heard me praying and reading from the siddur they laughed at me and said, "No, that's how the Germans say it, but now you are a Hassidic Jew." And I thought this was correct, and I started to read like them.

On Simchat Torah, I drank way too much with them and was sick, and my life had made food loathsome to me. I lay on my bed senseless, and when the wine had gone out of me, I began to think and worry about my end. "Can it be true," I asked myself, "That this is how the Jews of the exile live? Can they spend all their days in drunken joy? If so, why don't the Jews of Germany do the same? Isn't the dear man who lives on my father's estate wise and learned beyond compare? He is rich also, so why doesn't he do these things? Besides, he told me that the majority of Jews of Russia and Poland are greatly learned. If this is what they do and this is how they live, when will I learn?" So when I returned to my senses and went into their company I asked them, "My dear shepherds, I want to ask you what will come of me. It wasn't to drink that I converted, but to learn Torah and know the Lord, because ignorance isn't piety."

"Idiot," one of them answered me, "We don't need to learn. Doesn't the Rebbe learn our portion for us? What can we learn and what would we know if we studied? Isn't the Torah full of secrets, hints, and hidden things, so we could never understand it."

"Not so," I answered them, "Doesn't it say in the Torah itself that it is not in the heavens?" They laughed at me, but their answers had pushed me far away from them. The next day I took a parting blessing from the Rebbe and from the rich man with whom I had made the pilgrimage, and one man who wasn't a Hassid advised me to travel to Dvinsk, and so I did. I came here, and I didn't err in my destination. Now I know that the Lord has placed me on the true path. Lo, I spent ten months in the company of the Hassidim, I didn't learn anything from them except for how to drink,. Now I have been here about eight months and I have learned all of tractate Baba Metzia and have started Baba Batra, and in the Bible I have studied the early and late commentators. I'd never prayed to advance so far in learning in such a short time. I am so happy in my teacher and in my Rebbe. I know that you have dedicated your strength and your time on my behalf. Truly you have done the work of the Lord, and for all of my days my soul will be tied to your soul and the souls of your family. And what you did for me, honorable lady," he turned to my mother z"l, "During all the days without end that I lay confined in bed, you defied description. Like a tender mother to her only son you watched over me for a month, you didn't rest or remain still, nor spare your own health until I returned to myself. So this is the story of my origins," he concluded happily, "And now I'm going to Horowitz's house because those honorable people have prepared a family gathering in my honor this evening, and dedicated it to their guests."

Behold this was a great dear man who left all the pleasures of the world behind him and came to be absorbed into an oppressed people, to be tormented and suffer with them as part of their part. Twenty-two years ago I met his wife in Vilna, a dear and upright woman with a little daughter. She told me that they'd lived in the city of her birth in Russia in peace for a few years, but then the riots and the pogroms came there and they were happy to have managed to flee amidst the upheavals and come to Vilna. She and the girl remained in Vilna while he traveled to Riga to get work, and more I didn't hear of him. I'm sad for you, dear man, you were without a doubt driven from there also, because you are a Jew. He, Reb Yitzchak the righteous Tzaddik ben Avraham our father, who cast off a world full of all good and brought upon himself sorrows and troubles, and was happy with his lot because he was a Jew. Behold, this is the power and spirit of Israel. A grandfather who was sunken and concealed was restored to greater majesty and brought out of the deep abyss. The Prince will raise the lost and the dispossessed and set them in the highest place.

# 2.

# A Girl Can't Become a Gaon?

by Sarah Faige Foner of the House of Menkin

# ⋍ A Girl Can't Become a Gaon?[1]

*Sarah Faige Foner is a 65 year old woman, learned in Torah, Talmud and Hebrew Literature. She speaks beautiful Hebrew and has written several Hebrew books. She lives in Harlem, NY, and dedicates all of her time to the study of Hebrew literature, biblical and modern. In her free time she collects donations from her acquaintances, and she gives this money to Hebrew schools, in order that it be possible for them to teach poor children for free.*

In the beginning of the reign of Alexander the Second in Russia, in the year 1855, I was born in the town of Zager. My father was learned in Torah and wise, and he studied Talmud day and night. My mother also knew Hebrew, and every Saturday afternoon she studied the Parsha of the week, including the commentaries of Rashi and Ibin Ezra.

For those of you who didn't know, my young readers, in past times parents taught their sons Torah and Talmud, but not their daughters. A daughter was only taught to read from the prayer book and to write letters in Yiddish. The daughters were busy all day with housework, and the parents thought it superfluous to teach their daughters Torah.

How did it come about that they taught me Torah and Talmud? These are the events I desire to relate to you.

It happened in my childhood, when I was five and a half years old, that my mother said to me, "Sarah Faige, go to Miriam with the little house (Miriam poon'im shtiebeleh) and tell her to come to our house to help me prepare the meal, because we have guests coming.

---

1. Translation appeared under this title in the Winter 2000 edition of Woman's League Outlook Magazine. Original Hebrew story appeared in "Shaharut — The Youth" September, 1919 Vol 6. Jewish Youth Publishing Co. N.Y., N.Y.  Z. Scharfstein, Editor.

But if you find her in prayer, take care not to interrupt her — wait until she finishes her prayers then tell her my message.

I hurried to do my mother's bidding. I passed through the shuk[2] which was full of wagons in which the farmers from the nearby villages sat and sold chickens, eggs, lentils, and all sorts of grain and vegetables, and I crossed the street with the Beit Kinneset and arrived at the bath house. Not far from the bath house stood a small and poor house, whose teetering walls were supported with wood posts, and whose straw roof was rotten and had many breaches. In this house lived Miriam, who earned her bread by helping women to bake and clean and to do all sorts of housework.

I opened the door and found Miriam standing and praying. Her head was wrapped in a wide, multi-colored kerchief. The kerchief was tied on both sides of her head, and therefore her head looked as big as a bucket.

I stood to the side without disturbing her prayers and listened closely to every word coming out of her mouth. She was reciting the Shacharit[3] prayer, and after the prayers she said in Yiddish, "May blessings and success fall on my little head (kepeleh), Amen, Selah."

When I heard her last words I wanted to laugh out loud, but I was afraid that she would tell my father that I laughed, so I restrained myself. But as I walked home together with Miriam, strange thoughts and ideas began to trouble my heart.

Miriam, I thought to myself, is a simple woman, and she recites her prayers as she was taught by memorization, without understanding the meaning of the words. When she was a little girl, her mother taught her to recite, "May blessings and success fall on my little head," and on these words she is returning even today, without comprehension. A prayer like that is T'filah Shav[4] and I don't want to turn out like her. When I get home I will ask my father to teach me to read from the Siddur, in order that I will know how to pray properly.

---

2. Outdoor market.
3. Morning prayers.
4. A technical term meaning a prayer that cannot be fulfilled.

When I got home I said to my mother, "Give me something to eat, mother, because I'm hungry."

"Good," said my mother, "But first say the blessing."

"I don't want to say the blessing," I answered in tears.

"What's this my ears are hearing?" my mother said anxiously, "You don't want to say the blessing?"

"No," I answered, "I want to pray from the Siddur, not from memory like Miriam."

And so I told her what I'd heard and my mother laughed good heartedly and said, "In a little while your father will return from the Beit Midrash, and I'll ask him to buy you an Aleph-Bet and to teach you to read. Now say the blessing and eat."

I obeyed my mother, said the blessing and ate, then I went out to my girlfriends to play a game.

While I was playing with my friends outside, I saw my father leave the Beit Midrash. I abandoned the game and ran to greet him with a "Good Morning," took his Tallit and Teffilin from his hand and said to him, "Daddy, buy me an "Aleph-Bet" and teach me to read Hebrew."

"It's not yet time to teach you reading," he answered calmly, "Wait another year or two and then you'll begin to learn."

When I heard his words, I broke into sobs and ran to my mother and said to her, "Mommy, Daddy won't buy me an "Aleph-Bet!"

My mother approached my father and told him what I had related to her about Miriam "of the small house." My father laughed freely, stroked the hair on my head and comforted me that in the evening, on returning from the Beit Midrash, he would bring me the Aleph-Bet that I so desired.

For the rest of the day I was very excited, and I told all of my friends that today I would start to learn. I felt in my heart that I was being elevated above them all, because they would grow up simple and I would be learned. With the setting of the sun, I sat on the porch in front of our house and waited impatiently for my father to come.

Suddenly, I saw my father in the distance. Like an arrow from a bow I sped off running to greet him and extracted from his hand the Aleph-Bet. Then I happily returned home at a run, to deliver the good news to my mother that my father had brought me an Aleph-Bet.

About this time, our guests arrived, and these were my Uncle Reb Yediya and his son Aryleh. This young man was an "Ilui," remarkable in his many aptitudes, especially in his memory and his erudition in Talmud. If a person wanted to test him, he could take a closed Gemora and position his finger on a certain spot on the cover and say, "What are the words that are printed in this place on page thirty-one?" The youth would stand and tell him the words written there without having to think very hard and without any mistakes.

When I saw these important guests, I didn't have the courage to talk to my father concerning the Aleph-Bet, but I heard my father in the course of his conversation with the guests tell them what had happened to me and what I requested from him. The guests laughed kindly and told him that I was justified.

The next day, after I ate breakfast, my father sat me on his knees, spread the chart of the Aleph-Bet on the table and began to teaching me the first two letters, repeating them a second time and a third time. This wasn't to my liking, and I asked him to read for me the names of all of the letters, till "Tav." My father did as I asked, and I concentrated well on each letter, and the names remained engraved in my memory. When my father finished reading, I repeated before him the names of all the letters forward and backward, without errors. My father was amazed to hear the names of all the letters come out of my mouth, and he read me also the names of the nikudot.[5] I learned these also and began to join the letters with the nikudot, "Ah, Bah, Gah, Dah, . . . ."

"I have to go to work," my father told me, "Go and play with the girls and when I return for lunch I'll continue teaching you."

My father left and I went out and sat on the small bench on the porch, and I began reviewing the Aleph-Bet diligently, until I knew

---

5. Vowels, literally points.

it by heart. I entered the house and asked my mother to give me a Siddur, and by myself, without help, I began to slowly read the first prayer, "Ma Tov-ooh." I read it one time, two times, a third and a fourth, until I knew how to read this prayer fluently. From time to time, one of my friends came over to ask me to play with her, but I answered proudly, "It's not the time for play now, but the time to learn from the Siddur."

When my father came home for lunch, I opened up the Siddur and read before him the prayer "Ma Tov-ooh" fluently and well. He was astonished and hugged and kissed me, and he wanted to go out and tell our neighbors about this wonder. Just then, the door opened and my uncle came in, so my father called me and instructed me to read from the Siddur.

"She learned this in a half-day, from morning till now," my father said.

"I'm sorry that she's a girl," my uncle answered, "If she was a boy, she probably would have been a Gaon[6] in Israel."

"A girl can't become a Gaon?" I asked innocently.

My uncle and father burst out laughing, and I was ashamed and humiliated. I hid in the corner and didn't want to sit down at the table to eat.

After a couple weeks, my father delivered me to the Cheder,[7] and I sat there with the boys and studied together with them, even though they were several years older than me. Every half year I passed from one form to the next, until I had acquired knowledge of Tanach and Talmud. When I finished there I began to read every Hebrew book I could get my hands on. When I reached 25 years old, I wrote a Hebrew novel, and this was the first of my books to be printed, *Love of the Righteous.*

6. A great genius and scholar in Jewish law.
7. Traditional one room religious school for boys.

# 3.

# Letter to HaYom, 1866

*A letter from Sarah Faige published in HaYom, the first Hebrew Daily Newspaper, No. 67, 1886 Riga*

The principal of the school "Gymnasium Alexander" issued an order to all of the Jewish students in all departments that they must learn to understand Hebrew. When they stand for their examinations they will be examined in their Hebrew subjects as in all other subjects. If they are knowledgeable in all subjects, and only in Hebrew are they lacking, they will not pass on to the next form, but remain in their places from the year before. Like sharp arrows these words have pierced the hearts of the young men, the majority of whom barely understand Hebrew at all, and Tanach[1] — of what interest is that! Now every student in the school will want to know the name of the angel who taught Joseph seventy languages in one night, in order to invoke his name and energetically beseech him that they be delivered from captivity and be able to pass their tests. But because this is a secret blocked from them and the name of the angel they will never know, they are compelled to come into the midst of beings of flesh and blood and seek help from Jewish men in order to be educated. This sorrow has come to the students of Riga and who knows if the decree won't spread to other cities. Therefore, I find myself obligated to write to expose this matter publicly, in order that this "evil" be promoted, and that they should always have before their eyes the saying of the wise one, "To despise a thing is injurious to one."[2]

*Sarah Faige Foner*

---

1. Bible.
2. Proverbs 13:13.

# 4.

# The Children's Path

*or*

# A Story from Jerusalem

⁓

*A wonderful story to draw the hearts of youth, set in the days of Herod, King of Judah in the time of the Second Temple. For children learning the Hebrew language.*

by Sarah Faige Foner of the House of Menkin

*Printed in Vienna, 1885*

# ꝰ A word to the reader

Honorable Readers. I wrote this story in memory of the honored name of the tzaddik and leader, the prince of God who was amongst us. He was Moses Montefiore, may he rest in eternity. Behold, I saw that as long as this lofty leader was in the vigor of life, all the writers and authors sent him their books and wrote articles in his honor, filling their mouths in praise and admiration of him. They knew that they weren't doing this for free, but that he would pay every one in full coin for his trade. At the time when I also did this, and sent him my story "A Righteous Love," this friend of God and man had almost closed his eyes and returned his soul to the God of recompense, to enjoy the good fate he could expect. Then followed many days of lamenting and mourning Moses, but now he is almost forgotten from the mouths of all the Hebrew writers, each of them wandering off in his own direction,[1] this one hating that, like the scholars of Babel. There are also those who undermine and destroy others who don't direct their fire along with them, testifying falsely and bare-headedly, each man condemning and reviling his brother. When I realized this I cried out and said, "Where is his eminence, that esteemed man who was apart from and conspicuous above the myriad.[2] All the sorrows of your people were also your sorrows, you took notice and rescued them. While many rich men lay sprawling on their divans[3] and didn't give anything to the remnants of Joseph, you went over, you and your gentle wife so like you in her righteousness, journeying completely over the seas, the roar of their waves and breakers were like a

---

1. Isaiah 47:15
2. Song of Songs 5:10
3. Amos 6:4

game to you. From Damascus you ransomed thousands of your covenant from the gates of death and removed the fetters from their souls. In Morocco you changed the condition of your people from shadow to light, and wrote yourself an eternal name, and more and more. Who can list all the good deeds and kindness you did for our people and our fathers." In order to place before young people the praise of an exalted man, I present this lofty man so that your children will ask tomorrow, "Who is this excellent man?" and you will tell them about all the charity and kindness Moses did in the eyes of Israel. Then the hearts of the youth will be filled with the love of their people and their kings and they will follow in his path. This story is set in the holy mountains with excellent people who learn Torah and wisdom, serve in the army and work on the land. They all appear in this story, since the actions of this lofty leader promoted the holy city and people like these. Therefore I wrote this story to honor his name and eternal memory. I hope that the honorable readers will not judge me guilty and say that I did this only in order to receive a reward, because Moses is dead and who is there like him who knows and understands this precious language? I will also present the letter he sent me for my story, "A Righteous Love," which I published five years ago while I was living in my youth in the house of my father, of blessed memory. I hope to produce an appetite in the community of wise readers that they will approve of my work as they did my first story. Then I will seek, with the help of the Lord, to also bring to the publisher the rest of the stories that are with me in manuscript. Aside from the second half of "A Righteous Love" and this story that I will place before you now, I also have four large stories written in pure and easy language that will cheer the hearts of the readers. I hope that with open arms you will gather them into your homes, as is the wish of the Author.

## Letter from the Honorable Sir Moses Montefiore

Sir Moses Montefiore, Bart.

With the help of the Lord, Ramscott, Monday, Parsha Devarim, 1881

Blessings and salutations to the lover of the language of our holy Torah, a dear modest maiden in her deeds and praiseworthy in her wisdom, Miss Sarah Faige Menkin of the District of Riga, Russia.

Included in this letter you will receive my gift of four pounds sterling for the book that you sent me. You will please be kind to inform me and confirm for me that the money arrives safely in your hands. May the Lord in his great mercy speedily have mercy on all the remnants of Israel.

As a soul pleading for the good of his people,

Moses Montefiore

## In Memory and Thanks

To the prince of God who was in our midst.

The honored minister and elevated man who stood by the right of his people for more than 100 years and saved them many times from sorrow.

Moses Montefiore, resting eternally.

Presented with sincerity and thanks on behalf of her people,

*The Authoress*

*"Then they remembered the days of old, of Moses his servant.
Where is the one who brought them up out of the sea with
the shepherds of his flock?
Where is the one who put his holy spirit within them?"*

— *Isaiah 63:11*

# One – The Village of Yochani

In the Village of Yochani in the land of Judah there lived a man for many days. On account of this, he was called Yochanan the Villager. This man had worked the land since his youth, and he was wholesome, straight and God-fearing. Each day in the morning, he rose from his bed before the sun began to shine and put on his garment. He went out to the field and prayed a short prayer, that the Lord should send blessings on all the works of his hands so that he should be able to support himself and those of his house. After this he returned home and ate the breakfast that was prepared for him by his wife and companion, then he returned to the field to work and stand guard. Thus he did all the days of the summer. During the winter he wove open wicker baskets[4] from reeds or poplar in preparation for the days of the Holiday of the First Fruits. All the poor pilgrims (the rich would bring gifts of gold or silver in place of first fruits) bringing offerings in honor of the Lord God, bought baskets from him to present their first fruits before the Lord. Neither did his wife sit in idleness, but she prepared all the needs of the house for herself and for her husband and children; also the flocks and herds were under her hand. In the long nights of the winter she spun and wove the fleece from the sheep, and she sold it at such a high price that the man was greatly enriched. This man had also four sons, Natanel the first born, Y'honatan the second, Oved the third, and Atzel the fourth.[5] When they were little children they went to their father in the fields or to the servants with the flocks, but as they grew they became divided in

---

4. Genesis 40:16

5. Natanel – Given to/by God. The other three brothers names: Y'honatan – God has given, Oved – worker, Atzel – lazy

their opinions and thoughts, each one by himself. Their father constantly reproached them about their undertakings because they hated work and loved idleness, but they always answered that they were yet young boys and they needed more time to become accustomed to work.

# ✑ Two – A Conversation Between the Brothers

The sun shone with all her splendor and glory on perfect Zion. She cast her majestic rays also on the towns and villages that surrounded her, as if she were saying, "From Zion and from all her beauty the Lord will also appear to you, and with her blessings He also blesses you." In the village of Yochani the day was different from all other days. All the workers from the fields and the flocks came and gathered at Yochani's house, and a few from the surrounding towns came to his house also. An elderly priest came from Jerusalem to say the blessing over the bread and take his portion of the shearings of the sheep. That day was a holiday for Yochanan because he sheared his flock and set aside the Terumah[6] of his fields. Rachel, the wife of Yochanan, stood by the pots to prepare the meal for the guests. The priest arrived, and all those sitting rose from their places and received the elderly priest with honor, and he blessed them all and sat at the head. And it happened that after they ate and after they drank, every one of them returned to his place. Yochanan went to see off the priest and to cause him to pass through his fields that he should bless them. There he saw his sons arrayed, the four of them, under one of the trees, and he went slowly after them and hid under a different tree from whence he could hear all of their words. "Listen now, my brothers," said Natanel the first born to the rest of the brothers, "Did you know that in the time since our father took us to Jerusalem for the

---

6. Special tithe for the Temple

Festival of Matzot, I decided to become a Rabbi and head of the Rabbinical Court in Jerusalem? At first I longed to be High Priest when I saw all of the honor bestowed on the High Priest from all of Israel, like a god he was thought in their eyes. But when one of the young men of Jerusalem told me that the High Priest can only be one who is a descendent of the priests, and as our father is from the tribe of Shimon, I therefore decided to become a Rabbi and the head of a Yeshiva. Then I saw the two great Rabbis, Hillel and Shamai, one the Nasi and the other the head of the Rabbinical Court, and how their students sat before them in terror and fear, sitting at their feet,[7] it almost took away my breath. More than this, I saw people come to Hillel that he should judge them because they have a quarrel and suit, then Hillel said, "God of my people! Why do you quarrel with each other, are you the children of Cain that you wish to murder your brothers? Are you not the children of Avraham, Yitzchak and Ya'akov who lived in peace even with those who hated them? When there was a quarrel between the shepherds of the flocks of Avraham and the shepherds of the flocks of Lot, Avraham told his nephew to choose for himself a place to dwell as was goodly in his eyes, while he would remain in his place in order that there be peace." The plaintiffs, on hearing the sweet language of the exalted man, addressed each other in peace. I stood then next to my father and watched him without pause, and he said, "Perchance thy face is a lamp,"[8] and he passed two fingers over my right cheek. "And what do you say my son? Do you think it better to be a Rabbi like me or a tiller of the soil like your father?" My cheeks reddened like scarlet and fear and trembling seized me on seeing the importance of the answer. I was like a stupid brute then and I couldn't respond with a single word. When I return for the yearly Festival of the Harvest in Jerusalem, I will go to the house of study and fall before his feet and I will plead with him that he teach me Torah in order that I become a Rabbi like him.

"Why don't you want to learn Torah in the house of study of

---

7. Pirke Avoth I:4 – literally, wrestling in the dust at their feet
8. Psalms 90:8 – verse continues – "in the light of which secrets are exposed"

Shammai?" Y'honatan asked him when he concluded. "Is he not also a great Rabbi?"

"The young men of Jerusalem told me," said Natanel, "that the students of Hillel outnumber the students of Shammai, because Hillel is extremely humble and receives every man in joy. Shammai is very prickly, and if a man doesn't impress him in speaking to him, he will drive him away with rebukes. I am very dismayed by rebukes, and on account of this I will be a Rabbi like Hillel and not Shammai."

"It is different with me," said Y'honatan, "When I walked in the beautiful and splendid streets of Jerusalem, I saw from afar a great gathering of many people. I asked of them, "What is this?" and the people told me that in a little while Herod the king, in all his beauty and splendor, would show himself to us. Then I saw in the distance people dressed in expensive clothing with coats of mail[9] on them and golden swords girded at their hips. Some of them rode on horses and some of them went on foot and all of them ran from every direction and shouted, "Clear the way for our lord king. He will soon show himself to us, because he is on his way to the Temple to go before the Lord in the festival gathering of the people." Each man jostled his neighbor to see this fine view. Many of the upper class of Jerusalem ran before him and spread blue and purple cloth on the road from the palace to the house of the Lord, in order that the soles of his feet not tread on the ground, but on the blue and purple cloth. In their passing they cried, "Long live the King, Long live the King!" and the earth split at their voices. The king acknowledged them all with a beaming visage and went on. All of the generals dressed in armor and swords accompanied him on all sides, and they are in the king's presence always. He spoke with them, bestowing honor on them, and all of the people were jealous of them and also honored them. Therefore I decided to become a general and intimate of the king. Next time I am brought to Jerusalem I will go to one of these generals and beseech him that he take me into his service. So I have decided," said

---

9. 1 Samuel 13:5

Y'honatan, "And I hope that in the near future I will be a great general like those generals I saw in Jerusalem."

"Verily you are correct in the choices you have made," said Oved. "Natanel, he will be a Rabbi like Hillel, and Y'honatan will be a great general and intimate of King Herod. But with me it will be different. Behold when our father brought the tithe and Terumah to Jerusalem, the priests received him with love and honor. When my father said, "What am I that I am so valued and honored by you," they said to him, "Who is deserving of honor more than you? Did not David, the King of Israel, say, "He will that you will eat and rejoice and it will be good with you."[10] How could we not honor a man who has won himself two worlds by his toil." Therefore I will be a worker of the land like my father and I will eat by means of my toil and I will also win myself two worlds." Then the two older brothers rose and hugged their third brother and they said, "Be happy, our brother, in your lot, because he who works his land will eat his fill." And he said to them, "Also you my brothers be happy in your lots, rise and be successful, and the Lord God will be with you." They embraced again, each man his brother, and they swore to live in harmony, even in the time that their status should separate them one from another. In their great happiness they forgot that they had another brother, the youngest of them all, that hadn't told them what he desired to choose for the days of his existence. Natanel the first born spoke to his youngest brother Atzel and said, "Pray tell us your mind, Atzel, what will be with you?" "With me there won't be a thing," answered Atzel. "Behold my father is a very rich man, so why should I stint myself any pleasure. Shall I be a rabbi? Would I not be required to sit day and night without giving sleep to my eyes or rest to my eyelids for long days, and then only maybe would I succeed in becoming a rabbi, because not all students are ordained. If I aspired to become a great general like Y'honatan said, then I would have to serve in the army and go down to war, then maybe the hand of an enemy will reach me and his sword will take me before I become a

10. Psalms 128:2

general. Or, should I become a servant of the earth like my father, is this good? Do not the consuming dryness by day and the frost by night[11] rob the sleep from his eyes? Sometimes, when he hears tortured cries of the shepherds with the flocks of sheep and cattle, he strings his bow and runs into the midst of the flocks to shoot at the wolves or the lions, taking his life in his hands. Therefore, my soul also finds this repugnant. Behold, my needs are provided[12] for every day that I may do as I have done until now, leaping from mountain to mountain, hill to hill. I will play with the shepherds and the flocks and I will be free always, and I will go wherever the wind bears me." The brothers began to argue with him and rebuke him on his path, because he was up to no good and his end would be bitter. But he had set himself apart, and who could bring him back? Their father remained hidden under a leafy tree the whole time the brothers were talking, and he saw all and heard all of their words. When they finished speaking he returned to his place and didn't tell them that he had heard, but on his youngest son he looked now with penetrating eyes. And he chose for himself the part[13] of voiding the bad intentions of his son that he not be lost for eternity. But who can stop the flood of desire in the hearts of youths when they follow their own ideas, whether good or bad?

## ᔕ Three – The Festival of Succoth in the Days of Herod

The Festival of Succoth arrived and all of Israel gathered to come and see the presence of the Lord God, to celebrate the Festival of Succoth, and to hear the king himself as he read the Torah before the assembly. Yochanan the villager and his four sons also went up to Jerusalem. Natanel went to the house of study of Hillel the Nasi and

---

11. Genesis 31:40
12. Isaiah 33:16 – literally, bread is given
13. Deuteronomy 33:21

said, "Please my lord, my teacher, my rabbi, our teacher of Torah, I am the son of Yochanan the villager, but the deeds of my father are not right for me and I will never be a farmer. Only a rabbi like you shall I be, and in your path I will go if you do not reject me from your presence and teach me Torah." "Good, my son, good is the thing you have chosen," said Hillel. "The Lord blesses Zion that from her will come out Torah and you will go up, and up, and up and become great in Torah and posses a name like the names of the great ones in the land." And from that day on Natanel was a student of Hillel the Nasi. And his second brother Y'honatan was taken to serve in the army. Oved and Atzel, the remaining sons, returned with their father to the village Yochani. Oved began to work the land of his father, and the Lord blessed all the labor of his hands and he succeeded in all he did, but Atzel remained idle all his days.

## ✍ Four – The Death of Yochanan

Many days passed and Yochanan grew old. And he came to the end of his days and summoned his sons. Natanel came with fifty students who heard their lessons from his mouth because so great was Natanel in the Torah of the Lord. When he came to his father he fell on his neck and kissed him. And Natanel's students spoke to Yochanan saying, "Happy are you Yochanan that you merited this, you sowed in charity and reaped in kindness."[14] Next approached Y'honatan, his neck and breast were spread with gold medals that he received from Herod the king for his heroism and mightiness of spirit. A thousand men came with him to honor him and to honor his father, because he was a general of a thousand. He fell on his father's neck and kissed him and took out a letter from his pocket. As his men stood by to hear the words of the letter, he read,

*Behold I send you your son that he cheer your spirit in these,*

---

14. Hosea 10:12

*your final days, as you have asked of me. But, do not delay
in returning him to me because I need him very urgently.*

*Herod, King of Judah*

The old man embraced and kissed his sons, weeping from great
happiness, and afterwards Oved and Atzel also came and stood by
their father. And Yochanan said to his sons, "Hearken me now my
children. Behold the day of my death has come, now listen to me as
I proclaim my words. All the time you dwelled with me I took care
of you and you were not lacking a thing. But I also chastened you
when I saw that you were straying a little from the straight path, and
you in your good nature lent your ears to my admonishments and
you went in the correct path. When you took counsel under the tree
and each one spoke about his desires, what you chose to be, I heard
all your words and determinations and I didn't seek to restrain you. I
knew that it's not in the power of man to stop the flood of desire in
the hearts of boisterous youth, more so when I saw that everybody
chose for himself a good path, except for Atzel the youngest. Behold,
I return in thanks to the Lord. You have settled in the right path, and
behold, you have become men before my eyes."

"But what can I do with Atzel who will continue to give himself
to his wicked tendencies and his evil ways? If he continues doing as
he has done, in his end he will be cut off. One last piece of advice
occurs to me. I will divide my estate in five parts and every one will
take his part, and to Natanel there will be double as is written in the
Law of Moses, because he is the first born. But the portion of Atzel
will be under the hand of one of you and you will appoint a trust-
worthy man who will work Atzel's fields faithfully. And each and
every month he will give Atzel all that he requires for himself and his
household, and the remainder will be brought under the hand of the
guardian[15] to be kept in trust. In this manner he will be able to exist
as any man lives and not turn to evil or crime. But, if you give him
his portion, then he and his inheritance will be lost forever, as if I had

---

15. Epitropus – Greek word for legal guardian used in Talmud Bavli

not charged you."

And they all answered, "As your words we will do, our father, your command is holy to us," and afterwards he blessed each one with his blessing. Also his son Atzel he blessed and commanded to go in the path of good and to hearken the voices of his older brethren. He finished charging his sons and he drew his feet up on the bed[16] and died an old man. For seven days his sons mourned him and they buried him on his estate. Then each one of his sons returned to their work.

## ⤻ Five – The Breaking of the Will by Herod

Many days passed after the death of Yochanan and nothing new occurred. Natanel earned a name as good as the greatest names in the land. From the entire land of Israel many people came streaming to hear lessons from his mouth, and his name was very esteemed. Y'honatan rose from height to height because he showed Herod his fierce courage and the king raised Y'honatan high. Oved worked his land and was a man of worth. Atzel went in crookedness and apostasy, and every month when he received from the trustee his legal portion, he would lose it in some bad matter. His wife and children were left lacking everything and then it was incumbent on Oved to be a support for Atzel and his family. He was worthless and a drunkard, always going to his brother and quarreling with him that he should give him his part of the land from their father. Then he would no longer be under Oved's hand and he alone would manage his portion and not a stranger. But Oved didn't regard his words with favor, because his father had commanded him before his death not to give the inheritance into Atzel's hands.

One time Atzel came to Jerusalem when Herod was out riding with his servants, and the beautiful Miriami rode on his right on a

---

16. Genesis 49:33

pure white she-ass.[17] All of Israel, from the least to the greatest, went around them shouting and cheering because king Herod had proclaimed throughout the land of Judah that he would return the crown of the High Priest to Aristobolus, the brother of the Queen. He would serve in the Sanctuary in place of Hyrcanus his father, in order to cheer the hearts of the people mourning for the honor of the Hasmoneans, who had almost expired from our midst. Herod sent him from the palace of the king to the Holy Temple to restore him to the appointed office,[18] because these were the days between the full moon and the tithing. The Queen rode to the right of the King and Aristobolus, the brother of the Queen, sat to the left of the king. The sons of the king, Alexander and Aristobolus, rode to the right of the Queen. Y'honatan rode to the right of the children of the King to guard them because they were then seven and eight years old.

Atzel saw his brother Y'honatan from a distance and broke through to him. He grasped him by the back of his neck and cried aloud, "Bitter son,[19] why do you transgress the commands of our dead father! Here you sit on the heights of the world and do not give your waiting brother his inheritance. You stole my land from me, the inheritance that our father left for me, and I am dying from hunger and a lack of everything." All the people gazed at the two brothers in wonder and the sons of the king stared at Y'honatan in contempt[20] and cried in a regal voice, "Is it true, Y'honatan? Could you have done even one of these things to your brother? Will you be a retainer of our father the King and will you ride beside us? Will it be so?" One of the servants of the king approached Atzel to remove him by force from his brother, but Herod gave him a sign to desist. The Queen looked at the King in supplication, as if she feared lest he command that Atzel or Y'honatan be slain because they delayed him in the street. Y'honatan was stunned to the point where he could not

---

17. The donkey was the choice royal mount in Biblical times, not the horse
18. Palhedrin – a Greek term for an official office
19. Proverbs 17:25
20. Ezekiel 25:15 – literally, with despite in the soul

get a word out of his mouth in his awareness that this thing had occurred before Herod the King. But Herod, on seeing his fear, said cheerfully, "Shame on you, a leader and a mighty man of valor. In the field of combat you stood your ground and weren't cowering in the rear, nor did you retreat. Now you are dismayed before your brother and aren't able to remove him from your sight. ("Release me and I will fulfill your desire," said Y'honatan to his brother bitterly, and he put him aside and stood before the king.)

"It is true, my Lord King," replied Y'honatan to the king in answer and fearful respect, "That when I stand on the field of combat, my thought is to fall or to triumph. But here my courage vanishes, for fear of the splendor and royalty of my King is always upon me. The command of my dead father is strong on me. My regrets are kindled[21] towards my lost and unfortunate brother who has acted perversely since his youth and fell in love with idleness, but if I now transgress the command of my dead father and return to him his inheritance, then it will be lost forever." The words of Y'honatan found favor in the eyes of the king and he said, "Verily your father commanded before his death not to give Atzel his inheritance, but to feed him with his allowance of bread in order that his hand not raise to do evil. However, I will keep the words of the wisest king of all men, "Remove dross from silver when setting out to smelt a vessel."[22] Therefore, you will give him his inheritance and he will do with it as is good in his eyes. If he improves his ways, it will benefit him, and if he sins, he will be sent away for his crimes." The words came from the mouth of the king, and a couple of his servants took Atzel and brought him to the village of Yochanan and gave him his inherited fields and the flocks that his father left him before his death. The king and his nobles continued on and came before Temple Mount where they all dismounted from their horses and went on to the house of the Lord. Many priests stood there to receive the king and the new High Priest, son of Hasmoneans, to whom were given all the proper-

21. Hosea 11:8
22. Proverbs 25:4

ties and advantages that wise men attribute to the High Priest: grace and beauty, richness and honor, wisdom, might and breeding. The wise men raised a cheer to greet the king and the High Priest Aristobolus. The High Priest remained in the Holy Temple to dwell there until after Yom Kippur, in accordance with the law, and Herod the King with all his nobles returned to their palaces.

Atzel, when he came to the inheritance of his father, saw first to expulsion of all the servants and the overseer that his brothers appointed. He took new servants to work his fields and he went about idle as had always been his habit. When his servants saw that their lord wouldn't watch his inheritance, but he stretched out his hand with mockers,[23] they also withdrew their hands and didn't keep it as was fitting. Oved saw this from a distance and his heart pained him. He sometimes went to the fields of his brother and shouted heatedly at his servants, on seeing that the fields of Atzel were grown over with thorns and covered with nettles[24] and that his flocks were scattered on the mountains without shepherds. But the servants of Atzel always answered him that he was not their master, and that he couldn't command them. Then he returned in low spirits to his labor and to his brother he said, "Thy badness will chastise thee."[25]

## ☙ Six – Atzel's End

Not many days passed and the times changed in Jerusalem. Those who feared the Lord praised Herod with their mouths and honored him with their lips while whetting their eyes against him. Their hearts were distanced from him when he wrathfully pursued the family of his wife, the Hasmoneans. The servants of Herod, knowing that he was very fearful of insurrections, ingratiated themselves and brought him evil defamations. He listened to their lies, and began to interro-

---

23. Hosea 7:5
24. Proverbs 24:31
25. Jeremiah 2:19

gate and search out every man to see if he was faithful to his king. Many times he disguised himself and went to drinking houses and was able to speak with poor people about the burdens of king and his conduct. If he found a man speaking wickedly, then he sent his servants to seize him and torment him cruelly[26] that he would inform on the rest of the rebels. So he did many days.

One time he heard one of the rabble say to the rest of his companions that were with him in the drinking house, "Go open the door because Atzel the son of Yochanan the Villager is coming here." Atzel arrived and Herod recognized immediately that he was the brother of Y'honatan who had stopped him in the street while escorting the High Priest to Temple, and he bent his ear to hear their conversation. He heard that Atzel was a rebel against the king, because he spoke revolt against Herod and his family. He cursed the king on account of his promoting his brother and raising him high, and on account of his instructing to return to him the fields that had been under the hand of his brother. His fields were now entirely spoiled and he was ashamed to seek refuge with his brothers because he hadn't heeded their advice. Therefore, he had no other choice but to weave together the mobs to rebel against their king or to form a marauding band outside the kingdom. They struck palms with him that he would go at their head and they would follow him. Herod went on his way and commanded his servants to be on guard, and they seized Atzel and his men as they went into ambush in order to fall on travelers in the forest of Lebanon. They brought them before the king and the Sanhedrin, and the king spoke before them.

"A man was in Abel,[27] Sheba son of Bichri, and he raised his hand against King David, and no man dwelled in his house until he was put to death. This man, Atzel, was the son of an honorable man and a brother of honorable brothers, but he has gone in apostasy from his youth until now, following his heart. He didn't listen to the voices of his parents, nor to his teachers did he lend an ear. Behold he was

---

26. Jeremiah 30:14
27. 2 Samuel 20:18 – Abel is the town Sheba ben Bichri fled to

wholly evil amongst the community and finally he lifted his hand against King Herod, not him alone, but he incited and pushed many others with him. If a king renounces his honor it is not renounced.[28] He determined[29] to be a marauder outside the kingdom, and faithful witnesses will be found in this matter." After the interrogation and investigation, the Sanhedrin found the man liable to the death penalty in this matter. But before they determined their judgement, it was seen that one of the Sanhedrin rose from his place. And he said, "Make your judgement without me because I am the brother of this man." The listeners gazed at him in astonishment and he went out. As he passed before Atzel his brother recognized him, and he cried, "Save me now, my brother, from bitter death!"

"A brother cannot redeem a man, nor pay his ransom to God,"[30] said Natanel and went out.

A momentary uproar rose in the court, then the still silence returned. The sentence was fixed that the next day he would receive his punishment, he with the rest of his cohorts on his estate in the Village of Yochani. The servants of Herod took the prisoner and returned him to the jail pending the next day.

Y'honatan, his brother, exited from before the Sanhedrin with the rest of the generals. In low spirits, he met his brother Natanel in the corridor, and he said, "What do you say, my brother, about the end of our brother?"

"His end was destined from his beginning," answered Natanel in tears. "But what is our guilt that we saw with our own eyes the sorrows of our brother, yet didn't raise our hands to save him?" asked Y'honatan. "God will surely chastise us that we didn't continue to reproach him on his ways." Behold, so end all bitter sons that don't listen to their parents and teachers and hate the learning and the labor that sustains their masters in honor, and who love idleness. On

---

28. From Talmud Bavli, Kiddushin 32a – "If a father renounces the honor due him, then it is renounced, but if a rabbi renounces his honor, then it is not renounced" i.e., the king can't let him off the hook.
29. Psalms 83:6
30. Psalms 49:7

account of idleness they go from stumble to stumble until they are thrown down forever,[31] and they will be an everlasting abhorrence[32] to themselves and their entire family.

Not so for children who pay attention and are diligent in their studies and quick in their work. They become worthy and ascend from height to height, and every place they come they will earn respect and multiply honor on their houses. They will cause the hearts of their parents to rejoice and bestow honor to their children after them.

The End

*Riga, 11th of Cheshvan, 1885*

---

31. Jeremiah 23:12
32. Daniel 12:2

# 5.

# The Treachery of Traitors

*When you are done spoiling, you will be spoiled*
*When you are done betraying, you will be betrayed*

— *Isaiah 33:1*

by Sarah Faige Foner of the House of Menkin

*Printed in Warsaw, 1891*

# ⌒ A Word to the Readers

I applied myself to study the history of our people, and I saw that these events needed explaining. What did Ptolemy expect, and what did he get? Behold, he was the son-in-law of the High Priest and his wife was a daughter of the Hasmoneans who without a doubt was beautiful and wise. How extraordinary that he should kill her. Could he marry another daughter of Israel like her? If a man is angry with his wife, will he destroy his whole father-in-law's house? What was the political situation immediately following the death of the High Priest Simon, such that the king of Greece came with a mighty army and laid siege to Jerusalem? Therefore, I decided to shed light on these events.

The history of our people is known to every reader, that Ptolemy was a Hellenist, and how the aristocrats during this period inclined to the laws of the non-Jews more than they were inclined to the laws of Israel. All of them chased after honors, including Ptolemy. Based on this we can quickly come to understand the thoughts of our people's historian. Ptolemy killed his wife because he had set his eyes on the daughter of the Greek king who had enmeshed him in her seductions, as we will see in this story. He slew his father-in-law along with his brother-in-law because he wanted to destroy all of the Hasmonean seed, in order that he alone would inherit the throne. In all the evil that he did, he was confident and sure that the king of Greece stood on his right, and maybe it would have been so had not the youngest son, Yochanan, escaped. When the Greek king saw that there was another son of Simon left and that the children of Israel would take him as king over themselves, he angrily expelled Ptolemy from his presence. King Antiochus himself went up against Jerusalem and besieged her, as is written in the book of Josephus.[1] On these foundations I base this story, and I hope that the community of readers will find pleasure in it. I chose this time period because it is rich in meaning and drama.

— *The Author*

---

1. The Josephon, a Hebrew history adopted from the Latin histories of Josephus, which was in common circulation

# ➳ Chapter One

Next to Mount Modein unfolded a large valley which was lovely to behold. To one side appeared Mount Modein, and to the other side, a high hill extended out a great distance. The hill was covered in vineyards, and the vineyards were interlocked to one another by their vines and branches to the point that whole hill looked like a single vineyard. To the third side was built a large and handsome house, and everyone who passed it would recognize that the rich man who lived amongst the pleasing fields was their lord. In the courtyard were built stalls for horses, asses and camels, and also sheds and pens for many sheep and cattle. To the fourth side of the valley, gardens, orchards and fields stretched into the distance. Everybody will quickly recognize that a very rich man was the lord of the house. Do you also, honorable reader, wish to know the name of this rich man? Here I will tell you his history and what happened to him from this time until the day of his death. The name of the master of the house and everything that you see around it was Aviazar. This man is pure and righteous, God-fearing and removed from evil. Even though he wasn't learned in Torah, for all of this he loved the Lord, with all his heart, his soul and his might, and he observed the Torah of the Lord like all the great and learned men of the Lord. On the days of pilgrimage and holiday he went to the holy city of Jerusalem to seek Torah from the mouths of the learned, and the lips of the righteous priests taught him knowledge and fear of the Lord. He never delayed in bringing the Meiser (tenth part) and Terumah Omer and First Fruits before the Lord, and the servants of the Lord warmed themselves from the fleece of his sheep. The poor always found the missed gleanings and the Peah[2] in the fields of Aviazar. When the priests of the Lord gathered in his house, he would make for them a feast and celebration. Aviazar, his wife, his son and his daughter all waited on them and served them, and they did this willingly in perfect joy and satisfaction.[3] At this time, as occurred every year, the ruler and high priest of Israel, Simon the son of Matitiyahu, would go with his sons and all the great and important people of the city to the tomb of Matitiyahu his father, to visit him on the anniversary of his death. Since the priests were not permitted to approach the tomb, but only those of Israel.[4] Aviazar and his son Yehuda always went out to greet the high priest. They would bow before him and request him to detour into their vineyard and rest a little, a wish that was never denied. Many wondered about this honor that was given a villager and they didn't know the explanation for this, but it was obvious that they weren't family because Aviazar was of the tribe of Benjamin.

"Please look, my son," said Aviazar to Yehuda his son, as they stood in his great vineyard that was planted on a fertile slope. "From afar those look to me like an assembly of people are gathering and standing in rows next to our second vineyard below. Go and look and tell me who they are."

The youth ran off and returned in a moment, and signs of joy were visible on his face.

"My dear father," cried the youth in great excitement, "Behold the high priest with all the dignitaries of the city stand there and converse."

"You saw well, my son," Aviazar said joyously. "The anniversary is here, the day the high priest Matitiyahu expired and gave up his breath."[5] As he spoke, he ran in excitement to where they were assembled. But when he saw everybody gathered around the high priest lis-

---

2. The corner of the field left for the poor
3. Psalms 16:11
4. Priests are prohibited from cemeteries and contact with the dead, Israel here refers to the twelve tribes
5. Lamentations 4:10

tening to his words, he also stood at a distance to listen to the words of the ruler of Israel.

"Pray remember my people, people of the Lord, what the Lord has wrought for you in your lives. This very place we are now standing was not ours, because the enemy overcame us and took our land from our hands, not even allowing us passage for the soles of our feet. In this place stood an evil man from the aristocracy of our people, and he sold himself to do great abominations. He sacrificed a pig on the altar of a graven image, an appalling abomination.[6] This man was an inflammatory enemy of the Lord, and a disgrace to the living God. Therefore, the Lord, God of Vengeance, roused the spirit of my father. All the zealots of the Lord formed an army, and they struck the enemies of the Lord and took their vengeance on them. From that time on, we went forth from slavery to freedom, and we stand here as free men this day. The Lord also set shepherds on his people as he saw fit, and my father led you with knowledge and wisdom. My brother Judah exposed his body unto death for our holy city and our people, and I will do the same until we god-fearing are revenged on all our enemies who rise against us. God forbid that I should abandon you even a moment, only be strong and brave! Serve the Lord in wholeness and seek him with all of your heart, then you will be redeemed in eternal salvation. Do not bow before our oppressors if you see that they are many. Remember this place, where with a few men and the help of the merciful God, my father put to flight a nation as mighty and numerous as the nation of Antiochus the Wicked. Many times my brother Judah was destined for terrible misfortune, and all of Israel with him, and every time the Lord saved them. Many times I have despaired of my life, and the Lord helped me. Now the Lord has widened our borders and made great our name, and with the help of God here we stand this day on the heights of success. But guard well in your souls lest you destroy what our fathers built, because then you will be forever in hardship. Do not

---

6. Daniel 11:31

make a covenant with the inhabitants of the land, and do not lust after the palaces of the idolaters that surround us, their daughters, their slaves, and all that is theirs. If you make a covenant with them you will become their eternal slaves. The fate of lifelong slaves, if you don't know, is that as long as his master is pleased, he serves him. When the days come that the master is no longer pleased, the slave is driven out or put to death. So will happen with you in later days if you don't hearken to my advice."

"The Lord is our God, and you are our King!" cried the crowd when the high priest finished talking. "You are the light of Israel, you rule over us, you and your son and the sons of your son forever." So cried the assemblage in a great voice, except for one man who was mute and reflective. And who was this one? How extraordinary! It was Ptolemy, the son-in-law of the king, and the expression on his face showed that he didn't like the words of his father-in-law or the acclamation of the crowd. Yochanan, the young son of Simon, saw this and despised him in his heart.

And it happened that when the king rose to go on his way, Aviazar went to greet him. He bowed to him and said, "Please my lord, prince of God, make me a sign of affirmation, and honor me by visiting my vineyards and blessing your servant Aviazar, because through your blessing, many will be blessed."

The high priest answered him with a nod of his head as a sign that his wish would be fulfilled, and then he and the whole assembly continued on. But Ptolemy blocked his way, and said, "Please don't my lord and father-in-law. It's not proper for the high priest to go to the house of a villager." To Aviazar he said, "Remove yourself from the path, hollow man who chases after honor. How did you embolden your heart to request a thing like this?" Aviazar was humiliated by the words of Ptolemy, and he retreated backwards, but the high priest said to him, "Do not fear good man, peace unto you, because your ways are as wholesome as those of your father. Why should I not accept your offer? Behold I will fulfill your wish." And to his son-in-law he said, "God forbid, my son, that you should be sharp with a pure and upright man, whose heart is as his father's heart. His father was among the first that followed our father to take the vengeance of the Lord and his people from the hands of those who hated and pursued us. His tomb is beside the tomb of our father, and this is his son Aviazar, a neighbor of our father. Who is it that gives us honor and greatness if not He who makes equal the great and the small, and why did He set a king over His people? Are we not all children of one Father, and after everything is finished, our spirits and souls are all gathered to Him. How can a man be proud over his brethren?"

Ptolemy didn't say another word, but he devised evil thoughts in his heart. The high priest and the people that accompanied him turned to the vineyard of Aviazar, but Ptolemy with a few men that were part of his intimate circle set off on their way.

"I pray thee, dear father," said Yochanan the youngest son to his father, "I pray thee, don't keep bringing your son-in-law Ptolemy with you. Is he not always rebelling and finding ways to diminish you? And that's not enough for him, but he also refuses fulfill your wishes. He is emboldened with evil and he intends to violate your intentions and your council. I see this nature that he inherited from his fathers, to chase after honors and to seek office."

"He dresses himself in pride with our father," spoke up Hyrcanus, who until now had walked and conversed with other people.

"That he dresses himself in pride when he is with our father is very proper, because his father-in-law is the high priest and king while he isn't even a plain priest, but why act haughty with the villagers who are people of his standing?" said Yochanan in jest.

"Leave off speaking mockery," cried the father to his sons. "You! Do you also seek to diminish a man?" The sons were shamed by the words of their father and didn't say any more. Many of the people whispered and reinforced the words of Simon's sons. Everyone who loved of the Hasmoneans hated Ptolemy with a consuming hatred, but they didn't speak because of the respect they had for Simon.

The high priest together with all the people rested in the vineyard of Aviazar, blessed him, and continued on their way, but Simon's youngest son remained in the house of Aviazar.

## ⌁ Chapter Two —
## Yehudit and Her Mother

The sun faced the evening, husbanding the remains of her strength and gathering all her luminance about her. It was as if she wished to make reparations to all those now enjoying her rays, who had held back from them during the heat of the day. Many of the people had hidden themselves in their houses and closed and bolted their doors after them, in order that she shouldn't burn them with her heat. Now she was setting a little, but she cast her light on the tips of the towers and the trees and her skirts stretched out over all the square that was around the city like she was speaking to the creations of her making.[7] "On your behalf, creations of God, on your behalf I went out from the city to dwell in the fields, the vineyards and the villages. In order that you know that I am the messenger of the God of Zion, and I treat equally the small and the large, the city dweller and the villager. You villagers carried out much labor today, and your work is seen throughout my lofty house, people of the earth. You didn't close your doors and bolt them after you, but you stood there and suffered before me. Now come and enjoy the bounty of peace, because you know no jealousy and there is no hate in your eyes."

A dry wind[8] from the heights blew from every side of the valley, changing the fields to cities and the vineyards to nobles' palaces. All of the fields were filled with men, women and children. The respectable sons of Zion and esteemed daughters of Zion went out to breathe the air. The farmers and the villagers returned from their work to refresh themselves and rest from the labor of the day. Some walked carrying their sickles in their hands, and some came and went singing because they carried sheaves. Even the shepherds strolled and sang, because the day was retreated and the night called them to rest, and the bleats of their flocks were heard into the distance. The vine-

---

7. Habakkuk 21:8
8. Jeremiah 4:11

yards filled with people from the heights of Zion, sitting and drinking from wine bowls and eating the blessed fruits of the earth.

Yochanan, the son of Simon the high priest, sat in one vineyard that belonged to Aviazar, but he didn't eat and didn't drink. He just watched between the rows of the vineyard as the crowds passed before him. He looked, and behold! Amongst the daughters of the shepherds walked one maiden who was lovely as the moon and beaming like the sun. Her face was inscribed in purity and honesty, and her eyes sparkled like the stars in the sky as they searched in every direction, until she beheld her mother standing at a distance at the entry of the vineyard. She ran to greet her and to hug and kiss her, and she said, "Greetings, dear mother. I saw our king from a distance today, long may he live, together with a great assembly of Israel walking with him to Mount Modein. Without doubt this must be the anniversary of the death of his father the high priest Matitiyahu. I wanted to run home and help you in the house, but I couldn't abandon the flock that is under the supervision of Boaz and his brother Ustus, lest they all scatter in the hills without a shepherd."

The mother laughed at the words of her daughter, and she said, "Blessed is the Lord of Zion, Yehudit my darling daughter. Peace unto you. I did all of my work today without you, and it wasn't heavy on me, but what's this my ears hear that you were watching the flocks? Have your parents made you a shepherdess? Won't your father be wroth with you if he hears about this, because your parents didn't bring you up to watch the sheep. Secondly, didn't the high priest with his two sons and many of the dignitaries of Israel honor us today by visiting our vineyard? You weren't there and didn't see all the honor we merited today from the friend of God and the people, our King, because he spoke to your father and blessed him and all his house."

"God forbid that I should violate your instructions," replied the maiden, "But didn't you instruct Yehuda to go to the harvesters and supervise them, that they leave the gleanings as is proper? As there was a fresh breeze this morning, so I went with him, and thought that I would return in a little while. But when I arrived there, I saw the flock scattered over the face of the pasture, with only old Rueven sitting a ways off and unable to do a thing. I asked him, "Where are the shepherds?" He answered me "Go to Boaz's house and you will see what is there." I went there and behold, Boaz was lying on a sick bed. His brother stood beside him but he didn't know what to do. I ran to the fields and picked herbs, and I also milked one goat and gave him a drink. I boiled the herbs and I ordered his brother to give him one spoonful to drink every hour, and I also ordered him not to leave the bed of the sick man all day. And I promised him that in the evening my dear mother would also come to visit him, because maybe the drugs that I prescribed him wouldn't help and it was important to call in a doctor greater than I!' As she spoke a gentle smile was visible on her lips that added more favor and charm to her beauty and splendor. "Ustus said to me: "How can I sit all day next to my brother! Won't the flock disperse without a shepherd?" So I promised him on my word that I would watch them all day, and what could I do? Truthfully I was very sad that I was too late for their visit, but for all that I am satisfied because I saved a man from harm, and who wouldn't have done as I? Besides this, it escapes my reason to understand how it is shameful, my dear mother, to herd sheep? Wasn't Rachel the Matriarch a shepherdess?"

"It's not shameful my daughter, only we don't put such labor on your shoulders. There is always the danger that you will ruin[9] yourself with the gentle daughters of Zion, for if they knew that Yehudit the daughter of Aviazar was herding sheep, then they would abhor[10] you in their souls."

Yehudit laughed and said, "If what happened to me today were to happen to them and they didn't do as I, then my soul would abhor them, even though they are the daughters of ministers and aristocrats."

"You are right my darling daughter," said the mother. "The Lord will recompense according to your deeds, and your heart is whole with the Lord and the people. Now pray know that the son of the high priest, young Yochanan, remains in our vineyard by his fathers

9. Proverbs 18:24
10. Zechariah 11:8

permission until tomorrow."

The maiden blushed from happiness and asked, "Where is he?"

"In the vineyard," the mother answered.

"If so, let us go home, because it's not proper for us to stand here," and she didn't know that Yochanan watched her closely and listened attentively to everything she said.

"How beautiful and wonderful she is, attractive and wholesome like no other! In her beauty and wisdom she resembles my aunt Yehudit when she was young," said the youth in his heart. Then he turned and went to sit on a bench that was made for resting, and he submerged himself in the refuge of his thoughts.

## ᔌ Chapter Three — Yochanan and the Children of Aviazar

The night came and went, and the dark curtain that covered the light blue skies rose slowly to reveal them. The first rays of the sun[11] began spreading their brightness and awakening all those who were sleeping and drowsing.

The whole household of Aviazar rose to do their work, but Yochanan, the son of Simon, remained lying on his bed in the summer house in the vineyard. Aviazar closed the vineyard in order not to disturb the man from his sleep. Yehudit and Yehuda, the children of Aviazar rose also and they went to another vineyard which was near the first.

"Pray tell me, dear brother, what is the appearance of the young priest, this son of the high priest? Does he look like his father, who always seems to me as an angel on high?" asked Yehudit.

"He is a beautiful lad beyond compare," answered Yehuda.

"May the Lord grant that I see him and speak to him face to face, then I would be happy," said Yehudit at the end of the walk.

---

11. Job 3:9

"Sit here," said Yehuda, "until he rises from his sleep, and then you will be able to see him."

"I will go home and I won't again come here as long as the young priest will be here, because it's not proper," said Yehudit on second thought, even though every limb of her body trembled from longing to see the son of the king.

"Pray pardon me, lily of the valley," a voice was heard speaking from behind them. "Pray pardon me. If I am disturbing you then I will leave your father's house immediately. But tell me please, my innocent one, what wickedness you find in me that you distance yourself from me even while I seek to be near you."

Yehudit and Yehuda were stunned when they turned about and saw that Yochanan, the son of the king, spoke such good and pleasing words to them. Yehuda was mute and didn't answer a word, but Yehudit stood firm with a brave spirit and said, "God forbid that you, a prince of God, should think such about your maidservant, the daughter of your servant Aviazar. As great as the respect for your father and our ruler's household is in the eyes of all Israel, so it is in our eyes. How could your coming to us be for me anything other than a boundless honor? Why does my lord speak words like this? If it is good in your eyes, then remain with us many days. We will always be at the ready for anything you command."

"If you await my command, saffron of the Sharon, then the instruction I lay upon you is that from this day you will think of me as a brother. And I, like a brother, will think to the welfare of his dear sister."

Yehudit blushed and was mute, but Yehuda said, "And how is your sister, the wife of Ptolemy?"

"Alas, my sister is miserable. She is wretched like no other because despite her anger and wrath she was made Ptolemy's wife."

"And who compelled her like Mount Sinai leaning over the children of Israel,[12] that she be married to a man that her heart despises?"

---

12. "A mountain like a washtub." Talmud Bavli, Shabbat 88a. God encouraged the children of Israel to accept the Torah at Mt. Sinai by tilting the mountain over them

"Our father."

"This is an incomprehensible wonder to us," said Yehudit and Yehuda as one. "Does he not rule men justly, and not place any yoke on a man, much less his children?"

"My father did this for peace," said Yochanan. "After the defeat of the army of Antiochus at the hands of my grandfather Matitiyahu, wars began with all our enemies near and far, large and powerful wars. New destroyers continually sprouted from the midst of our people. Verily my grandfather slew a man while he was offering up pig fat to an appalling abomination, and many rose up in his place who did no better than him. My grandfather and my uncles Judas and Eliezar pursued them in hot anger, but even as they pursued them, they multiplied and spread."

"The evil ones will always flourish, like the poisonous herbs in the furrows of the fields[13] and the more one uproots them, the more they sprout," said Yehudit and turned red.

Yochanan laughed and said, "You are correct, honorable maiden, and you have given voice to a parable[14] that was unknown to me. As the Lord favored you with kindness and beauty, He also included wisdom and knowledge."

"If only my sister had been a man," said Yehuda. "By now, without doubt, she would be studying wisdom and would be a wonder in Israel."

"If she had been a man," said Yochanan, "She wouldn't be able to make happy the man that she chooses! But let us return, please, to our discussion. When my father rose in the place of his father and brothers to be the priest and also the ruler, the first thing he did was to make peace with those who pursued honor, as my father always called them. All of the evil done in Israel is done only for the sake of honor. It was their desire to make themselves rulers over the people of the Lord and to strip their skins from them. This was why they

---

13. A clever play on words, which without vowels can also be read "like the head on the demon Ptolemy"

14. Psalms 78:2

wanted to deliver the city of God into the hands of the Greek king, because he promised to raise them to be under-lords and lieutenants. In the cause of peace, my father gave his daughter as a wife to one of these pursuers of honor, and this was Ptolemy. Then everyone knew that only towards the sinners and the rebels that angered the Lord did my father turn his hand to strike them with the vengeance of the Lord of hosts. As to those who sought peace for their people, my father entered a covenant with them. But the eyes of a man will not be satisfied, least of all the eyes of Ptolemy. Verily he will not say that it's enough of an honor to be the son-in-law of the high priest. To increase his honors he requested my father to give him permission to war against our enemies, so the land that he would conquer would be his to govern. But my father refused to provoke war with those who didn't do us any harm and who didn't violate our borders. This answer raised the anger of Ptolemy to a murderous pitch, and my sister told my father that she was very frightened for our lives. Her heart told her that he plots evil against us, because many chieftains of the people come to his house and hold friendly council with him. But my father calmed her heart, and said to her, "Do not fear. Are you not his wife whom he loves with an eternal love? Furthermore, it's not in his power to do anything to us." From these words you can understand that my sister is very wretched." Yochanan wished to talk more, but Aviazar came and requested Yochanan to come to the garden hut to take refreshment, and he was astonished to see his children talking to the son of the high priest.

# ⤳ Chapter Four — The Feast in Antiochia

The palace of the king of Greece[15] in Antiochia was a wonder this day. It was even more splendid and glorious than normal days,

---

15. Greek Syria, the Seleucids

because it was a holiday for the king. All the great and respected chiefs of all the foreign lands that were vassal states came to the festival. Great crowds flowed from every direction. From the poorest of the people to the loftiest citizens, all came to stare at the magnificence inside. The guests went inside, and those who weren't invited stood without and searched for some occasion they could talk about.

Behold, here came a carriage harnessed to four horses, and the horse's gear was of pure silver, and the carriage body was of welded silver.

"Look, Sabinous! Here is King Litira, son of the Egyptian Queen, arriving at the feast of the king."

"And what's the wonder in this, Giganus? Kings visit kings. Had King Litira come to you, you would have cause to wonder."

Giganus laughed and said, "You are a great clown for jesting, but look there, look! A chariot is traveling this way, and it exceeds the splendor and glory of Litira's carriage by a factor of ten. Who is sitting in it?"

"We will go and look," said Sabinous.

"Stay where you are, because if you lose your place you won't see a thing." The chariot noisily and rapidly passed in front of them. The two speakers stared in amazement and said to one another, "The chariot glitters with silver and fine gold as only seen with great kings. Who is he?"

"Maybe a king's son comes from a far nation, and wishes to take the king's daughter, Helena, the most beautiful of women."

"This can't be right, because Litira loves Helena and she also loves him." The chariot stopped, the driver opened the door, and from it emerged a young man of beautiful countenance, tall like a date palm and sturdy like an oak. On his face shone pride and a haughty heart, and his black eyes sparkled like stars on a bright night, beaming rage and hatred together, as if he was prepared for war. But when he stepped from the cab, one of the great ministers of the Greek king ran to greet him, and they hug and kissed one another.

"I am happy and overjoyed, Ptolemy my friend, that you fulfilled everyone's wish. Come now, come my dear, because the King, Queen and also the beautiful Helena are waiting for you with pining eyes." When Ptolemy heard the name Helena, all the sorrow fled from his face and he struck palms as a token of thanks for the warm greeting that had been delivered, and the two of them disappeared into the hall of the palace. Sabinous stood shocked and astonished, and said to his friend Giganus, "Do you know who this rich man is, with the chariot more splendid then the carriage of King Litira? He is a Jew. He is Ptolemy, the son-in-law of King Simon of Jerusalem.

"If that's the case," said Giganus, "Then there's no wonder in all the richness we saw on his chariot. Are they not the champions and men of the Lord? They have subjugated many peoples and taken their silver and gold from them. Many are the lands that have to pay them tribute, so who has money now if not the Jews? The brothers of the king, Yehuda, Yonatan and Eliezer, caused many of our citizens to fall wounded. Now we are all happy that we are at peace with the Jews. But what is Ptolemy doing here?" asked Sabinous, as if to himself. "Is he not a Jew, and the Jews will not worship the gods, neither do they know idols or masks. They say, "The God of Zion is greater than all the gods, and He gives strength and daring to those who serve Him faithfully." I was one of the King's soldiers who camped around their city, and we saw that God fought for them. Look over there," said Sabinous, "There in the great palace stand the two greatest gods, Jupiter and Adonis covered in fine gold, with many candles placed around illuminating them from all sides. And here Ptolemy sits in the chair on the right hand of the king. This honor was never given to a Jew."

"The ways of the Lord are miraculous," said the king to Ptolemy. "Who would have said[16] to the kings of Greece who were your adversaries that they would now seek after your peace and well being."

"May the Lord grant it be so, and let the hearts of all my people turn to peace as your own hearts," answered Ptolemy.

The king examined Ptolemy, but didn't say a word. Ptolemy continued to speak, "My father-in-law, the king, wants to cause all those

---

16. Genesis 2:17

who serve the gods to pass from the earth."

"Who will hearken to him? Who will command me to choose a new god for myself?" the king asked Ptolemy.

"His sword and his arm," Ptolemy answered the king.

"Pray tell me about this, my friend Ptolemy," said the king, and he drew his chair to Ptolemy's, lest anyone overhear their words.

Upon seeing that they were having a quiet conversation, all of the ministers rose from their places and wandered about the great palace to its length and breadth, in order not to interrupt them. "Pray tell me. Will it be from the great temple in Jerusalem and at the service before the Highest that this profanity will go out? Is it conceivable that Simon the high priest will desecrate his oath and end the peace in the land? From the first, I assumed you came here because you were angry at your father-in-law, but I tell you that a man like Simon will not act perversely."

"And what he did to the children of Edom was not wicked?" Ptolemy asked the king.

"His love for his God compelled him to this."

"Let us assume that," said Ptolemy, "But pray imagine, my lord king, what you would say if your beautiful daughter or handsome son were to give their hand to common folk, children of low families. Would you approve of this?"

"God forbid that I or my children do a thing like that. I will not give my children to any but the mightiest rulers of earth."

"Imagine now, my lord king, that the brother of my wife, the king's son, has picked for himself the daughter of a villager to marry. The villager has no name, beyond the fact that his father slew many of the soldiers in the army of Antiochus in the days of Matitiyahu. The king told them to cleave well to one another, because the maiden found favor in the eyes of Yochanan and his mother, Hagbira."

"Maybe the king did this for the peace?" the king asked Ptolemy, "He is a good man, and this could be very useful in buying him the hearts of the people, more so than majesty and force."

Ptolemy shook his head and said, "My lord king! For the scorn and disgrace he will pour on me through the giving of my wife's brother to the daughter of a low family, I will never pardon him. I will always look at him as a man who has stripped my honor from me."

"Pray relax, my friend," said the king to Ptolemy, "And what is the honor of your father-in-law to you? Do I not respect your honor greatly, because I see that honor is dearer to you than any fortune, and you will receive the respect due to a king in my house and in my land." The king rose and Ptolemy after him, and they went into the ballroom. King Litira took Helena, and after them all the beautiful wives and daughters of the chiefs of Greece went out to dance. Helena sat to rest and the king took Ptolemy by his arm and sat him next to his daughter, who received him with grace and enchanting lips, as if they were already old acquaintances.

Helena, the daughter of the King of Greece was so very beautiful and lovely that she was beyond compare. With her bewitching lips she could lead mighty men astray, and malice and cunning dwelt together within her. Her father had previously instructed her to ensnare Ptolemy, and she went out to dance with him.

In the arms of the beautiful Helena, Ptolemy forgot his God, his people, his country, his wife and his family. The daughter of Greece was all he could see, and she understood his thoughts and assisted him on the way to destruction. She put her arm about him and brought him out to the garden of the king to converse. There she enticed him with great skill, and with smooth words she pushed him until he sold himself to do every abomination.

Ptolemy, on seeing that nobody was with them, got on his knees and said, "Beautiful Helena, daughter of the heavens! Could I possibly hope that you will say the words that will make me eternally happy? It never would have occurred to me to think this way, but your goodness and the loveliness of your speech taught me how to speak of things like this."

"Away with you, Jew," cried Helena laughingly, "Does not my father swear by the name of the god Jupiter? He would never give me to a man who hasn't placed on his head the crown of a king. If you will do this, then I will be yours, because I also love you."

Ptolemy's face glowed with happiness, and he said, "Listen to me now, daughter of the heavens! I didn't hope to hear this from you, but now I will swear to you by the greatest God of all the gods that I am yours. Pray know that the throne of Simon, my father-in-law, the throne of Judah, I will overthrow to the ground and I will lay the dead at your feet. By the God of Zion I swear to you, that I will put an end to the entire family of my wife, just for you."

"If you do this thing, I will be yours forever, and my father will give you a mighty army that will help you to the throne. But promise me on your word that if you become the king of Judah and Jerusalem, you won't compel me to serve the God of Zion, because I fear the gods of my father." They continued talking, and the king came to the garden and saw them in friendly conversation, and he said, "I am happy, my daughter, because I see that Ptolemy has found favor in your eyes more than all the ministers and King Litira."

Helena laughed and said, "Know now my dear father that I did a great thing without asking you, but I hope that you will agree with me. I chose this honorable man Ptolemy for myself, to be my husband, and he will make me the queen of Judah. Therefore, if he requests from you soldiers and armies, don't withhold his wish from him."

"I will fulfill both of your requests," answered the king.

Ptolemy parted from the king and his daughter full of happiness and cruel murder.

## ⤳ Chapter Five — Helena Before the Assembly

After Ptolemy set out on his way from the palace of the king of Greece, the king summoned all of his great men along with King Litira, and said to them, "Hear me now, my brothers, my people! I have a great thing to tell you, but first swear to me lest you make it known to anyone before the proper time. Pray know that what we were never able to achieve with our swords and our bows, neither us nor our fathers, has now been obtained by my daughter using only her wisdom and beauty." Then Helena, the daughter of the king of Greece, came in and spoke to them saying, "I will be glorified over you, great men and heroes of Syria. Many are the lands and peoples you have conquered and the kings you have captured. But at Jerusalem your champions were slaughtered. There the shield of your heroes was vilely cast away[17] and you were smitten and retreated back. You fled before the Jews, fleeing the sword and the slaying. I, a young maiden who has never held a sword and scorned the javelin, never worn armor and helmet, I will deliver to you all of the champions and great men of Jerusalem, even the King of Judah. You will be revenged on him for the blood of our heroes that was spilled by his hand, and by his father and brothers."

All of the listeners wondered, and they said, "If you will do this thing, princess, you will miraculously subdue a people. Kings will rejoice in you and queens will praise you, and as the temple of Minerva marks that she was a woman of wisdom, so in the days to come will the temple of Helena stand for wisdom and courage. Tell us how and by what means are you able to do this?"

"I delved into the heart of Ptolemy the Jew. He cares only about modern things and he hates the old. He utterly hates the laws of his father-in-law, and he has complained in the ears of my brother many times saying, "How happy are the people of your land, because the king and the priests are two different factions. Not so in my country, the king is also the high priest, and his family has the great priesthood, the captains and the government. All the treasure that our heroes amass is brought under the hands of the priests, and apart from the priests, no man is free to act.[18] What will be our end? Did they not call us Hellenists? Because the aristocracy of our people made common cause with you, my father-in-law and my brothers-in-law were out to destroy us. But my father-in-law made peace with us, and what is this peace? From all the cities and lands of the people we

---

17. 2 Samuel 1:21
18. Genesis 41:44

conquered, did he give us even a single city to rule over? Because he gave me his daughter to wed I should forgive him for all the evil he did to us?" So spoke Ptolemy and when I heard this I said to myself, "Here you have caught a traitor to the land of his fathers." In accordance with my council, my father invited him to the feast. This evening I stole the heart of the Jew, and he swore by the God of Zion that he will throw down the throne of Judah to the earth and place the dead at my feet. He will destroy his father-in-law and all his wife's family, the Hasmoneans, if I will only be his wife. I swore to him on this matter, and I hope that Jupiter won't think this a sin when I profane my oath, because after he does all these things, my father will send his whole army there to capture the city. And if Ptolemy comes for his reward, I will laugh and scorn him as is fitting for a fool and wicked one like he. I will say to him, "Shame on you, traitor to his god, traitor to his land, traitor to his people, traitor to his wife. Do you imagine that the daughter of a Greek king is like you? If I was to be yours, then I would also be called a traitor, because who knows? Maybe you would become wroth with me, and therefore my father, and then you would do to my father's whole house what you did to the house of your wife. Thus I will speak to him, and I will laugh at his distress, because I am for this honorable king." As she finished speaking she approached Litira the son of the Queen of Egypt and gave him her hand. King Litira and all of those who listened to her words applauded and cheered. They swore further on the matter saying, "Any man that reveals this secret to Ptolemy will be killed and all of his possessions confiscated." Replete with joy, laughter and happiness, King Antiochus and King Litira and Helena left the palace assembly.

# ⤳ Chapter Six — The Day of Atonement in the Days of Simon the High Priest

The sun came out in her glory to illuminate the earth and cast admiring rays on the beautiful perfection of Zion. There the splendor of the Lord in His holiness washed over the people who arrived and congregated to bow in the holy temple and to offer endless sacrifices. A multitude of priests stood in two rows, the high priest came in with his bull, and the bull was positioned between the vestibule and the altar. The high priest lay his two hands on the bull and confessed. Afterwards he brought out two lots and called to the Lord, and the people responded, "Blessed is His name." He tied a sign of warning to the head of a goat to be sent away and stood it by the house of the messenger. The second he ritually slew in front of the slaughterhouse, and he did all the work according to the laws until it was finished. Our glorious house was full of men, women and children from end to end. The priests stood in their service, the Levites in song and melody, and the ushers stood at their posts. The songs the Levites sang in the Temple could be heard throughout the streets of Jerusalem. The high priest was dressed in the garments of the Day of Atonement and he prepared himself to go into the Holy of Holies. He spoke words of encouragement to the people saying, "Hear me now my people, people of the Lord! Behold the Torah of the Lord is with you and you will love its statutes. Don't you know that our enemies and the enemies of the Lord are all around us? You know that all the nations have sought to cut off our name from the face of the earth since the day we were first called by the name Israel. Pharaoh was the first to make his yoke heavy on our fathers, and this last one, Antiochus, was mightier then he. Had not the Lord our God been with our fathers, and if not for his great mercy and the able deeds of our fathers who returned to the Lord with all their hearts and souls, we would be nearly finished from the earth. According to your will,

I rose in the place of my father to be priest in the place of His dwelling. Fear and trembling enter me and quaking engulfs me, because woe to us if we secretly transgressed the word of the Lord and didn't seek forgiveness and atonement for all of our sins. Now my brothers, my children and my people, call to the Lord with all of your hearts that He hear our voices from within His sanctuary and we not be destroyed. This is the eighth time that I have prepared to enter the Holy of Holies, and on none of those occasions has my heart been as afraid and anxious as this day. Do not think, my children, that my heart is afraid on my own behalf and on behalf of my father's house. God forbid, for I am no better than my brothers who were all devoured by the sword. It is on your behalf, my people, children of the living God, on your behalf I melt in tears. The Lord knows what will happen with us this year, and He knows who will return, because merciful and forgiving is the Lord. On this great day you will atone for all of your sins before the Lord." As he completed his words he vanished from their sight, but the sound of ringing bells that were on the borders of his garments were heard, so that all the people knew that the high priest had come within the Holy of Holies. The weeping of the people was stronger that day than any other Day of Atonement. But Ptolemy stood amongst all the people, he in whom we know ripened all the great evil that would come in this year to the high priest and most upright man and all his house. Ptolemy didn't cry and didn't take the words to heart.

And as the weeping of the people swelled as he went into the Holy, so multiplied the joy as the high priest came out of the Holy of Holies whole and uninjured. All the dignitaries of the city and all the people escorted the high priest to his home. There they rejoiced in great happiness and celebrated their good spirits, and they ate and drank and pleased their hearts. When the rising tempest of people in the house of the high priest lapsed into silence, he said to Yochanan his youngest son, "Was Aviazar here also?"

"He was, dear father, and he is still here now, but he stands at the side of the house and blesses you from afar."

"Approach me, Aviazar, my friend," the high priest called to him.

Aviazar approached with great respect and bowed towards the high priest, and blessed him and waited for him to speak.

"A month ago I sent you my words by way of Yochanan, my son. Did you receive them?" the high priest asked him.

"I received them, my lord high priest," answered Aviazar fearfully.

"Why didn't you answer me?" the high priest continued the questioning.

"I am humbled, my lord and king, by all the honor and respect that your servant has already been allotted. How could my heart overflow to believe also in this great honor that has never been merited by the majority of the great families of Israel? I am from the youngest of all the families of Israel, and I am reckoned amongst the toilers of the soil. I haven't entered the courtyards of kings and lords, except to go before you and your father. I always ran after him under swords and slung stones saying, "May the Lord grant that my life ransom the life of my lord." When the high priest Matitiyahu died, I exchanged my inheritance with my uncle, even though the value of my inheritance was twice that of my uncle's. Despite that I rejoiced on the purchase and the exchange like on a fortune, because now I am close to the deceased high priest. I commanded my son that when I die he should bury me in the corner of my vineyard, where it presses up against Mount Modein. But this matter ..." — Here Aviazar sank into silence, but the high priest understood his embarrassment and said to him, "Pray hear me, Aviazar! Does not your own mouth answer that you were a friend of my father's in his life, and you wish to be a friend to him also after your death? Why can't you believe that I also choose you to be my friend in life and in death? I have also carved myself a tomb in Mount Modein. Now we will make a covenant, the two of us, and you will give your daughter to my youngest son Yochanan to be his wife."

Aviazar's face paled, then reddened like scarlet from great happiness, and he said, "If these words emerge from the mouth of the high priest, without doubt it is the word of the Lord. I am your servant and I hearken the word of the Lord and your voice, my lord, and accept this great honor that is not for men of my standing."

"And why not for men of your standing?" said the high priest to comfort him. "Honor belongs not to us but to God. He will give it to those who are worthy before Him, and take it from those who make themselves vain. He despises the proud and raises the oppressed. Before Him the noble is not recognized before the meek. Only the eyes of men are never satisfied, and they always seek a fig tree on the land that the Lord apportions them. But you, my friend, the Lord removed from you all the lusts of mankind and you distance yourself from honor, therefore it pursues after you. The Lord gave you a son and a daughter through whom there will be many blessings, so why not recognize their value? My son's mouth is always full of praise for your son, because he is greatly learned in Torah, wisdom and fear of God. He is also a champion in war who bows down before no man. Why should he not inherit honor? And your daughter is pure in conduct and God-fearing, and she is a refuge to the poor and downtrodden, providing for them on their sick beds. One time she remained to watch a flock in place of a shepherd in order that he rest and ease his illness. Is she not suitable to be reckoned amongst the daughters of Aaron? What can you object to? Now you will tell your daughter that during the four days between Day of Atonement and the Feast of Tabernacles she will celebrate her marriage with my youngest son Yochanan."

Aviazar went forth from the house of the high priest and delivered the wonderful news to his wife and daughter, and their hearts grew faint because they couldn't believe it. Ptolemy had lived in the house of his father-in-law until this time, but when he heard all of these things, he left the presence of his father-in-law in a rage. He said, "We are seen by your words as kinsman to the rabble, my word of honor if it's not so. Verily you said He will make low the proud and raise the humble, and so it is. You make contemptible the majesty that you dress us in, and I will be raised in your place."

# ⤳ Chapter Seven —
# Feast and Mourning

Woe, cruel pen! You will not rest nor be quiet until you complete this history and these shocking stories. They will anguish the souls of those who read them, yet they are the events of our people's history. Every story about the people of our nation is written not with ink, but with blood, the blood of those martyrs for the Lord. They will be a support to the children of Israel who say, "In darkness we will live amongst the heathens." They were trapped and outnumbered in these massacres. The innocent are cruelly murdered from the world because they are not wary of evil men, believing in their loyalty and giving their confidence to those who intend ill for them. The anointed of the Lord, Simon the high priest, listened to the voice of his son-in-law the sycophant. With words of peace in his mouth, Ptolemy invited Simon to a feast, at which he was preparing to ambush and kill him.

Ptolemy and all his Hellenist companions arrived at the house of Ptolemy during the morning watch and waited there for the arrival of the high priest with his wife and sons. They welcomed them with open respect and love, and with hidden hostility. "I give thanks and blessings to you all for accepting my invitation," said Ptolemy, "But to you, ma'am, the greatest respect," said Ptolemy to his mother-in-law with a smooth tongue. "How good and pleasant this day will be, because you also, Hyrcanus and Yochanan are present. But Yochanan, why didn't you bring your wife Yehudit, who is the loveliest of women?"

"I didn't want to bring her here, because she is a villager and she shouldn't be spoiled by the aristocracy of Judah."

Ptolemy stared at Yochanan with a penetrating look, and said, "Even in my house will you express your words like sword thrusts, Yochanan?"

"Do you invite guests to your house to shoot burning arrows and death at them? Then you say, "Wasn't I kidding?" Ptolemy! Is this what you will do?"

"It's contentious of you, my son, to quarrel with the husband of your sister!" cried Simon. "Have you forgotten that he is greater than you in both years and wisdom?"

Yochanan left him for the other room, and Simon the high priest said to Ptolemy, "I was very happy, my son, that you brought the aristocracy of Judah here to make a covenant of peace, as you asked of me. I am always for peace, even with those who are for war. Now that they seek peace, I give to you the five cities that we conquered from the inhabitants and all the possessions within them. Just be whole with the Lord and with His land and His people."

"As your word, my lord, we will do," answered Ptolemy and the rest of the Hellenists who were gathered in the house of Ptolemy at his wish.

"Will the elders of Jerusalem also come here, my lord father?" Ptolemy asked his father-in-law purposefully.

"I didn't bring anybody, aside from my two sons," answered Simon. "My son Yochanan said I should bring the elders of the city and also their men with him, but I refused him, for what are men and servants to me? Am I not in the house of my son?"

The cruel heart of Ptolemy was dreadfully exultant on hearing from the mouth of his father-in-law that he was caught in the trap.

They all sat around the great table to eat and drink to their heart's content. They praised the good deeds of the high priest and they all conducted themselves benevolently as if seeking peace. Hyrcanus sat on the left hand of his father and Ptolemy on his right, but Yochanan didn't want to sit at the table and he found a pretext in saying that it was too hot for him. In truth his heart was afraid and anxious because he knew the wicked heart of Ptolemy.

Thus it happened that as Simon the Righteous sat tranquilly and without fear at the table of his son-in-law, the evil servants of Ptolemy rose up at the command of their wicked lord and slew this righteous innocent for no crime he had done. So ended the life of this hero who had fought many mighty wars and always triumphed over the enemy. No man could oppose him and he succeeded in all that he tried.

Behold, he fell at the unclean hands of an evil man who utterly separated himself from God. And when Hyrcanus saw that the blood of his father was spilled on the earth, he said, "Slay me together with my father, and maybe I will revenge my father's blood vengeance." He grabbed the sword from the hand of one of the assassins and slew many of them, then he also fell to the earth, killed by the sword of Ptolemy. Yochanan, when he saw all this, quickly fled from them saying, "Here I am one and they are many. If I oppose them, then they will kill me like my brother and I won't be able to revenge the blood vengeance of my father and brother." He fled to Gaza and Ptolemy pursued after him, but didn't catch him, and he fled to the city of Ragona and stayed there a couple days. When Yochanan's whereabouts became known in Jerusalem, they sent all the elders of the city and all the to bring him to back to Jerusalem and anointed him King and high priest in place of his father. Then he went out with a great army to war against Ptolemy and revenge from him the blood vengeance of his father and brother. Ptolemy went and closed himself up in a fortified city, and he took his wife and his mother-in-law with him. And it came about that when Ptolemy saw Hyrcanus[19] storming the city to destroy it, he took his wife and mother-in-law and hoisted them to the top of the wall. He commanded that they be bound, and tormented them in a cruel manner. Hyrcanus was very distressed and he decided to withdraw, but his mother called to him saying, "Don't, my son. God forbid you move away from the city before you exact revenge on the enemy of your father and your brother. Pray, my son, remember your father, the most straight and righteous of men. He was the last of his father and brothers, the right pillar that the whole house of Israel was supported on. If the pillar falls, then what is supported on it will utterly collapse, if you don't hurry to rid the land of the awful wickedness of Ptolemy. Do not soften your heart because of the cruelty of the wicked one who tortures us. Would he not return to his evil path? Verily he will kill us dead, and we can live

---

19. *[Original footnote]* When the elders of Jerusalem named Yochanan ruler in place of his father they gave him the name of his older brother Hyrcanus on account of his bravery.

no longer after our honor and our skin is stripped from us. So what are you waiting for! Here I command you, my son, the command of a parent. Don't look upon our torture. Destroy the city and revenge the blood vengeance of us all. Be cruel this day and you will be merciful the rest of your life." When he heard his mother's words, he started to storm the city as before, but Ptolemy increased the cruelty of the torments in an awful manner and the young man didn't know what to do. He wept from the rage in his heart and he said, "Lord God of hosts, who dwells with cherubs. You know the innermost thoughts of every man and You know that it is in my grasp to take blood revenge on this man. You oblige and command us to do this vengeance, because the earth will not be atoned for blood except by the blood of those who spill it. But I am greatly distressed seeing the torments with which he tortures my mother and my sister. Therefore, I pray to You with all my heart, Lord God, excuse me from the wheels of justice. Woe, my miserable mother and sister. Where will I take consolation for your bodies covered in the desecrating blows of the wicked one who offered his hand in peace and violated his covenant. Woe! Wicked one son of evil. Whether I kill you or whether I don't kill you, you will be an object of abhorrence forever. Know that the blood of my father and my brother and my mother and my sister all call out to me from the earth, but I am not able. Shall I wait until Judgement Day arrives for him? No! No, I cannot wait. Come, my brothers! Behold the blood of the Hasmoneans who redeemed you from all suffering, who saved you and your fathers from robbery and murder, who expanded your borders until this day. The blood cries to you to take revenge on this ravenous man and bloody son-in-law." At his word they all approached to break the city walls by force, but the wicked one continued to do his singular work[20] until the blood poured from the women, and he called to Yochanan and said, "Hear me, Yochanan. If you don't withdraw from the city then I will cast them from the wall and their skulls will explode on the rocks." And his mother cried, "Don't withdraw, my dear son. These torments are

---

20. Isaiah 28:21

beloved to us in our knowing that you, my son, will take revenge on the man who destroys us. Even more so, because I see that all the people are taking your orders."

"In love and willingness we obey the commands of your son, honorable lady!" called the multitude of people around the walls. "Oh, woe! Woe to us. Woe to us that we have seen you so, wife of the high priest, whose honor is dearer to us than our own lives. We are all prepared to die together on behalf of this son of yours if a hand be against him. He is our king, and he will minister in the Holy in the place of your husband, because all of Judah and Israel anointed him to be king over them."

"You will be blessed by the Lord, my children," the mother of the king called courageously from atop the wall, and she suffered the torments without crying out, in order that her son wouldn't withdraw from the city. "The Lord bless you all who served me in this great happiness. Bless the Lord who showed me this consolation before my death, because I leave a son sitting on the Hasmonean throne after them. Woe to you, completely wicked one. Torment us, but these consolations you will not steal from us anymore, and he will demand our blood from you."

The walls of the fortified city were starting to breach under the iron rams that struck them, and Hyrcanus thought that in just a short while, the blood of Ptolemy would be flowing down like the blood of his father. But that very moment Ptolemy approached the women and swore he would push them from the wall. Then a great and dreadful war was stirred up in the heart of Hyrcanus, a war that no sensitive man could withstand. He cried to the angel of death, "Stop it, because I can't look upon the blood of my parent and my sister. Would doing this bring my father and my brother back to life?" And he cried to Ptolemy, "Leave off and I will withdraw from the city. But don't say in your heart "Behold I am saved, Yochanan withdraws before me!" It may be that my sword will not take you, but if you don't die from our hands, do you imagine you will live? Remember well the words that I speak to you this day. Behold the day is coming that you will say, "Better I should die than live." The blood of the

Hasmoneans will pursue you always and overtake you when you rest.[21] Woe, traitor! Traitor to the living God! Traitor to his people! Traitor to the land of his birth! Traitor to his wife! Woe, my sister, dear soul. Woe, my mother. I see your blood dripping to the ground, yet God lacks hands to save you." When he finished speaking he withdrew from the city in depressed sprits. But the wicked traitor Ptolemy said to his wife and his mother-in-law, "You wished to deliver me to Yochanan to be killed by his sword, therefore you will both die." He slaughtered the daughter of the high priest before the eyes of her mother in cruel murder, then he slew also the mother, wife of the high priest. So the lives of these good and dear women were ended by the warring hand[22] of the wicked aristocrat. He ran after foreign honor and set his eyes on a strange woman who manipulated him. But his day would also come.

## ✏ Chapter Eight — From Mourning to Joy

The darkness passed and the heavy clouds that covered the splendor of the skies gathered and left, and the light of the heavens began to shine on our Holy land. The sun began to spread her light to all who awaited her, and brought with her a healing balm to heal the bruised hearts that hadn't been shined on for a very long time. And what is the name of this good balm that heals the sick and redeems the imprisoned? Is it not time, because the Lord changes the seasons. Truly the Lord caused his people to mourn by taking the crown from the head of Simon the high priest. That righteous man, a Hasmonean and the son of a Hasmonean, had governed his people in righteousness, justice, kindness and mercy. He had inherited from Aaron, his forefather, the quality of loving peace and pursuing it. Through all of this he didn't abandon his people and won't ever abandon them, for

---

21. Judges 20:42
22. Psalms 39:11

he gave them his son Hyrcanus in place of his fathers, that there would be a just man to govern them. The holy city of Jerusalem was filled with joy, the joy of the Lord, and from all the cities they came to celebrate the festival of Succot. There was joy and happiness in the palace of King Hyrcanus and all the dignitaries of the city came to cheer the king and high priest. These days were days of happiness and rejoicing for all the Jews, because the days of celebrating the Temple of Foundation[23] had arrived. It was now four days after the young high priest went into the Holy of Holies to do the service of the Day of Atonement and emerged whole. This day, the joy in Israel was multiplied more, because after Ptolemy slew his wife and mother-in-law, his hope had been that he would go to Antiochus and take the king's beautiful daughter as his wife. Ptolemy had hoped that her father would give him a mighty and numerous army to lay siege to Jerusalem and destroy it, and to take the kingdom by force from his wife's brother. His hope went for naught because when he went to the king and told him all he had done to his wife's family, the rage of the king was roused to a murderous pitch, and he said, "Out of my presence, traitor! You would be my son-in-law? My daughter would be the wife of a man as sinful and soured as you! Not many days would pass before you did to my daughter and to all her father's house as you did to your wife, the daughter of the King of Judah. Was she not also the daughter of a king, and of the most beautiful daughters of Zion? My daughter requested of me that I never let you see her face again, because fear seized her when she realized all the great abominations you did to your wife. She has given her hand to the son of King Litira who rules in Prifaliya."

When Ptolemy heard these words, he drew his sword from it scabbard and sought to stab the king in the belly, but the servants of Antiochus grabbed the sword from him and the king expelled him from his city and from all his kingdom. And he went to Tyre and he dwelt there.

The king went out with a great army and all his camp, and he laid

---

23. The stone at the top of the Temple Mount is know as the foundation stone

siege to Jerusalem and sought to make a breach. When Succot festival arrived, Hyrcanus sent messengers to Antiochus and requested him that he make a truce for all the days of the festival and not interrupt the worship of the Lord. This suited Antiochus and he greatly honored the messengers. He sent his own messengers to Hyrcanus, the king, with words of peace and faith, and sent a sacrificial bull to the temple of the Lord, and the horns of the bull were gilded in gold to the honor of the Lord. The priests waved the bull in a wave offering to the Lord and they raised it on the altar. The messengers of King Antiochus returned to him whole and well satisfied as is written in the book of Josephus — "And these were the events that made the festival happy and joyful for all the Jews, and they forgot the evil that had occurred to them."

But one person who should have been happier this festival than all the rest of Israel was sad spirited. She was Yehudit, the daughter of Aviazar, the wife of Hyrcanus the king and high priest. When the tidings came to Jerusalem that Ptolemy had slain Simon the high priest, her father Aviazar couldn't bear this great pain. He sobbed bitterly over the loss and became bedridden, and after a couple of weeks he died. And Hyrcanus the king decreed that Aviazar be buried on Mount Modein next to the tomb of Simon his father.

And Yehudit, despite all the honors that she received now, took no comfort and was depressed and mourning for her father, because he would never see with his own eyes all the honor that the Lord granted to his beloved daughter.

## ᔒ Chapter Nine — The End of the Wicked

In Prifaliya, which was ruled by King Litira, a man lay on his sick bed. His face was white like the face of death, and his hands shook with occasional tremors. The seal of death had come to his flesh and was plain upon him. A little longer and he would be redeemed from all the wounds and injuries that tore at his brain these many years. Were they not the pangs of conscience, the final chastisement that comes to every sinner and criminal at the end of his days? Next to his bed sat an old man. This man was not of his family and not of his people, but a man of a foreign nation. His office was to stand watch next to the bed of the sick as a kindness to the common people. The watchman said to himself, "May the Lord grant that this be the last day for this lunatic, who continually relives his old deeds, as if he did good and he can find some delight in them. Were it not for the orders of the king and queen to watch him until the last moment of his life, I would have already put an end to this sad and shameful life which is a burden to us all."

"This man lies on his bed with his eyes shut as if he fears to open them, and he speaks these words: "God in heaven! How awful is death to one loaded with sins and transgressions. How heavy it is for the sinner to die as he confronts the memories of murderous deeds done for imaginary honor, and in a moment he will dwell with his creator.[24] He delivered up his very soul to the king of destruction, and he sold himself to every abomination and every murder and robbery. He didn't think then that feelings of regret would later conquer his heart and burden him greatly, or that the voice of rue would cry constantly in his ears, "Be gone with you! You will not come into the midst of human beings anymore, because your honor is in ignominious disgrace and you rage for the imaginary prestige you trafficked in. Behold, so is the end of every evil-doer. He can't even die like everybody else. Not so is the fate of someone who keeps himself from sin and is innocent of robbery and murder. The heavens always rejoice over such a one, and if such a man sees death before him, he will go calmly and confidently to greet it, because that man is given a vision of life until its end. As a merciful mother takes her playful child and puts him to sleep at her breast, so death will take him in its arms to sleep at its bosom. He will be laid on a silk couch and put to sleep in the cradle of eternity. But I, I! Where am I? In a foreign land,

---

24. Job 39:28

lonely and naked. Far from everyone, far from the Lord, even should I cry my prayer with eyes closed. Far from the land of my fathers, far from my people, without a wife or children. Here my life will end, here I die! Here, who will cry for me, who will shake their head. Nobody! If my people hear of my end they will rejoice and praise the Lord God as they rejoice at the fall of an enemy. And why shouldn't they rejoice? Was I not worse to them than all of their enemies? Woe, woe to me for what I did! I brought destruction to the dwelling of the upright. I spoke of peace and faith and they believed in my peace, but with a sharp and polished sword I pierced them. I pray to you, high priest with the holy anointing oil on your head. Have pity on my soul and torture me no longer. Here you stand before me in the precious white garments you wore on the holiest day of the year. In one hand you hold the censer to light the incense, and with the other hand you cast flaming coals on my head, burning me with your fire. You shout in my ears, "See now, murderer! See the blood that you spilled like water on the ground! You made me blemished,[25] and I won't be able to go before the Holy to atone. Therefore your sin will not be atoned for even when you die, because your fire won't be extinguished and the worms devouring you won't die, and you will be an everlasting abhorrence. Woe! How true were the words that Yochanan spoke: "Hear me now Ptolemy. Behold the days will come to you that you will say "May the Lord grant I expire from this life." The blood of the Hasmoneans will pursue you always and prevent you from resting. Woe, traitor! Traitor to the living God! Traitor to your people! Traitor to the land of your birth! Traitor to your wife. He raised his hand against the sanctified of the Lord." A curse be on you, Antiochus. A curse be on your daughter that incited me to do these abominations and afterwards jeered me. The highest authority prepared this awful instrument of torture for me when I was sent to this cursed land and always saw that snake before me. It was the beautiful Helena who led me astray to do all this. Every day I see, I ask the God of Zion whom I angered to hurry and speed my end. But she, she is the statue of jeal-

---

25. The priests, just like the animals they sacrificed, had to be physically perfect to go before God

ousy[26] that in order to acquire her I came to this awful condition today. Truly I am not alone now, for here are my father-in-law and his son and my mother-in-law and my wife, all of them standing around my bed and their blood dripping on my back. They are full of anger and seek to tear me to pieces. See, pray. See them all coming here to watch the end of their enemy. See, pray. Is his fate not inscribed, so what more could you want? Surely the God of Zion arranged this, that I didn't fall dead then to the hands of Yochanan. If only he killed me then, but now the suffering is hidden from my eyes."

Another watcher of the sick approached the bed and said, "And what will be the end of this sick, insane person? How long can he live?" The other watcher of the sick waved his hand against him as a sign to be quiet, and he also approached the sick bed. He saw that now the final moments of life were drawing close.

Ptolemy raised his two hands and put them over his eyes as if he desired to hide before his pursuers, as if they spoke to him from the ground. He said, "Forgive me, forgive me, righteous people and sanctified of the Highest. Do you not see the end of Ptolemy, the son-in-law of the high priest? Pardon me for all the evils with which I wronged you in malice of my heart and in awful murder. Maybe you will also forgive me . . . ." He didn't complete these words because the shackles of death set about him. The first watcher ran to tell this to the king and queen, as they sat eating and drinking to their hearts content. The watcher of the sick told them of all these things, of all the awful visions that haunted Ptolemy, and of all the things he said in the heat of his soul. The queen Helena answered with these few words: "Surely the hand of his god was punishing him. Thus is the end with all traitors, traitors to their gods, their homelands and their women."

*The End*

---

26. Ezekiel 8:3

# 6.

# The Love of the Righteous

*or*

# The Pursued Family

⁘

*Through six sorrows you will triumph,*
*through seven no harm will come to you*

*— Job 5:9*

Written by the maiden
Sarah Feiga the daughter of Joseph Menkin of Riga

*Published in Vilna, 1880*

# ⟜ Introduction

I have observed many of the things that are done under the sun and I have seen that this is a cruel time, with every calamity and trouble. This period has conceived and given birth to evil episodes and terrible incidents, a rod of punishment to those who pass under it.

As I stand frightened and horrified by this awful vision, I am yet astonished at this great wonder: That people boast about their kindness and compassion, but stand ready to support these goings-on and enjoy the sight that is before them, like the Spanish when they put a man on the rack.

I approached to see, "What is this?" I cried, "What is the name of this play before me? Is there also religious fanaticism in this praiseworthy country, where every man walks safely in his path without anyone able to discern nation from nation? Why does a man pursue his neighbor in unremitting hot anger? The wails of the oppressed and the screams of the broken are heard on every street and corner. Is there no salvation from the hand of hard-hearted oppressors?" When I examined the actions of these people I found that this wasn't religious fanaticism, but the intellectual jealousy and hatred which underlie every calamity and trouble. The jealousy and hatred established between knowledge and stupidity are greater than that of religious fanaticism. The foolish angrily pursue the wise and proudly crush them underfoot. They burn with zealous fire all those who gather wisdom and knowledge, never sparing them, never satisfied with their blood.

But the person who collects knowledge and understanding cannot look upon the excitement of evildoers and the conduct of a fool without admonishing them on their ways. The fool who hates knowledge and truth is wroth with all who love them. He realizes that he cannot speak out in public,[1] while his neighbor is praised there in everyone's mouth. His hatred grows and he doesn't pay attention, because at that moment he will be enjoying himself at a splendid banquet. The wise man will sacrifice his time and his moments of rest on the altar of knowledge. While the fool lies stretched on his couch, with eyes closed so as not to see the light, the wise man will give no rest to his eyelids until the morning light. He will keep watch over the gates of wisdom in order that he may later be able to disperse the clouds of darkness and lift the black veil that covers the eye of the land.

While the fool supports the hand of fate for the sake of tormenting a tortured soul, a considerate man applies himself to rescue the suffering and save them from distress.

How can one not praise a man like that? But for this the fool will burn with hatred, the utmost hatred, and pursue him with all his strength.

As all this passed through my thoughts, I said, "Who knows whose hand will be the upper and triumph, the hand of knowledge and truth or the hand of stupidity and lies?"

There were many times when it seemed that the magnificence of impudent stupidity and the might of lies would conquer.

But in the wink of an eye, knowledge and truth destroyed and broke all the fortresses and towers that had been built and prepared over many days by the forces of lies and stupidity.

Therefore I decided to try my strength and the strength of my pen, meager and weak though it is. I will bring together a collection of all those souls I saw as they passed before me in my imagination. I will stand them on the parade ground and dress them up according to their worth and their actions, and I will set each one in the place that befits him. I will place words in their mouths in order to show their conception. The plot of the story I have dressed in garments of love, because it is love, along with peace and tranquility, that is the objective of every person and the desire of every human, without which

---

1. Proverbs 24:7.

there is no joy on earth.

When I stood all of these souls in their places as on the theatre stage and I saw that they were in my hand, I judged each one according to his actions and I hope that I haven't erred in my judgement. Every man is requited according to his actions and rewarded according to his conduct.[2] I have called this story "The Love of the Righteous" or "The Hunted Family." By means of their upright love and the wholeness and truth that was between them, this hunted and smitten family returned to their place from which they had been driven and pursued in hot anger. Set in the days of Napoleon the Third and the Ninth Peace in the years 1851 to 1870.

---

2. Job 34:11.

# ❧ Prelude – Italy

I will take you, honorable reader, to a fine and pleasant country, a land of green and plenty. The skies and earth appear brand new to the people there. She is blessed from ancient times.[3] Is this not Italy, delicate and beautiful? You will go with me to Milano, the praiseworthy city, and there your eyes will behold every precious thing. The walls surrounding her are built of white marble, four thousand five hundred different statues encircle her like a crown, adding even more to her glamour and splendor. When you first step over the portal of the city, she will draw you in after her like an electrical force with the strength of her loveliness. Now imagine for yourself the beauty around the inside of the city. Every place your eye alights you see luxurious adornments, the tips of her towers and spires reach to the sky, her streets are splendid with pleasure palaces that the eye is not satisfied with seeing. Throngs of people from every land flow to her, until each man is pressed against his neighbor. She is the richest of the cities of Italy from the trade of many nations. The number of inhabitants found in her and her suburbs is around four hundred thousand. All of them make up her mix and do her work, going about with happy hearts and cheerful faces from seeing the majesty and splendor that is within her. Even the sun there is noteworthy in its beauty, shining and beaming as if making an effort to add more to the loveliness of the city. The violet sky spreads over the heads of the crowds, and from morning to evening their tumult is like the crashing waves of the ocean. Finally, the time of rest arrives for those labor-

---

3. *[Original footnote]* The blessing of Yitzchak to his first born – "From the fat of the land will be your dwelling." (Genesis 27:39) and our wise ones of blessed memory said "This is Italy." Breshit Raba 80:67 and Yalkut Shimoni.

ing within her, to relax from the noise and commotion of the day in order to regenerate the strength to greet tomorrow.

But imagine not, reader, on seeing the beauty of the city with her riches and good fortune, that the sun of fortune shines on every street and corner. Know that even there are found dark places where a ray of light doesn't enter (they cover and bolt the doors). Although we can take in the beauty of the enchanting city in a glance, we move on, because this isn't the aim of our story. We will only attend the places from which the light is absent. There we will find pleasures and delights for our spirits, for we won't be sitting in darkness. The light of Torah, wisdom, Haskalah, kindness, beauty and uprightness are found there; these are our treasured possessions. There I will guide you and bring you in order to meet and esteem, as I do, the worthy family who dwell there. You will also say that all that glitters is not gold and all that is earth is not for the plow, because gold may also be taken from dust.

# ◌ Chapter One –
# First Acquaintance

The time is January 1st 1861 at six o'clock in the evening. This is the season when winter strives with spring, because winter doesn't want to quickly give up his place where he has pitched his tent for weeks and months, and go wandering off into exile through different lands. Despite this, little by little the spring robs him of his rights, and shows him he is not a prosperous citizen here, for the sun stands on the right of the spring and destroys by day the nightly labors of the winter. When the spillways and canals are barely frozen, the sun comes along and melts them back to water. But the winter will not be frightened or intimidated and makes a firm stand.

The day and the night also struggle, because the one doesn't want to give up his place to the other, until the hand of one becomes daring and goes forth forcefully, driving the other before him, and day concedes to night.

At this moment as the sun is going down and the stars are yet hiding their power, a woman walks abroad. Her figure is wrapped in black garments and a black veil conceals her face along with netting over her head. But who is she? We cannot know, as she has covered her face, but her bearing and her refined step inform us that she is of the loftiest daughters of the land. She walks and gazes at each passerby, perhaps she will meet an acquaintance, then walks on. Suddenly she hears a voice addressing her. "Pardon me, dear maiden, for stopping you in the street!" The maiden lifted up her lovely eyes from behind her veil,[4] to see who was speaking to her, because these few

---

4. Song of Songs 4:1.

words pulled her heart after them. Despite her face being covered by a veil, her eyes sparkled like stars leaving their orbits on a clear night.

"Behold, for two years now I have been following your steps in order to speak a word to you, but you have always turned away from me. Did you imagine me a wolf waiting in ambush that all innocent kids must flee from him? Why are you walking alone in the evening on this quiet street, far from the commotion of the city and people?" The maiden gazed at him for a moment then tried to walk on, even though she knew he was a respectable man.

"Pray mistress, answer my words, then afterwards you will go on your way."

"In the dark we cannot discern between wolves and men, because sometimes we meet a wolf in the guise of a man, and therefore we must be cautious."

"If this is what you are looking upon, honorable maiden, then you will not be able to tell even by day. A wolf in ambush to catch an innocent kid will not come to the flock in the form of a wolf but wrapped in the skin of a sheep in order to deceive. I sincerely hope that you don't think me a wolf, and now that you know me a little, you will answer my words."

"When I went out from my father's house it was yet day," answered the maiden, "But I tarried at the house of my friend Goldberg. I thought certainly the stars will shine and light the way for me, but to my heart's anguish, they are all hidden under the clouds that I must walk in darkness. But sometimes a man will walk in darkness and it will be light for him like a bright day, yet under a bright sun like in our city of Milano a man walks in the dark like the middle of the night."

"In this, you speak correctly. The stars hid when you appeared because they are frightened that your glow will dim their shining, and therefore they disdain to compete with you."

"Leave off this speech, sir, because flattery is hateful to me."

"I also hate flattery, but I cannot hold the truth captive under my tongue."

"Have I spoken as you? Didn't I say that the stars were hidden because it was their will to darken the way for me."

"What do you need with a multitude of stars? May not a single star light the path for you and be your guard and shield in order that you travel safely on your way?"

"See now, sir," said the maiden, lifting her eyes on high, "Are they not all hidden? Therefore your imaginings are empty."

"Believe me, mistress, if you promised the stars not to shame their glow, then they would all come to you bowed down, their noses to the earth, as they did to Joseph."

"Have you forgotten that it was in a dream they bowed to him? Do not answer in dreams, for a dream comes from a multitude of interests.[5] So it was with Joseph when he dreamt his mute dream and his brothers interpreted for him, 'Shall you reign over us?'[6] He was thinking the whole time of being a king, and therefore he saw in his second dream the sun and the moon and the stars bowing down to him."

"Believe me, mistress, that as they bowed to Joseph in a dream they will bow before you in the end, if you only promise not to darken them by your glow."

A scarlet blush suffused the face of the maiden, and she turned her shoulder to go, but he blocked her way and said, "Pray mistress, answer my words."

"Behold, this is known to all," said the maiden, "That the majority of the heavenly bodies are dark. They only receive their light from the sun and without her they wouldn't illuminate anything. And what have they to do with me or I with them? Can I fire the heavens, am I not of the earth? Can we lower the planets to the earth and distance them from the sun? Would not both they and I then be dark? And if they sought later to fly upwards, then in the end they would fall back because others would have taken their places. Therefore, leave them in the sky to receive light from the sun and illuminate each other and not come to me, because I am on the earth, from which I was taken and to which I shall return."

---

5. Ecclesiastes 5:2 — continues with "and a fool is known by a multitude of words."
6. Genesis 37:8.

As the rejoicing of a wise man grows who has been working years on a thing and suddenly his reason brings him a new invention, so grew this man's happiness on hearing these energetic words from the mouth of the maiden he loved and for whom he had been longing. He was no longer able to contain the stormy spirit inside him and he cried out, "Gentle Finalia! So much I have heard about you. Now that I finally meet you I see your integrity, your precious soul and your intelligence lift you above every man. How happy will be the planet which descends to you from the heights of the skies, distancing itself from the sun to receive your bright shining. Could you truly believe, gentle one, that I cruise the streets just to exchange words with maidens? It is because I already know you and praise of your honorable name is always on my lips. But every time I meet you and seek to talk with you, you always find a strategy to elude me. Today, I saw you passing this way, so I kept watch on the street the whole time for your return. Now, honorable maiden, do you not know that the earth is also a planet like all the planets in the sky, and she also receives her light from the sun? If only I succeed in my ambition that you will call me by the name of a planet I will be happy, because surely you would be my light and in the end I wouldn't fall."

"What suits you is the name Victor," said the maiden, "Because you are always daring. Your words compelled me to reply to you and stand in the dark of the night speaking with a strange man with whom I have not been acquainted."

"For all that, you haven't answered my question that will remove for me all doubt and confusion and give me ground to stand on."

"My answer will not gladden you."

"Why?"

"Do not counsel me to answer your question."

"What will be will be! I'm not afraid of anything."

"As I said earlier, sometimes a man will walk in the dark at midnight and despite this it will be light for him, and sometimes a man will walk under the sun on a bright day groping for the wall as if blind.[7] The sun

---

7. Isaiah 59:10.

of good fortune has descended from my father's house, which was previously exalted. Surely you have heard that I am the daughter of a French Baron, and so he is. Woe, the name "Baron" is all that remains to my father of the riches and honor that were apportioned to his estate under the skies of France. When fortune smiled on the entire land of France, he was among the leaders. Now the sun has set and destroyed most of the leaders, taking also my father's honor and his soldiers."

"Do you know, gentle Finalia, if you were to mark my faults,[8] then these words must be thought crime and a sin. But you must know that with all my heart I bless these events, because if your father retained his standing now, I wouldn't be able to hope for such happiness as this. Now I hope that the sun will send me a ray and illuminate me with the light of life."

The maiden didn't answer his words in order to put an end to the conversation.

"Why do you refrain from speaking?"

"Leave me be, sir, and I will be on my way, because my parents will worry about me. I will answer all your questions for you another time."

"Is this your answer? Indeed I am a fool, because a fool in his speaking will be thrown down,"[9] said Victor.

These words of complaint hurt her pride, and she said, "Tell me, sir, who can stand up before humanity?[10] This is the first time I have heard such words from the mouth of a man, and because I do not answer everything that you come up with, you find occasion against me? Should it be counted a crime and a sin if I know that a man of war comes against me, shooting at his target and not missing, so I set up a shield for my heart lest he wound me with a sudden arrow? Now allow me to go, because my parents will worry and the vision is for an appointed time."[11] When she finished speaking she said "Good-

---

8. Psalms 130:3.
9. Proverbs 10:8.
10. Psalms 130:3 – "who can stand . . . " is the second part of the Ps. 130:3 citation given above which begins "If you mark all our sins, Lord, who can stand up." i.e. nobody is perfect.
11. Habakkuk 2:3 – continues "but in the end it shall speak."

bye," and left him.

Victor stood for several moments like a driven nail, unable to budge from his place. His eyes alone followed her passage, his gaze flying after her as the dark light cast from the street lamp further increased the grace and elegance of her lovely bearing. "She is a daughter of the heavens," he thought to himself, but suddenly he awoke from his inward trance and said, "What a fool I have been to let her go off alone after delaying her until now. I will go after her to protect her, because my peace depends on her wellbeing." He didn't tarry in fulfilling his words but strode energetically after her until he caught up, and he said, "Did you imagine, dear maiden, that I would let you walk alone in the dark of night and not watch over you? Know that I will always be your guard and shield, for you I would go through fire and water." The maiden didn't answer him, but he took in her glance and understood that her heart was full of thanks. "If only you will permit me, dear maiden, to give you my arm?" Again she didn't answer him, but she didn't remove her hand from his arm and he felt a slight trembling throughout her body. "Tell me now, gentle one, when will we see one another again, for when you said, 'The vision is for an appointed time,' I determined to ask you this."

"Your question will remain without an answer, but this I can tell you. In a little bit we will reach my father's house and I will part from you."

"This answer does not gladden me. I want you to set me a time when we will meet again, and I won't move from this spot until you answer."

"If so, choose as you see fit and I won't go back on your words."

Victor's face shone with happiness and joy, and he wanted to converse further but the look in her eyes compelled him to keep silent, and she said, "Here is my father's house."

"Remember now," he said to her, "and don't forget. Thursday, six in the evening at the appointed place," and the happiness was again apparent on his face. Made joyful by a sweet, new hope, these two lovers parted, and he remained in his place watching after her until she was hidden from his eyes by the hallway of the house.

# ⌒ Chapter Two –
# An Upright Dwelling

On one of the streets of Milano, you can see a small house at the end of the street. The house consists of four rooms, not splendid like the rest of the homes in Milano, because the shine of silver, which beautifies everything and brightens the darkest places doesn't appear there. Nonetheless, the rooms were fastidiously clean because the efforts of a gracious woman uphold the honor of the house. In this house the reader will find the honorable Adelberg family. The four rooms of the house were arranged thusly: The first room was the kitchen, containing a table, a chair and a cupboard where all of the cooking utensils were kept. The second was a bedroom containing two beds with sheets as white as snow, and over them were purple bedcovers. Even though they weren't new, one can see that they had been very expensive, and by their great value, everyone can under-stand that they were the remains from happier days in a house grander than this one. The third room was the daughter's, and in it were found a bed, a small table, and a cabinet in which the daughter kept her clothes, her books, and her ink stand. These last were her whole life and being, and she was always engrossed in them. There were also some splendid and pleasing flowers that gave witness to the diligent hand that grew them, and these were the prized plantings of the daughter who put much effort into caring for them. The fourth room was for dining at meal-time and for receiving guests when one of their friends would come to visit. It was also the library for the Baron because there he would sit and meditate on his books.

"Dina," called the man sitting at the library table with a book open before him. The man was around fifty, with gray hairs sprinkled about him. Even though he was handsome, with a large forehead and broad temples that encompassed half his head and long eyelashes that added to his elegance, he was obviously a troubled soul. Recent days had weighed heavily on him and his household, leaving after them the tracks of their cruelty and the signs of sorrows and distress on his face. He is Baron Meir Adelberg.

"Dina," called the Baron and lifted his head from the book to see if his wife had heard his cry. When he saw her standing on the threshold of the room he said, "Dina, has Finalia still not returned?

"Yes," she said, "But she won't tarry there late, nothing is wrong. While I don't know the reason, she is surely in the house of her friend Henrietta where she has remained until now."

"You know that this is against my wishes, and it is not her way to sit in a stranger's house all evening. How can she return home alone at this hour?"

"She won't go out alone because they will send their maid with her."

Adelberg sighed and said, "You know, I'm finished here so I'll go out to meet her."

"Don't be nervous," said Dina, "We'll wait a little longer and maybe she'll come."

"You know, Dina, that I don't want her going there. What can the friendship of a rich girl bring her, if not a pining heart."

"Do you imagine, my dear, that our daughter Finalia is like all the girls who only set their sight on silver and gold? If she occasionally visits the house of this rich man, she isn't going to see his silver and gold. It is their daughter that she loves, because she also has a wise heart and education, and therefore she finds pleasure in talking to her."

"Why does she sigh every time she returns from there?"

"She sighs about the evil things that touch her soul."

"Is the heart of the rich man's daughter so oppressed? If only I had remained in my earlier glory in the city of my birth, then my daughter would be different. There I thought I would seek for my daughter a man of high office, also educated and learned in wisdom and knowledge and removed from being god-fearing. But when fortune turned her back on me, all of my hopes disappeared and passed away.[12] And what can I do? But the daughter of Goldberg, whose father has said he will give her a dowry of one hundred thousand in

---

12. Nehemiah 1:12.

silver, does she also have a heavy heart?"

"She, more than our daughter, because our daughter is always happy and cheerful. If she hears me give an occasional sigh, she says, 'Please, dear mother, don't sigh. You are tearing my heart to pieces because I can't stand to hear sighing,' so I am forced to laugh at her words. It isn't so with Goldberg's daughter. She is always complaining about her bitter fate in the ears of our Finalia. Her father intends to put an end to her youth because he wants to give her to a man whom she hates. But her father has chosen him because he has a great fortune and also a famous genealogy. He always laughs at the new customs, saying, 'A maiden cannot know whom to push away and whom to draw near. I am her father and I will choose for her what is good for her.'"

"So he is also not a native born Italian?" asked the Baron.

"He is a Galician," said Dina. 'He came here poor and destitute, but he is skilled in trade and succeeded greatly."

"Trade?" the Baron laughed mockingly, "Isn't he a moneylender?"

"Is that not a trade?" asked Dina.

"God protect every Jew from tradesman and merchants like these. For fifty silvers a poor man will pay interest for two years, and afterwards the moneylender will take as pledge the last garments for his skin that cruel times have left him. In taking them the moneylender will say, 'You haven't yet repaid me my money,' even though the interest he has been paid is five times the principal. Why else does hatred for us grow in different lands if not the business of usury? Once there appeared in my theatre a terrible play that drags our honor through the dust. And what did we see there? A rich Jew who sought the flesh of a poor man for interest, and everyone laughed and clapped their hands. The moneylenders put a sword in the hands of those who hate us, with which to terrorize and demean us. On whose account were produced the conflagrations in the lands of Spain and Portugal if not the usurers? When I was on my land, I was much richer than Goldberg, but I didn't put out my money for interest. Don't you remember that I loaned the widow of General Wallom ten thousand in gold interest free, and that she didn't return my money.

Despite that my fortune was none the worse. But many of us speak about this moneylender as if he were fervent and god-fearing."

"Truly he is god-fearing," said Dina. "He has already been living here in Milano for many years, but he hasn't changed his dress, his customs or even his language. He will even wed his educated daughter, who is accustomed to going about with native Italian girls, to a Galician Hassid."

"Your mention of the Galician Hassid has reminded me of something to tell you. Yesterday morning I met Zevchiel the matchmaker, and he said that he has an honorable matter to discuss with me and asked when he might find me at home. I imagine that man Yechidiel has sent him to me, because he has seen our daughter in Goldberg's house."

"You're right," said Dina, "Finalia also told me about this, but she made light of his dreams and his words, even though he is very rich. I'll be back in a minute," she said, and ran off to the stove even though she hadn't finished speaking, because the meal was nearly ruined. Just as she intended to return to her husband's room, the sound of footsteps was heard in the entrance hall.

"Pray go and see who is here!" cried the Baron, "Because I hear footsteps and it may be Finalia."

"And if it's Finalia, what then? Should I go to welcome her because she is so late?" Dina said angrily.

The door opened and Finalia came in with a glowing face and addressed them as her custom, "Greetings, sweet parents. Certainly you were worried about me because I am late?"

"Why are you so late?" the mother said in complaint, "Your father wanted to go out to meet you. So where were you?"

"I tarried in Goldberg's house," said the daughter, "And afterwards – afterwards – their maid brought me home." Her face reddened with these words because it was the first time a lie had escaped her lips.

"Tell me Finalia," said the father, "Are you familiar with that man who always goes to the house of Yediya Goldberg?"

"Surely you are asking about Yechidiel ben Dalia, a Galician Hassid," the daughter said.

The father examined her and understood that she despised the man in her heart. He asked her a second time, "Do you know this man?"

"If so?"

"What do you say about him?"

"He is like all the Galician Hassidim," said the maiden and gazed penetratingly at her father, as if she sought to plumb the depths of his heart, but he paid no attention to this and continued speaking.

"It happens that yesterday morning I ran into Zevchiel, and he said that tomorrow evening he would come here to discuss with me matters that concern you."

"Concern me?" asked the maiden, and she began to tremble and shake as she recalled that this very evening had been her first acquaintance with Victor, and she thought this time had been the happiest in her life. How could she be hearing now that Zevchiel would be coming tomorrow to speak concerning her. Maybe Victor would hear and be distraught. "And what have I to do with him?" the maiden resumed speaking, "He made his intentions known by way of Henrietta, but I laughed at his words and his ambitions. Woe to a fool and idiot such as this who thinks that his money will always gild his stupidity. God forbid that I should transgress his commandments and worship the golden calf. I won't bow down before strange gods and I won't covet the gold that covers them."

"Will you also find occasion against every man, my dear Finalia?"

The father wanted to say more, but Dina came in and arranged the table for supper, and she said, "Don't wait to talk until after you've eaten because in a moment the bell will sound the hour ten."

"Can the time already be ten?" asked Finalia in wonder.

"This evening has cheered you up greatly, Finalia," said the father. "Even though I don't know how, that the hours pass like minutes for you proves it to me."

The maiden blushed slightly then recovered and said, "And do you know what this happiness is, dear father? Maybe it's that you told me how tomorrow Zevchiel and Yechidiel are coming here," and she turned to leave the room.

"Where are you going Finalia?" said the mother, "Aren't you eating?"

"I'm not hungry, eat without me," said the daughter and left. Dina brought the meal to the table and the two of them sat to eat.

"So what do you think?" said the Baron, "She abhors him very much."

"What do I think?' said Dina, "She knows the man and his limitations and that's why she abhors him."

"I won't push her, but I imagine that the choicest jewels will do their work with great effect, because he is very rich."

"You are mistaken, my dear, mistaken! You do not yet know your daughter who keeps her feelings locked away, because her heart is as bold as man's, and money means nothing to her."

"That may be," said the Baron, and the discussion continued throughout the meal.

But let us see what Finalia is doing now. She lies on her bed and she thinks about the new things that have awakened and ripened in her heart this evening. The arrow of love, which had yet to reach her heart, was suddenly fired at her by an educated man who took aim against her and didn't miss the target. Even though we saw the innocence and uprightness of her being this evening, we can't deny that her heart has been captured in a trap prepared by the hunter. Such is always the technique of the best hunters. They do not stalk lions or bears with their nets, nor do they spread their snares on trails for ferocious beasts, but for innocent kids. Kids that don't attempt to flee even the breadth of one step. These are gathered in the nets, and afterwards they moan under their hard yoke and heavy burden. A precious soul like Finalia, who was always cheerful in her lot and who never complained even in the worst time, she can almost be recognized as one of these. Here she is, lying on her bed powerless, her eyes full of tears and her pure thoughts jumbled. She was thinking, "Is he truly a man and not something come down from the heavens to laugh at me and see if I would also spurn a heavenly creature? I have never encountered the beauty of his wisdom and understanding and his rare soul and delicate feelings, so how can I believe that he is a creature of the earth? Therefore I will forget this evening because it surely was a day dream or a vision. But no! Didn't I hear him pressing me to answer his questions? And he also said that Thursday at six in the evening we would meet at the appointed place. So I will wait until Thursday, but I wish I knew what he was doing now! Maybe he is also obsessed with me. Maybe he will think that I am thinking about him." A scarlet blush covered her face with these thoughts. Her heart was like a stormy sea, her head like a struck anvil. She covered herself with a blanket and slept, and sweet dreams flew over her head in their thousands. And in every scene and every image she saw Victor, because from now on she was obsessed with him whether she was dreaming or awake.

## ⇌ Chapter Three – The Baron Adelberg Argues with the Matchmaker Zevchiel

"Where are you going, dear father?" asked Finalia, on seeing him put on his coat.

"I've been called to the court."

"To the court! Why?"

"I don't know myself, but don't worry, nothing is wrong. If Zevchiel should come, tell him to wait for me. Don't quarrel with him or call him to account as you always do with fools such as he for being a dog of the heaven."

Finalia didn't say a word but closed the door and took a volume of the works of Schiller from the book cupboard. She read about the destruction of Troy, and she was very angry about the deed of Paris who stole the beautiful Helen from Prince Menelaus, her husband. When she saw his horrible end, she thought, "He is struck by his own hand." But afterwards she thought, "What was his sin? Didn't love cause this? How awful love is, blinding the eyes of the wise, and not considering the evils and disasters brought about by it. But who is the man who can control and hide away his feelings when they rise up?" She supported her head on both hands and sank deep into thought, until there was a knock at the door.

"Who's there?" asked the maiden, rousing from her reverie, as she heard the door creak under the pounding of a wild hand striking it.

"Open, pray," she heard a voice like thunder. "Open, pray. Why have you locked the door when I come on your behalf? Do you imagine that burglars or thieves in the night will come to your house? Would they find it worthwhile?"

"Who are you?" she asked, angered by the scorn poured upon her father's house.

"I am Reb Zevchiel, the Matchmaker," was the answer, and he continued to pound and push at the door. When she opened it, he fell inwards grasping the door handle in his hand. He entered and asked her in complaint, "Why have you locked the door?" She didn't answer this, just told him to sit and wait for her father. Zevchiel sat his full length on a chair that lacked the strength to contain this heavy weight and groaned under its burden. She sat back in her place to read the book that was in her hand.

"What are you studying?" inquired Zevchiel.

"One of the books of Schiller."

"Who is this Schilner?"[13]

Finalia laughed inside and said, "He is one of the great German authors, and his name is praised by all of the educated."

"And why should a daughter of Israel read through worthless books as these? What can she find in them?"

"Everything is found in it; wisdom, ethics and proper conduct."

"You make me laugh, that in a heathen book, which is an abomination to every man who calls himself by the name Israel, is found wisdom, ethics and proper conduct." Finalia didn't know whether or not to disabuse this fool on his foolishness, but to her relief her father came and rescued her from this disgusting man.

---

13. Original misspelling intentional.

"Why did you return so quickly?" she asked her father.

"I didn't find the Minister of justice at home, and his servant told me to come tomorrow morning."

'Was it to his house you were summoned, and not to the court?"

"To his home."

"For what reason?"

"I don't know."

"Behold, Zevchiel is waiting for you," said Finalia, and went to her room.

"Greetings, Reb Meir," said Zevchiel, and rose from his place when he saw the Baron at the threshold of the room, and he extended him his large, powerful hand, such that the small, soft hand of the Baron was so entirely concealed that one couldn't tell it was there.

"Pray sit," said the Baron, and seated himself in a nearby chair.

"I've come to talk to you concerning your daughter," said Zevchiel and continued. "It's no secret to any of us that wisdom is a defense and wealth is a defense, but money can answer any problem. Don't we often see wise and intelligent men going to bow to a rich fool for the few pennies they will earn by the sweat of their brow? The rich man will dress himself in pride and haughtiness as he weighs the money into their hands, and who is responsible for this if not the money. When a man sits in prison for some wicked deed he has done, who will untie his bonds if not money? Who is granted honor and prestige in every street and corner and in the city bourse, or in the temples and the community assemblies, if not those with money? If a hall lacks the room for all those gathered, the rich will be seated, and few are the wise and intelligent men who will interfere with them. If a man comes to speak honorably concerning his son or daughter, what is the first question, but money? I am a native of Galicia and I was engaged there in the business of matchmaking for thirty years. There I was born and there I grew up. I have only been in this city for three years because Yechidiel brought me, but it is my desire to return to my land and birthplace. Here there are few people who fear God and that great man, elevated above his brethren, who the King of the world delights in honoring. He was chosen, with his seed after him, such that a three year old boy and a two year old girl will speak great secrets. They are the children of God, and from just speaking of them a holy fire is kindled within me." As he spoke he became so enthusiastic that he practically went out of his mind.

The Baron, even though it was hard for him to listen to the words of this man who opened his mouth in vain,[14] controlled himself and was happy that Finalia wasn't there. He nodded his head even though he didn't listen to the half of it.

And Zevchiel went on, saying, "Everybody knows of the great acts of the Tzaddik of the generation are without bounds. Happy is the man who sits in his courtyard to guard the mezuzah on his door, because the dust of his house will make atonement for every transgression and sin. Anybody who touches the doorknob of the house of the Tzaddik is guaranteed that he will not die without confession. He is always in the secret of God and he knows the higher knowledge. We have seen that there are many in every time who do not believe in the Tzaddik, and their end is bitter. If they bind themselves to him with all their hearts, with all their souls and all their strength, then they will be quickly saved, because he has the ability to change the appointed time. Therefore, my advice to a man with daughters as beautiful as Achsa bat Caleb,[15] even if he has a great fortune, is that a man can do no better than to marry daughters to men of Galicia."

The Baron, when he heard these last words of Zevchiel, grew very angry and stared at him in haughty pride and scorn on account of the insults to his honor and the honor of his gentle and praiseworthy daughter who he saw in his imagination on the heights of happiness. And he said, "Know, pray, that you aren't correct in saying that harsh and bitter will be the end of a man who doesn't believe in the Tzaddik, or that cleaving to him will bring rapid salvation. A groundless falsehood it is, because a man is as sealing wax in the hands of his creator,[16] to do with as he pleases, and only he causes everything to

---

14. Job 35:16 – continues, "and multiplies words without knowledge."

15. *[Original footnote]* – Our wise men of blessed memory said that all who saw Achsa became angry at her husband because of her beauty: Talmud Bavli, Terumah 16a in Rashi's commentary.

happen, and by his hand every man's time is inscribed. A man cannot know what will be, even in his last moments, and if he can't know his own fate, how can he tell the future of others? We have seen many of the Tzaddikim of the generation gathered suddenly before their time, and they knew nothing about it beforehand."

Zevchiel leapt from his place on hearing this question as if he had been bitten by a snake, and he said, "This is known to all: A doctor cannot heal himself, and what I said to you about many becoming rich, it is true. The man Shmuel the merchant was incredibly poor until he went to the Tzaddik and complained of his bitter fate. The Tzaddik gave him a silver coin, and he started to trade with this coin, and now he is a rich man. Every year he brings the Tzaddik a thousand in silver for the redemption of his soul. Will you deny also this?"

"Let me answer you," said the Baron. "When Shmuel received the present from the Tzaddik, and all of his faithful heard the Tzaddik tell him that he would become rich, they spoke to each other saying, 'Certainly we are all obligated to support him with enough money to start in business.' So he succeeded to the point where he became very great. And you ask me 'Where does this success come from if not the Tzaddik!' I will speak a further truth, that when the Tzaddik tells a man, 'You will get rich this year,' he doesn't tell him, 'Be on guard and watch yourself carefully that you don't cheat in your business, because it is forbidden for us even to swindle a foreigner.' And as the Tzaddik doesn't command him in this, he doesn't keep from it. When he trades he will only attempt to get rich and will do deceit and fraud in his business. Even if he doesn't lust after money he will do this in the name of the heavens in order to sanctify the name of the Tzaddik. And many, many are those who will believe in the Tzaddik, and his followers will be fruitful and multiply like the grass of the earth germinating everywhere. And by his thinking, it's not enough, since he won't be punished for this and will still receive his reward. Now who will make me a liar and invalidate my words?"[17]

---

16. From a liturgical poem recited on Yom Kippur.

Zevchiel bit his lips between his teeth and said, "Will you also say about the Hassidim of Russia what you say about the Hassidim of Galicia?"

"They are different men and one can't compare them to the Galician Hassidim, because amongst them are found wisdom, intelligence and learning."

"Do they not go to the Tzaddik and bring him the fruits of their toil."

"We cannot despise them for this. Can we say about men like these who bring atonement money to the Tzaddik that they are narrow like the Galician Hassidim? Aren't they just fulfilling the custom of their fathers? But the Galician Hassidim make their Tzaddik into a god and honor him greatly. They don't say, 'God has made me rich,' regarding the wealth and possessions that they acquire, but attribute the power to their god, the Tzaddik."

"If that's the case, I have no further business in your house," said Zevchiel, "Because you are speaking heresy against the Galician Hassidim. I was sent here by the gentleman Yechidiel ben Dalia, because he desires your daughter and will accept her without a dowry. What do you say about this?"

"I can't answer you right now. I will ask my daughter, and if she wants ben Dalia, she will go after him, and if not, I won't compel her."

"An awful thing! Very terrible!" cried Zevchiel and leapt up from his place. "Have you ever heard of such a thing as a father asking his daughter about a match? Could we say about such a maiden that she is decent?"

The Baron laughed inside and said, "Know that the thinking of the men in this country is not like your thinking. After raising a daughter and teaching her wisdom and knowledge, a father will present a man before her and ask her if she finds him acceptable. Then the father will bless their union, and together they will enjoy a pleasant and pure life to the joy of God and man. But in the land of

17. Job 24:25.

Galicia, fathers trade in their daughters like horses or asses and do with them what benefits themselves, not their daughters. For a handful of pedigree, a father will deliver his beautiful and gentle daughter to a fool who doesn't even know how to speak, and he will make her wedding palanquin her grave. If she fears God and respects her father she will see that she is bound in iron manacles and she will bow her shoulders to suffer the hard yoke that her father burdens her with for her whole existence. If she is from the new generation, she will try to beak these bonds in accordance with the law. If this doesn't work, she will break them forcefully, like a thread is broken when it touches fire.[18] Her misfortune will lead her to follow after her lover, and finally she will deny her God. Surely I won't do this with my daughter. I will not say to her, 'I have chosen this one for you.' Instead I will say, 'Know, my daughter, that I have found this man to be good and straight according to my understanding. Do as your heart instructs you and I will bless the two of you with the father's blessing.'" Zevchiel said goodbye to the Baron and left.

## ⤳ Chapter Four – The Baron and the Minister of Justice

"Are you one Meir Adelberg, Baron of France?" asked the handsome and well set up man of thirty as he sat writing at his desk. But the moment the man standing in front of him began to speak, he rested his pen.

"I am," answered the man in question.

"How long have you lived in our city of Milano?"

"Ten years now."

"So you came in 1851, the year that Napoleon ascended to the throne of France."

"Yes."

"Does Napoleon know your current place of residence?"

---

18. Judges 16:9 – i.e., like Samson.

"If so?"

"That's for me to know."

The Baron's face paled a little and he said, "Do you imagine, sir, that I was one of the revolutionaries?"

"And what have you to fear on that account? Are you in France? Surely his rage cannot reach you here. Be so kind as to tell me why you abandoned all the honor that was your inheritance in your homeland and chose to dwell in a foreign land."

"It is as I said, sir! Don't imagine that I was one of the revolutionaries. It was only on account of my love for my country and my people that I left all the honor that was mine to be a wanderer in a foreign land."

"Did you journey from there with all the members of your household?"

"My son remained there, and he now wears the rank of a general on his shoulder."

"What is his name."

"Ludwig."

"I know your son because I am also a native of France; I grew up in her breast and played on her knees. For twenty years I was her playful child, but then a black cloud darkened the pure skies, until many of her children were forced to seek a place of light."

"Did you also, sir, leave the land of your birth on that night of rage, the night prepared for slaughtering all innocents."

"That is so."

"And may I know your honorable name?"

"I am Emil, the son of the Minister Asaf Maranya, and I studied together with you son at the military school. Here I am called Emanuel."

"So you, sir, are Emil the son of Asaf the Minister? How is your father?"

"At the moment, I don't know myself, but in the course of our conversation I will tell you everything." He rose from his place and opened the book cupboard and took out a letter. Then he sat back in his place and gave the letter to the Baron, and watched as his expression change.

"Why do you become agitated, Baron?" he asked.

"From the address of the letter I recognize my son's handwriting."

"Do not fear, all is well with him. Pray, read." said the Minster, "And you will recognize the feelings of a noble man."

And he read:

*Honorable sir,*

*I have heard, to the rejoicing of my heart and soul, that you are in that good land blessed with tranquility and quiet as befitting your honor. You are far from this bloody land containing only robbery and murder, where whoever washes his hands of such acts is sent into exile. How unlike the land you dwell in now, which is honestly ruled and where every man lives in peace and quiet. Be happy sir, and friend of my youth, that the times worked out well for you, I share in your joy and pleasure from afar. Not so is my lot here, and even though I wear a high rank on my shoulder, my heart is always anxious when I go out to do my work not knowing if I will return, because the profane at heart make their presence known. But I have nothing to complain about since I desired this. As heaven is my witness, it was not for my own honor that I abandoned my dear worthy parents and my beautiful and gentle sister, who if you stood her amongst lilies they would pale before her glow. For their sakes I took my life in my hands and remained here, because I thought, 'Here I will know what is coming. The provocation of my father towards the emperor is an offense marked before him forever, and the strong hand of the emperor can reach him from a distance.' Therefore I decided to be on my guard and position myself to hear what was said concerning my father's household which is dearer to me than my own life, and so I did. Now, noble sir, whose loving friendship has honored me since youth, I have made up my mind to petition you. Use your strength to guard and save the remnants of this family which previously shone like the firmament, who in exchange for her pure heart and her love for her land had all of her honor stripped from her. Therefore, I request you, be a shielding cherub over the remains of this family, over my parents and my only sister. Be informed that the ruler of our land has sent secret agents to travel to Milano and take revenge on the man he has doomed, in saying that he was one of the chief republicans.*

*Your servant who bows to you from afar,*
*Ludwig Adelberg*

When he finished reading, the Baron's face paled from sudden fear, and he stood silent.

"What do you say now," asked the Minister.

"And what do you say, kind sir," answered the Baron. "I'm sure that my son knows your gentility, and I hope you will be for us the guardian angel he requested."

"Certainly, I will exert all of my power to protect you and save you from all evil, no matter how serious the matter. Do not fear nor dread, because I will be successful in arranging you happiness without your moving, just speak softly in my ear."

The Baron wished to thank this noble man, but the Minister refused, saying, "Do not thank me. What I am doing is required of every man, and besides, we are brothers." As he spoke he extended his right hand to the Baron, then sat next to him on the bench. And he said, "Let me tell you what has occurred since that criminal night."

"Ten years ago, on the first of October in 1851, my father came to me at night and said, 'The time has come for us to part. Flee from this land to Italy, to the city of Milano, to the bosom companion of my youth, Julius Von Piemont. He is currently the Minister of the courts, and you will bring him this letter and it is certain that he will receive you with love and be a shield for you, for great was our love for one another. Do not delay even one moment, lest you perish. Do as you are commanded.' With this I asked, 'Are you and mother coming with me?' 'I cannot leave my people in this terrible time,' said my father, gave me his parting blessing, and went. My mother, even though she cried and moaned that it was hard for her to be parted from her only son, still counseled me to do as my father commanded. That night I left Paris, and it was as my father has said, because the Minister Julius loved my father and received me with open arms. Afterwards, he test-ed my aptitudes and found within me more than he had hoped. He made me an Italian citizen and changed my name to Emanuel. For a full year I lived in his house and worked in his service, and after this he made me sub-Minister of the city. Two years later I rose to be vice-Minister of the city. Then, two years ago, Minister Julius was elevated to the District Administrator. All of the townspeople liked me very much and they appointed me to fill his place, so I was promoted to this level. Aside from Minister Julius, none of the Italians know that I'm a Jew, because Minister Julius ordered me to hide this until the proper time. In 1854, Minister Julius received a letter from one of his supporters, written a couple months previously, saying that my father had been sentenced to transport to Cyan. They found that on the night of rioting he had conspired to alert two families of the nobility of France whom he had been commanded to arrest and send into that land of exile. They fled to the land of Russia where they remain until today. When Napoleon was informed of the matter, he passed sentence with his criminal hand to send my father there. My mother died, because she couldn't bear the hardness of that day the husband of her youth was fettered in irons, but after a year passed my father escaped from that desolate place. Even though I don't know where he is now, I can find comfort in my soul, because if he escaped from there then he must be alive. But seven years have passed and I haven't heard anything further concerning him. That is my story, so now, my friend Baron, be so kind as to tell me your history."

"I am yours to command," said the Baron, "But first I will ask you how Ludwig, my son, determined to write a letter like this without fearing lest it fall into the hands of his enemy, because at every step our enemies wait in ambush for us."

"Be at ease," said the Minister, "Your son was very careful in his actions. He sent the letter by the hand of a fast runner he knew to be a loyal and faithful messenger in his mission. Nobody else knows. I didn't even tell my faithful scribe."

Just as the Baron began to tell his history, the servant entered and said, "The District Administrator has sent to summon you, sir."

The Minister said, "I am called to go to the District Administrator now, but at another time, perhaps in a few days, I will visit at your home."

"I will be honored to receive an important guest as yourself under the shelter of my roof," said the Baron and he blessed him and left.

# ⤺ Chapter Five – An Eternal Pact of Love

"What's happened!" said the young man as he paced to the street lamp and examined his pocket watch. "What could have happened that she hasn't come yet? Could it have been a dream I dreamt? A dream that even when waking I will be satisfied by her likeness.[19] A dream that I will never wake from and forever continue in my slumber? If it isn't a dream, why hasn't she come yet? Is it possible for a maiden like her to lie?" As he spoke he examined his watch a second time, then said, "The hour is seven and I thought the midnight watch had already arrived. So time stretches out for a man who waits and feels hope kindled inside him, because all his inner being is focused on this point. Then the minutes seem like hours to him. But what if he fears that she was fabricating from the start? Can he hope even then? And if he hopes, that hope will consume his insides like a worm." So spoke the young man to his soul, and he paced about, looking off in every direction. At a distance she appeared to him as a black form, and thousands of thoughts rose all at once in his heart he as went forward with strong steps. When the two of them met he stopped in his place and said in a quiet voice, "Finalia."

The surprised maiden stood in her place and examined the face of the speaker, then she cried, "Victor. I hadn't hoped to find you here because I was so late after the appointed time, but it's not my fault. What time does your watch say now?"

"Seven o'clock"

---

19. Psalms 17:15.

"Is it truly seven? Then I am a full hour late for our appointment."

"Don't fear, my dear, you will bear no heavy sin for that. It is the nature of man that if he waits for something, it will afterwards be for him even more beloved and cherished."

Finalia looked at him with amusement, but also in complaint, and said, "Do you imagine that this is why I was late?"

"God forbid I should think so," said Victor, realizing he must weigh his words on a scale. "Didn't I say it only as a general principle? But from my great exultation I forgot to greet you properly. How are you, my dear?"

"I am well," she answered, "And how are you?"

"I'm fine," said Victor, "But I have no peace, because my heart and my tranquility were suddenly stolen from me as one. Yet I cannot make myself ask the robber to return her spoils to me."

"And if this robber returned the spoils that she stole, then the hero would be compelled to return the plunder he carried away," said the maiden, fixing her beautiful eyes on the speaker. Victor couldn't answer her, but gazed at her face enraptured by her great cleverness. So they walked and conversed until they arrived at a mansion with a tall tree planted before each window. Between every two trees was a wooden bench where the inhabitants of the house would refresh themselves during the summer.

"Be seated, my dear," said Victor, "The inhabitants of the house won't interrupt us."

Finalia sat down, and Victor sat himself near her. She set aside a little of the veil from her face to inhale the breeze, and she wiped a bit of perspiration from her forehead with a white kerchief. Victor lifted up his eyes and gazed at her, but he didn't say a thing. After a few minutes he broke the silence and said, "Please, dear, cheer me with your sweet words. Open your mouth and enlighten me with your words."

The maiden cast her eyes down to the earth and said, "When they wish to examine the power of a lodestone, those who investigate nature pass silver before it, but it doesn't attract. They pass gold before it, but it doesn't attract, nor sapphire does it pull toward itself.

But when they pass iron and diamonds before it, then these investigators will know its strength. It will only attract iron to itself. Not silver, gold, nor precious stones, so the wise investigators cannot use this means to separate between them."

Victor's face shone on hearing the wise heart of the maiden. He wanted to hug her in his arms, but he restrained himself and remained in his place, and he said, "Let me answer your hypothesis. The magnet doesn't attract silver or gold because they aren't of its kind, but iron and magnets are of the same substance, so when one meets the other, it will be quickly attracted and inseparable. But which of us is the magnet?"

"Do you have to ask?" said the maiden in complaint.

"Forgive me, gentle one," he said, "You are correct in your judgement."

"I will not forgive you," she said. When she looked at him she saw he was a little dismayed, so she went on, with a giggle, "I will not forgive you because I'm not angry at you."

Victor rose from his place and said, "Now, my dear, I can read your face like a book. Pray, listen to me. Let the two of us establish a pact, before the Lord. An eternal pact of love, that will not be broken nor forgotten to our last day. The good Lord will be our witness, and he will guide the generations to come."

Finalia rose from her place, and the two of them swore an oath before the Lord. A holy silence reigned between these two lovers, with neither of them wishing to break the sanctity of this moment. They stood gazing at each other, then Victor took Finalia's hand in his own right hand, and she sat back in her place.

"Tell me now, my dearest, who dared to delay your arrival, and I will have my revenge from him."

"Behold, I will tell you, but not in order for you to take revenge, because it is hateful to me to take revenge even on a mortal enemy. Yesterday a Galician Hassid came to us, and his name was Zevchiel the Matchmaker. He said to my father that a very rich man of the Galician Hassidim desired me, but I said that I knew this man and despised him greatly. Today he came in person to speak with my father, and my father sent him to me. If only you could have seen my face when I was forced to talk with him. That was a bad hour that I won't forget for the rest of my life."

"And what did he say?"

"He laid before me a bag of money and said, 'Please be agreeable and take this from me.' 'And what will I do with it?' I asked. 'You will find five thousand Liras here. Take it and do with it whatever you see fit.' 'And how can I take money from you for no reason?' I asked him. 'Please take it,' he said, 'And buy yourself the choicest jewels. Fasten them around your neck, and that will be my wages.' 'Presents are hateful to me,' I said, 'Therefore I can't accept anything from you.' He stood for a few moments and afterwards he said, 'Know that I intend to buy your love, I just don't know what it will cost. My fortune is very great and I will lay it all at your feet to do with as you please.' Then I grew angry at his foolishness, because he had come to boast and to glorify himself in his riches. I answered him, 'Know that with milk you can hunt only mice.' He answered 'I hope also to hunt doves,' and left."

"Why didn't you let yourself be persuaded by him?" asked Victor. "Isn't a great fortune like fortresses and towers to those who posses it? I would have taken pleasure in watching you from afar and seeing you adorned in sapphires and diamonds on the parapets."

"Victor!" cried the maiden in high feelings and pride. "Shall I compare the words of your mouth to the thoughts of your heart? Just a moment ago the two of us swore an oath in the name of the Lord, and I am certain your heart felt like mine. At that moment I felt a holy feeling in my breast, and I thought that it would be incumbent on each of us to sacrifice his very life for the other on the altar of love. How can you cause my soul to languish without cause?"

The fastest artist's brush or writer's pen couldn't fully describe the glory of her face as she spoke. Her beauty is known to us, her intelligence and her fine speech added further splendor to this. The pleasant evening that cheered all bodies of the creation added further favor, and the purity of her heart and uprightness of her character completed her beauty, so she appeared as a daughter of the heavens.

Victor was taken aback by this vision and retreated, then said, "Forgive me, my dear, that I dared to say such words. You have spoken justly, my dear. I would sacrifice my life and my soul on the altar of our love. You are my pure dove, a seal of perfection. Every beauty is portrayed in your face. May the Lord bring about the time that I can be satisfied by your image while waking as I have now in a dream. These moments have seemed to me as a dream, a vision of the night. In a little while we will part, so pray tell me what was the end of the matter with the Galician."

"He went out from my presence, but didn't leave my father's house until seven o'clock. I was unable to leave the house the whole time, and that's why I was late for the appointment but not for the date," Finalia laughed. "But what time does your watch have now? I imagine it must have reached the ninth hour."

Victor laughed when he examined his watch and said, "You're a little off," and showed her.

"The time is midnight!" Finalia said looking at it, then she rose from her place. "Pray arise now, and we will go."

Victor got up and they walked to her father's house, and he said, "I request that we see each other again on the Sabbath at three in the afternoon."

"Let it be as you say," she replied, and they parted.

# ⇒ Chapter Six –
# An Evil Conspiracy

"What news have you brought me today, Zevchiel?" The questioner was a man of around thirty years, tall of stature and healthy of flesh, but his heart was full of fraud and deceit. His eyes sparkled as he sought out any lies or deception, "Truly it seems you have been backsliding. You took the money I gave you and put it in your pocket, but your hands have made no progress. Know that money means nothing to me when it comes to her. I will give all of my fortune and possessions for her if she will only be mine."

"Be easy," said the man, "Be easy, Yechidiel, my dear. We will certainly accomplish this and will be able to overcome her."

"But when? Didn't you prophesize her to me long ago? Do you imagine I will wait as days become years?"

"Don't be dismayed," said Zevchiel. "Our wise men of blessed memory said 'Patience is worth four hundred Zoozim.'"[20]

"I'll be distracted if even in this matter they would prescribe patience, for how could I dispute them." said Yechidiel.

"So jump in a canal, but know that you won't obtain her by rushing."

"So what should I do, Zevchiel, my dear," said Yechidiel. "Advise me what to do, and if I succeed, then I will parade all my goodness before you." As he spoke he opened up his moneybox, took some money from it, and gave it to him. Then he said, "Know that if you do your job with diligence and alacrity, you will receive much more from me."

Zevchiel took the money from the proffered hand with disguised joy, in order that Yechidiel not see how great was his lust for money. And he said in his heart, "Aha! A deep gold mine has opened before me, one that I will mine the rest of my days. Even from 'The Good'[21] I won't withhold good." After placing the money in his pocket he turned back to Yechidiel and said, "Be sure that I will serve you with every bit of my strength. Everything you tell me to do I will do, that we will be successful."

"My thanks for that," said Yechidiel, "Although I already knew this, because a bribe is a precious stone in the eyes of its owner."[22]

Zevchiel pretended that he didn't hear, and said, "What would you have me do now?"

"Wait a bit, and I will teach you wisdom. But due to the great

---

20. A zooz is a Babylonian coin – this expression was the 1st Millennium equivalent of "Slow and steady wins the race."

21. *[Original footnote]* – Many of the Galician Hassidim call the Tzaddik "The Good."

22. Proverbs 17:8.

burning within me, I forgot to ask if you went to the Baron's house yesterday."

"I was there this morning."

"And how did he answer you?"

"He said that his daughter told him that she esteemed Yechidiel greatly, but she didn't want to speak further for the time being."

"This is what the Baron answered you?"

"Yes."

"And what do you say now?"

"I don't know."

"'I didn't hear' isn't evidence and 'I don't know' isn't an answer," replied Yechidiel in complaint to his friend. Zevchiel looked at the new master he had acquired for himself but could find no answer in his mouth. Yechidiel continued speaking, "Know that his words are not without significance. By the answer of the Baron I think he wishes to reject my suit, but do you imagine I will stand about with my hands in my pockets?"

"And what will you do to the father if he doesn't wish to give you his daughter?"

"Not from him, but from her I will take revenge, because she despised me. Know, pray, what I will do, because I will scatter all of my fortune about until she is mine. Then I will take her to my land, to the place the Tzaddik has desired for his habitation.[23] This will be for her a consternation because she hates the Tzaddik to her core."

"How do you know this? Have you met her?"

"I know her."

"Where did you see her?"

"She frequently comes to the house of Reb Yediya Goldberg to speak with his daughter, Henrietta. The two of them are like sisters in beauty and in wisdom, and both of them make jest of Hassidim and the Tzaddik."

"Henrietta also makes jest of Hassidim? And what about her father?"

---

23. Psalms 132:24 – original quote is "For the Lord has chosen Zion, he desired it for his habitation."

"She even laughs at her father because this is the instruction of Finalia, and Henrietta is like a monkey imitating her."

"And what is this strange name Henrietta?" said Zevchiel. "To my ears it sounds like the name of a daughter of Israel which has been changed to a foreign name in order that she not be recognized as a Jew, even though she is the daughter of a Hassid."

"Her father doesn't call her by this name, but only by her Hebrew name, Henka. She is enraged by this, but what can she do to her father? Know now that also to her the cup will pass[24] because yesterday I told her father that she was dallying with one of young sparks of Milano. The fool was stunned, and he said, 'I won't wait any longer. Now I know why she always laughs at the men of Galicia, because she is making contracts with the young men of Milano, who reject the word of the Lord and are removed from faith in the Tzaddik. Know what I will do to her. I will bind her as with rope, whether she likes it or not, and she will be the wife of the man I choose for her.' Thus spoke the father in his fury, and it's certain that he will carry out his words. Now picture to yourself if she is given to one of the Galician Hassidim whom she loathes in her soul. Will she not then be paid in full?"

"Hearken me now," said Zevchiel. "Maybe Finalia is also making promises to the young men of Milano, and due to this she told her father that she doesn't want to talk about it."

"You're right, my friend, you're right," said Yechidiel. "I ask you now to watch her always, and if you see it is so, go to her father and tell him."

"Can you know that the Baron doesn't already have this information? Or what if I told him that his daughter was making promises with one of the young men of Milano, and then he commanded her to present the youth before him? If he favored him he would say, 'Cleave well to him,' and bless them."

"If that's the case," said Yechidiel, "Tell me if you should see something and I will know what to do."

---

24. Lamentations 4:21 – quote continues "and she will be made drunken and naked."

"And what would you do?" Zevchiel asked him cunningly, in order that Yechidiel make known all the hidden secrets of his heart and be delivered into his hand, but Zevchiel couldn't conceal the crafty deception of his own heart.

"And what would you do if you were in my place," Yechidiel countered. Zevchiel saw that he was caught in a trap of his own slyness, because it hadn't occurred to him that such a young man could be greater then he in cunning, so he remained silent.

Yechidiel understood his embarrassment and said, "Why are you mute, my friend? Is it for this I opened my treasury to you? Speak as your intelligence instructs you, and don't withhold your goodness from me. You are always saying that you only seek my benefit." As he spoke he took a jar of strong vodka and poured a large glass, commonly know as 'a Hassid's quarter measure,' raised it to his mouth and emptied it. He poured another for Zevchiel and he said, "Drink now, my dear, because this liquor will cause you to forget all sorrows and turn the heart of a rabbit into the heart of a lion or a leopard."

Zevchiel took the glass from his hand, made the 'she-ha-kol' blessing in a loud voice, and tasted a little. Then he turned his face to Yechidiel and said, "L'chaim. May the Lord grant that we carry out your heart's purpose."

"We will carry it out,' said Yechidiel, as Zevchiel drained it to the bottom. "We will carry it out, because who will dare to set up a barrier against us? But you still haven't answered my question."

"I'll answer you," said Zevchiel in the heat of liquor. "If I was in your place, then anybody who interfered and barred the way for me would no longer glow with the light of life for setting roadblocks in my path."

Yechidiel saw that he hadn't missed the target in choosing this man to be his helper. He said, "I'm very pleased with you because you are a wise man and you watch your step. From now on, my treasury will always be open before you, but show me your great strength and be on the lookout. Neither will I sit with my arms folded. Today I will send one thousand in silver to the Tzaddik as redemption for our souls, because we have done business without asking the Tzaddik."[25]

"Do so, my friend," said Zevchiel, "And it will be guaranteed that you will succeed in your path. Pray don't forget to mention my name to the Tzaddik," and he parted in great spirits because a well of salvation had opened before him, from which he could constantly draw as he pleased.

Such is the way with every covetous person. When he knows he has found a source of money, he will close his eyes from seeing evil and stop his ears from hearing the cries of the oppressed. Thus he will pervert every wholesome thing. His eyes will not be satisfied with gathering the wages of sin, and his mouth will not weary of saying, "Give, give," until he persuades himself to spill the blood of an innocent with no reason other than to fill sacks with money.

# Chapter Seven – The Sabbath

"Isn't it pouring rain outside? Where are you going?' said the Baron to Finalia, on seeing her put on her cloak to go out, even though she hadn't yet finished eating lunch.

"I won't go just yet," she said and sat at the table. But could she remain in her place when she knew the appointed hour had arrived? Wasn't it certain that Victor was waiting for her, that he hadn't been stopped by the heavy rain? Could she be late again today? She rose and went quickly, and the whirling storm and the drenching rain were like a game to her, in her knowing that she would soon be in the arms of happiness. Before she arrived at the place, Victor ran to greet her and made much of her bravery.

"Come now, my soul's companion," he said, "And I will bring you to the house of my friend Albert, the beloved friend of my youth."

"Is he also a native of Italy?"

"How do you know that I am Italian?"

"I have great resect for all the people of Italy, on account of their

---

25. *[Original footnote]* – The custom in Galicia is that they will not carry out any matter of business, exchange or trade, without revealing their secret to the Tzaddik, so that he not withhold his light from them.

energy and their uprightness. I have found that you are as one of them, so I assumed that you are also an Italian."

Victor gazed into Finalia's face, chuckled pleasantly, and said, "Why have you never asked me about my background?"

"Why should I do that? This much I do know, that you aren't born of wood and stone. If you have parents and siblings then I will honor them, because your parents or siblings they are."

"In this you are correct," said Victor, "And today I will tell you of my origins," and as they spoke they arrived at the dwelling of Albert.

"I am honored to receive such respectable guests in my home," said a man of about twenty-five years to the arrivals. He placed before them chairs to sit, and both Finalia and Victor thanked him and sat.

"What is the title of the book you are holding," Victor asked Albert.

"The laws of Italy."

"What is his job?" Finalia asked Victor.

"He is the scribe of the Minister of Justice."

"Minister of Justice Emanuel Maranya," said Albert. "He has promised when he is promoted to the District Administrator he will place a higher position in my hands."

"The Minister of Justice Emanuel Maranya is being promoted to the District Administrator?" asked Finalia, turning her face to Albert.

"That is so, gentle one. Do you know the honorable Minister?"

"I know him," said Finalia, and if she had looked at Victor's face as she answered then things would have proceeded differently, because the appearance of his face changed and his strength abandoned him. He was forced to lean on the arm of the chair to listen further, and plunged deep into thought. "How could Finalia know the Minister of Justice, who according to many people is actually a Jew. Maybe he loves her? He has in his hands the means to take her by force, and her father would not prevent him, because he's a great Minister. He is also handsome and a fine picture of a man, and uniquely well educated, understanding, and rich. Beyond this he bears a high rank on his shoulder, and soon he will be the District Administrator. Who amongst all the maidens would not fall in love with a man like him? That is the nature of most maidens, that if they see before them a man with gold buttons on his jacket and a badge of honor on his chest, then they don't look any further. They don't examine his nature and his feelings. And with a happy heart and a willing mind she will go after him, especially a man like the Minister who has no second." These thoughts confused and spoiled his good judgement to the point he thought her a traitor who profanes oaths to the Lord. He wanted to put her on trial before him, out of angry male jealousy, because by his thinking she had betrayed him. But he pulled himself together a little and remained in his place to listen further. Such is always the way with men. When you see a maiden who finds favor in your eyes,[26] you will be like a slave to her, bowing to her with your noses to the earth. However, if she is caught in the trap you spread for her, how far you will distance her from delight, and she will groan under your hard burden. But haven't we seen the uprightness of Finalia and her faithfulness to Victor? Behold, he merely hears from her that she knows another man, and he thinks it treason. But let us not become dismayed and pass faulty judgement also on the honest men. Such is the nature with all of the most valuable objects; we follow with utmost care their every step. If a bit of dust gets on a valuable garment, it is thought a stain in the eyes of its owner, and he will clean it with all his strength until it is clean and pure. Love is what brought about these thoughts, a boundless love. He thinks that there is none like her in the whole world, and when he heard from her mouth that she knew the Minister, he considers it a transgression. But he quickly calms down, forgives her in his heart, and braces himself to hear more of their conversation.

"Please be so kind, sir, as to tell me how you know that Emanuel Maranya will be promoted to district Minister?"

"It's ten years now that I've known him, because when he arrived here he was like any of us. But he found favor in the eyes of Julius von Piemont, who loved his father, and he elevated Emanuel. But Emanuel didn't forget his comrades, and he improved everybody's

---

26. Here the author begins to speak to her readers as if they were all male.

condition to the best of his ability, Jews and Christians alike. When he was made the Minister of Justice, he took me to supervise his establishment, and yesterday he told me that Julius had summoned him and said, 'Know that the time has come when I can repay you for the life and kindness your father did for me. I will soon be summoned by the king to be the District Administrator in Venice, and I hope to put you in my place. You are liked by the citizens of the city, and if they will approve, I will write to the king, and I hope that my efforts succeed.'"

"What was the life and kindness Emanuel's father did for him," asked Finalia.

"He had taken twenty thousand from the state treasury where he worked and didn't have anything to repay it with. Then Asaf Maranya gave him the money. If the matter had become known to the leaders of the government, which was then a Republic, he'd have paid with his head. This he told me, and he also promised that he would give me a higher office than I currently have. But how do you know this man, gentle one?"

A scarlet blush covered the maiden's face on seeing that Victor was watching her and counting her words. However, she quickly recovered and said, "I don't know him, nor have I seen him even once, but my father told me about him because he met him last week and praised him greatly."

Victor's joy mounted on hearing that she hadn't seen the Minister, but despite this he was very unsettled by her words, because her father knew him, so maybe she would see him, and then? With her beauty and intelligence she could take the heart of a king. And he said, "Tell me, my dear. What is this love between your father and the Minister?"

Finalia gazed with her beautiful and sparkling eyes on the face of her interrogator and was silent. Victor looked back at her, but with complaint that she should hide a secret from him. Albert observed at both of their faces and decided that it was a delicate matter between them so he rose and went into the second room.

"Tell me, my gentle Finalia, how you can conceal something from me."

Finalia's face paled and teardrops like pearls ran down her lily cheeks, because she didn't know what to do. Victor, when he saw that she was unwilling to tell him, was strengthened in his desire to know. He held her hand and said, "Don't be afraid, my dear, for what could I do to you? But how could you hide anything from me?"

"Forgive me," she said when she saw she could no longer keep it from him. "My own life and also the lives of my parents depend on this matter. Napoleon has sent secret agents to hunt down my father and bring him back to France and present him before the throne of judgement. Now imagine if he should fall into their hands. But the Minister of Justice is protecting us, because my brother in Paris asked him to hide my father from the agents, and my brother and the Minister studied together in the military school in Paris. This is the secret that I wanted to keep from you."

"You have a brother?"

"Yes."

"And he is in Paris?"

"In Paris, he is a Colonel."

"How is it that he isn't afraid to be in Paris and to serve in the army of Napoleon?"

"Napoleon says that he will act according to the law and not punish sons for the sins of their fathers."

"Will I see you again this week?" Victor asked when she finished speaking.

"I cannot promise."

"Why?"

"Because I am afraid."

"What are you afraid of? Are lions outside?"

"Don't you know that there are men of whom we must be more wary than of wild beasts?"

"But what have you to do with men like this? Are they not far removed from you? Where do you get this from? How can you know men who are thoroughly corrupt?"

"How can I?" she asked. "Don't you know that men such as these seek to ruin and destroy only the innocent, and that they spread their nets at the feet of wholesome girls in order to catch them?"

"I don't understand what you are talking about, Finalia. Elucidate for me, please, that I may also know."

"You're right, because you must also be on guard against them. Do you know the matchmaker Zevchiel?"

"I don't know him."

"And the rich Galician, Yechidiel ben Dalia, do you know him?"

"Him I know, and one time I spoke with him."

"When?"

"Last year, when my master Max Ramaganius died. His daughter Celia inherited all of his great fortune because he had no other children. I had been working in the trading house for three years, and Celia was then a maiden of twenty years. She loved me very much, and one time she came to my work room and said, 'Excuse me, Schoenfeld, but I wish to have a few words with you.' I told her, 'Speak, and I will listen, because you are my mistress.' My answer strengthened her resolve and she said, 'Know that all the wealth and fortune I inherited from my father I would lay at your feet, if only . . . .' 'I have great respect for you as befits your honor,' I said to her. 'Respect like this I don't seek from you.' 'I cannot,' I replied, "Because I took an oath that my home would be without a woman until I save my only sister from the clutches of evil and redeem her from the hands of the wicked.'"

"Do you have a sister, Victor?"

"I have just one sister."

"And where is she?"

Victor sighed and said, "I will tell you and make everything known when I relate my history to you." Then he continued his story. "'Schoenfeld!' she said to me. 'How can you ransom her without any money? With my money, which I will put in your hands, you will be able to redeem her, because money will answer everything.' 'Fortune will not help with the worst of the heathen, these Jesuits,' I replied to her. 'If my plan succeeds then I will redeem her without money and without price. But in this matter, forgive me, and may the Lord send you a man as your own heart, one much better than I.' This answer aroused all of her fury, but she left without saying a word. The next day when I arrived at work, the head bookkeeper summoned me to go over the accounts. Then behold, I was free from the trading house, and they gave me a letter of release."

"Why didn't you desire rich Celia and her fortune?" asked Finalia.

"And why didn't you desire Yechidiel, the rich man?" asked Victor in complaint.

"Because I didn't want to profane my word."

"And I didn't lust after riches because I already knew you. I saw you two years ago when all of the people of the city gathered to receive that honored and lofty guest, his majesty our king Victor Emanuel. I asked my friends about you, and they answered me that you were the daughter of the French Baron, Meir Adelberg, who had fled from the wrath of Napoleon. Then I determined I would neither be still nor rest until I could say, 'You are the love of my soul. You will be mine forever. I have found what I am looking for.' So how could I give my hand to Celia of great wealth and little understanding? When I left Max's trading house I didn't know what to do, and that's when Yechidiel approached me and said he wanted to do business with me. From his words I recognized that his heart was full of deception and lies, and I was frightened of him, so I kept my distance."

"Do you have employment now?"

"I have."

"Where"

"In the business of Raphia from Granavich."[27]

"You work in Raphia's house? Do you know his daughter Emilia?"

"I know her."

"She is a beautiful and educated maiden beyond compare," said Finalia.

"So you know her?"

"I know her, because for three years we went to the same school."

"Did you know that she loves Albert, but her father won't agree to

---

27. *[Original footnote]* – Granavich is a city in Hungary.

the match because her stepmother wants her for her stepbrother, who is a rotten scoundrel. Now I will tell you about my origins," said Victor as they finished their conversation, and he called Albert to hear the story.

Dumbfounded and astonished, Albert gazed at the beauty of the maiden to the point where he didn't hear their conversation.

"Victor," the maiden said, "Let me finish what I started saying about how we must be wary of men even more than of wild beasts. Today, as I walked to our meeting place, I encountered Zevchiel, and he asked me where I was going in such a rain. 'That's for me to know,' I answered him and walked on, but he stared after me, and I fear that he was sent by Yechidiel to oppose us."

"Don't be afraid, because I will protect you."

"And who will reassure me that you can walk safely in your path?"

"Me? Why? Will they come against me with weapons? If it will be so, then my weapon will send them down to silence. I never go about without a gun."

"All the same, I ask that you be cautious of them."

"I hope that I won't meet them," said Victor. Then he began to tell his history.

## ᴈ Chapter Eight – Victor's History

"I was born in Rome, where my father was one of the rich men. His name is Aaron Schoenfeld."

"You are the son of Aaron Schoenfeld?" said Albert. "My father told me much about him, that he spread about his money to improve a little the condition of the Jews in Rome. Evil has come upon him, because he sought to call the Jesuits to account."

Victor groaned bitterly and said, "Many have heard about my father's house, yet you can know but a fraction of my father's good heart or of the troubles that befell him and his house. My father was a trader in notes, and many of the great men of the city, Jews and Christians alike, did business with my father's money. Eight people worked in his trading house and his success grew from day to day until 1853, the year the war of the Russians against the French and British began. Then came an end to all of our happiness and success, because the Granat brothers of Rome borrowed a half a million Liras from my father. They were supplying horses to the French army, and they mortgaged their property to my father as security, and in the end they were forced to flee. My father went to the city clerk and showed him the mortgage note that he received from the Granat brothers, and requested him to support his claim so the property could become his. 'Today I can do nothing,' the city clerk told him. 'But tomorrow I will go to the Holy Father and speak with him on your behalf, because the brothers are Jesuits. Come back on Tuesday and you will know the results.' Heavy hearted and displeased my father came home and told my mother of this disaster. He said, 'Be aware, my dear Esther, that if the hand of the Pope is involved I won't salvage any of my fortune. The Jesuits will do everything in their power in order to take possession of the property.' Thus spoke my father, and he wept all night. The women also wept about the loss of the money, even more than the men, but despite this, my mother consoled my father in order to calm him. But my father refused to be comforted, saying there was no bandage for his wound. I sat with my father and wept with him. My sister didn't understand what was going on and asked my father, 'Why are you crying?' My father answered her, 'We lost a hundred in silver today.' 'You're crying like this about a little money, dear father?' asked my sister in wonder. 'Surely you have so much money that to lose a hundred is nothing.' 'How do you know that I have so much money?' my father asked her. 'Zephia, the daughter of the sub-Minister told me,' said my sister. 'Yesterday, many men gathered at her house and talked about you. They said that you have much money, and that your fortune surpasses two million Lira.' 'Don't believe what they say because I don't have great sums like that,' my father told my sister. But to us he said, 'Know that evil has come against us. It is the nature of the Jesuits that if they lay their eyes on a man's money, especially if that man is a Jew, then they won't stop until the money is in their possession.' So spoke my father in bitter complaint all of the night. When morning came, it was my father's intention to go to the city clerk, saying that he wouldn't wait until Tuesday as he'd been instructed."

"But behold, a woman came and asked for my father. This woman had been my sister's nurse and had raised her until she was five. She wanted to remain in my father's house forever, but one day she returned from church on the first day of Easter and said, 'I am very distressed, Shoshana (my sister's name) my beauty, but I must part from you forever. I swaddled you and raised you, I bore you in my arms, at my breast you grew and on my knees you played. I said that I would never be parted from you, but things don't always go as we plan. A higher authority than us has put aside our wishes. He is the holy man who is elevated above all his people, who watches and numbers our steps. We go before him for judgement on bended knee for every hidden thing, whether good or bad. His words are sacred to us. Now, honored mistress,' she said to my mother, 'Pay me my wages and I will leave your house, for I can't remain here even a moment.' My mother asked, 'What's the matter, Eva, that you want to leave us now. If your salary is too small I will give you a raise.' 'Please, dear Eva, don't leave us,' said my sister and fell weeping on her neck. 'Why are you in such a hurry to leave?' added my mother. 'Because the holy father spoke in the great church, "Pietro en Vaticana" and said that it would be considered a great sin for any of our faith to work in the house of a Jew. The money earned in a Jew's house is an abomination for us, and must go to the holy treasury.'"

"'If that's the case,' said father, 'I won't delay you even a moment.' Afterwards he said to her, 'What will you do now? Won't you die of hunger since the wages I paid you will be given to the holy treasury? You don't have another place to work yet, so what will you do?'"

"'I don't know,' she said, 'But can I rebel against the holy words?' 'This won't be that,' replied my father, 'I will give you fifty in silver as a present, aside from your wages, and this will support you until you find a situation with people of your own covenant.' He gave her the money, and my mother also gave her clothes and leave to go. But before she parted from us, she said, 'Know that I will never forget the kindness you have done with me, and I will repay you for all the benefits you have rendered me in your time of sorrows. Because it is known to all that the Jesuits hate the Jews, especially the rich ones.' She kissed my sister Shoshana and she left. Indeed, two years later, at the moment my father was ready to go to the city clerk, she appeared suddenly. 'Eva,' cried my sister when she saw her, 'My dear Eva. Are you returning to be in our house like before, and to cheer me with your nice stories?' 'No, my dear Shoshana! I only came here at the last minute because I want to talk to your father.' My sister ran off like lightning to inform my father that Eva was here. When she told him that Eva wanted to speak with him, he was very frightened, because he knew that she served in the house of the city clerk. And he went to hear what she had to say."

"'Don't be upset, Mr. Schoenfeld, that I am interrupting you from your business, but this matter is very urgent for you. I have come to fulfil the oath that I swore two years ago that I would repay you for your beneficence to me. But don't let anybody know what I will tell you because it would mean my life.' 'Trust me,' he said, 'Your words will be hidden away with me forever.'"

"'Now, hearken me,' she said. 'Yesterday, my master said to me, "Eva! Don't go running off until I return, because I must hasten off to the Holy Father, and surely I will be kept until midnight. If a man comes here and asks after me, tell him to wait for me and give him a place in my room." So he spoke and he departed. At twelve o'clock, as I sat sewing a garment for myself, the door opened. In came a young man wrapped in a black robe that dragged on the ground and a black hat that covered his head and his face. From his dress I knew that he was an initiate, and it was a wonder to me that in the middle of the night an initiate should come to the house of somebody of such a different position in society. He asked after my master, and I told him that he wasn't there, and to wait for his return. My master returned after midnight, and he closed the door after them. I posted myself behind the door to hear what they would say. "Were you just now in the papal audience?" asked the initiate. "I was." "And did he say anything concerning the properties of the Granat brothers, for Schoenfeld intends to take them in accordance with the laws of the state."

"We spoke of this there, but Antonolla (he is one of the Cardinals who stands at the right hand of the Pope) said in retort, 'What are the laws of the land to us? We will act according to the law we have legislated for ourselves. This man, Schoenfeld acquired all of his wealth from us through multiplying the bite of interest. Therefore he will be made to vomit up which he has swallowed. If he wants to call us to account to bring the property into his possession by force, then we will give him what's coming to him. But we will also say that the church loaned them more than he, and holy money takes precedence over ordinary money, so the property will come under our hand. The brothers Granat wrote us from America that it was very distressing to them that their splendid houses should fall into the hands of a Jew who they hate in their souls. They wrote us to work according to our skills that the properties will fall into possession of the church.' So spoke the Cardinal, and everyone approved of what he said. Then they spoke to one another until the Pope arrived. The Pope sat on the throne gilded with the purest gold and everyone stood before him, but none was bold enough to open his mouth. Only the Cardinal, who always stood before him and who would fill his place after him, emboldened himself to break the silence. 'Holy father,' he said. 'Here is the city clerk who desires that you honor him by listening to a few matters which are very urgent to him.' When he finished speaking, he pointed at me with his finger and gave me a sign to approach."

"'Terrified and laid open by fear at the splendor of his majesty, I approached before him. After I greeted him as befitting his position, I said, 'Holy Father. I request from your Holy Majesty to inform us what to do with the property of the Granat brothers. Yesterday, a rich Jew, Schoenfeld, showed me a document which the brothers gave him as surety because he lent them a half million Lira. He will take their property for debt in accordance with the laws of the state, as it was written and sealed.' Silence ruled in all the great hall, and all eyes were fixed on me. The Pope stared at me for a few moments, then he said, 'Bring the Jew here and we will see. If it is true, then it is proper that he take the property for the money is his.' With faces blanched from fear and anger each man looked at his neighbor and was mute. 'Holy Father,' Antonolla cried trembling, 'Behold, the Granat brothers borrowed two million Lira from the church on their properties, then fled the country. Can the church suffer such damage as this?' 'Why did you loan them such a large sum?' asked the Pope. 'Because they were known to be amongst the faithful of the land.' 'How could you sign twice for one guarantee?' the Pope asked me, 'Without your seal no business is done.' Then I didn't know how to answer, but after a delay, I answered that I only signed one mortgage. 'If so, then one must be forged,' said the Pope, 'But tomorrow the sun will shine on the truth.' The Pope rose from his throne and the Cardinal went after him. When I wanted to leave, the priests prevented me until the Cardinal returned. He said to me, 'Know, my friend, that it is up to you to repair that which is crooked. You must prevent the man Schoenfeld from coming here, for it will do him no good.' Now advise me what to do," my master said to the initiate. "I am very sorry about this man Schoenfeld, because he is a good man, but these were the instructions of the Cardinal." I was also frightened because if you strive with them, what then! "You don't have to do anything," the initiate told him. "If you aren't able to tell him that if he fights with them they will put an end to him, then tell him this when he comes to you. That the Granats borrowed massively from the church, and so she has the senior right." This I heard from behind the door,' the woman concluded her tale. 'And now, Mr. Schoenfeld. Be on guard lest you come to blows with them because it will mean your life. See you have been warned and see what you must do, because life is dearer than any fortune.' She called goodbye to all of us, kissed my sister, and left."

"My father stood in his place without moving for a long while, and we were silent for we saw how great his pain was. After this, he asked us our advice on what to do, and my mother and I both warned him not to set his heart on seeking justice from this order of Jesuit priests, for whom robbery and murder was a game. But my father said that he could neither be still nor rest until he retrieved what he earned by the sweat of his brow and they had gobbled up. Then he went to the city clerk who answered him that the Granats had borrowed more from the church than they had from him, and therefore the church had the right to take their property."

"'If so,' said my father, 'Then I will seek another way.' He went out, and the next day when he approached all of the rich Jesuits whom he had already loaned money. They all said they couldn't pay him even the interest now. Then my father knew that they were all conspiring against him to steal all of his wealth from him, including the residue. In the end he decided to go to the Pope and petition before him and tell him about the robbery the priests had done to him, because according to Eva, he didn't know anything about it. Mother and I entreated him not to go, but he wouldn't be influenced by our words. On the day he had chosen, he dressed in his finest clothes, rehearsed what he would say to the Pope, went out and never returned." Victor choked up here and wasn't able to go on. He turned his face from Finalia to hide his tears. When he was ready to continue, he saw that Finalia was melting in tears, and he said, "Forgive me, my dear, if I don't describe for you the riot and confusion that was in our house when we realized that my father wasn't coming back. We were terribly frightened and my heart was torn to shreds, but I will depend on your intelligence that you will be able to imagine and feel the pain that made a nest in our depressed hearts. Our dear beloved father was lost from his children who loved him like themselves, and a beloved and pleasant husband was lost from a wife who loved and honored him."

"If it is so, tell no more," Finalia cried.

"Despite this," said Victor, "Despite this, the spirit within compels me to tell you all that transpired, in order to pour out the anguish pressing on my heart. My mother went to all of the places she knew my father frequented, but she didn't find him. She went to the court house and he wasn't there. She wrote to all of his acquaintances in vain. For a whole month she didn't get out of bed, only cried and screamed. Finally she saw that if she continued doing this then we would all be swallowed up, because we were also with her in her distress. We wept until we had no more strength to weep, so she was forced to get up and comfort us, saying, 'Don't cry, my children.

Soon the Lord will take pity on us and return your father and my husband, because he lives.' She had just returned from her madness, and we didn't want to provoke her spirit or contradict her hope, so we were mute. But when she went out we continued crying and we were inconsolable. But I won't pile up words, and I will tell you only the end of the matter. We were left destitute, because we were robbed on every side. All the time that my mother sat in the house and cried, the employees in my father's trading house took the remaining residue and said they were paying debts, and who was there to debate them? The little that was left to us in the house, including the fine cutlery, we sold to support ourselves. So we lived for a whole year."

"One time, the city clerk sent a summons to my mother, and we thought surely he had heard something about my father. In place of this, she found there a man with a letter of credit on my father for twenty thousand Liras. She said to him, 'Verily you cannot take my house from us for a debt, because you loaned the money to my husband and not to me, and I lost more than you. But I don't want the honorable name of the champion of my youth profaned in everyone's mouth, and even though I bear no guilt, I will sell my house and pay you.' And so she did. All of the city wondered at the simple heart of my mother and her faithfulness to her husband. This was the year 1856, and after another year passed, I saw the deficit in my father's household increasing from day to day. I said, 'I have studied accounting as is needed in a big trading house, but I don't want to seek work from one of these establishments here in the city of my birth. I will travel to Milano where I will find many friends who studied with me in school. I will tell them about my situation, and they will try to find work for me in a trading house so I can be a support to my mother and sister.' I came here, and this friend (here he indicated Albert with his finger) brought me to the trading house of Max Ramaganius, the father of Celia. I sent the wages from my work to my mother to support her and Shoshana, my sister, and so it was until 1860. Then, suddenly, I received a telegram from my mother, in which she said, 'My son. Make haste and come quickly, don't delay even a moment. The Lord has heaped trouble on our troubles and destruction to our ruin. My daughter, Shoshana, has also vanished, and no trace of her can be found.'"

"On failing knees I ran to the house of my master and showed him the telegram, and he gave me money and permission to travel. I was in Rome for two months but to no help or profit. My mother sat in pain and cried until she became gravely ill, and I was forced to bring her to a hospital. She screamed continually in a bitter voice saying, 'Let me search after the lost and oppressed until I either find them or my own grave.' When she began to recover a little strength, I left her and returned here, and so three months of affliction passed with no word concerning my sister. Then, as I was sitting in my room today, a letter was brought to me from the express house. When I opened it, I saw that it was a letter from my mother, with a second letter enclosed in it. First I read the letter from my mother, and she wrote in it the following:"

*Victor, my dear son and delight of my soul. Here are glad tidings from my daughter, your sister, that she lives. Read the attached letter and you will know everything.*

"I opened the second letter, and behold it was written with a lead pencil, saying:"

*My dear mother! This is to inform you that I am still alive, and I know very well that you are mourning for me without cease. You cry and wail and your face is reddened from tears, and your lot is worse and more bitter than mine. Because I am a girl of twelve, the hope sustains me that the Lord will quickly set me free and heal the wounds of my heart, because time works on youth like rain on grass. But for you, dear mother, and for the sorrows that time has cast upon you, I will not let my eyes cease from crying until I know you have found consolation for your great disaster. A small consolation I request from you is that you will not weep. Do not withhold from me this desire, as with a mother's love you never withheld from me what I asked of you all of the time I was with you. This way my you will cheer my depressed spirit, and I will hope that soon I will fall into your arms and together we will cry tears of joy. Maybe my father will also return to us and then our joy will be multiplied without bounds. But hear, now, what happened to me from the day the robbers stole my happiness and separated me from you, dear mother, and from my brother whom my soul loves. Do you remember the day that you sent me to post a letter to Victor? As I returned home, the sun was turning to evening, I walked occupied with a multitude of ideas and I thought, 'Who knows, but I might meet my father. Oh, how great my happiness would grow when I ran to tell you these wonderful tidings.' But suddenly, a Christian woman attacked me, and before I could see her face, she wrapped me up in her cloak to I couldn't move a hand or foot, and she lifted me up and brought me into one of the houses. When the covering was removed from my eyes, I didn't see the face of this huntress who had stalked me, and I looked in every direction to see where I was. Behold! My eyes blackened and my knees collapsed and I fell to earth from the fright to my heart, because I was in a nun's cloister. I cried and screamed and wailed, but I had nobody to hear. Finally an old woman entered, who according to my estimation was the governess (Mother Superior) of the house, because of the respect all of the nuns accorded her. She said to me, "Know, my daughter, that all your crying and screaming won't help you. You are ours, and you will live with us and learn our religion, and if you get along with us, you will be fine." "Don't speak such things to me," I answered her. "I am a Jewish maiden and I will be faithful all the days of my existence. Not you and not a thousand of your age will persuade me to give up my religion. Here I am in your hands, but all of your words will be of no help or use. Release me and let me go to my mother."*

*"You will not see your mother again."*

*"I will not listen to your words," I answered her in tears, and the woman went on her way. So I endured and answered them every day when they came to persuade me, sometimes with positive words and sometimes with threats. But I laughed at them, and when they saw my stubbornness, they imprisoned me alone in a cell whose only value was to chastise those who wouldn't hearken their voices. Despite this, they couldn't prevail over me, because the moral values of my father, in which he instructed me to walk in the way of truth, I hear even now as if he were speaking to me. And the teachings that my mother gave me I will not for-*

*sake forever. Last week, as I lay on my bed in the evening but wasn't yet asleep, I heard voices speaking in the next cell, and the voice was like the voice of Eva. I wanted to know what this was and whom she was talking to, so I put my ear to the wall, and hear the voice saying, "Believe me, Louisa. If the Holy Father hadn't promised that I would receive eternal life in exchange for this I never would have done it, not for any fortune, because I greatly loved the maiden Shoshana." "How did it come to your mind to waylay her?" asked the second. "Behold, I will tell you. On the last Easter, the priest, who stands by the side of the Holy Father preached, and he said that every Christian who had done a good deed for a Jew would go down to the lowest hell and not see the eternal light enjoyed by the righteous. With a bitter soul I walked home, and I wasn't able to eat or drink, and didn't know what to do. In the end I ran to the priest who always hears my confession and I told him that I once did a favor for a Jew. I cried before him to save my soul from destruction, and from the goodness of his heart he had mercy on me and said, 'Know that there is a cure for your miserable soul. If you will do this you will take away your iniquity and purge your sin. To the man you did a favor you must do a wrong, one that is much greater than the good you did for him.' So I thought, 'What will be the wrong that will subdue the good?' and the advice I was counseled was to waylay his only daughter, and so I did. I ambushed her and snatched her and brought her here, and with us she will remain forever." "You did well," said the second. "But pray listen," said Eva. "When I brought her here I went to the Holy Father and fell before his feet and confessed before him my sin and told him what I had done to erase that sin. Then he blessed me and said, 'If only those like you were multiplied amongst our people, then the crown would be returned to the Catholic religion as of old, in place of the depth to which she has sunken.'" It was a wonder that those hands were incited to do evil work in the name of this civilization, as I heard from the mouths of these women. I thought all the time about how I could get word to you but I wasn't able. But now Zephia, the daughter of the sub-Minister, has come because she is visiting her father's sister. When she saw me, she fell on my neck and said, "What are you doing here Shoshana? Have you forgotten your parents and your religion and chosen to be counted amongst the* nuns?" "God forbid," I answered her, and I told her all that had befallen me, because to my joy, none of the women were in my room. Then she swore to me in the name of our childhood love that she would bring a letter to you, dear mother, in order that you take a little comfort in the knowledge that I live. She promised me to fulfill my request, and she also told me that you, dear mother, are lying in the hospital. I know that this is on my account, and certainly you have cried a multitude of tears. Now live and be well, my dear mother. Also you, my dear brother, I bless with peace and I request that you not set your heart on doing something for me now, because you will do me no good, only harm. Take care of yourself in order that you can be a support to our mother. Be comforted, be comforted, and this way you will please the heart of your daughter and your sister.

Shoshana Schoenfeld

Finalia's eyes ran with tears and she asked, "How did your mother receive the letter?"

"In the evening, as my mother was sitting on her bed, a girl wrapped in dark clothing came to her room and asked after Mrs. Schoenfeld. When they showed her my mother's place, she approached her and said, 'Here is a letter for you, but I don't know who it's from.' She gave the letter to my mother, and when my mother wanted to thank her she had already vanished from sight. This is my story," said Victor.

After this, they all rose from their places and parted, because the evening had arrived.

## ✑ Chapter Nine –
## In the Middle of the Night

The night cast silence. The bustling avenues of Milano were emptied of people because they all lay in the arms of sleep. Even those who hadn't yet closed their eyes lay in their beds and didn't attempt to go out. Dark clouds covered the glory of the heavens, swallowing up those playful children who glorified in the light of the street lamps, which sometimes shone strongly, and soared upwards and sometimes descended downwards and disappeared as if it had never been. But the storm always came to help, lest the night be shrouded in secrecy. The darkness was occasionally broken by terrible lightning, which lit up the whole city. Following the lightning came the loud rumbling of thunder, which rattled the windows of the houses. But when the lightning vanished, the darkness returned to the city and the gloom returned to the avenues. Pouring rain sliced earthwards and struck the roofs, disturbing the silence. But we will see what occurred in the middle of the night between the lightning flashes and thunder such that even the city guard feared to leave their shelters. Behold, two men are walking and conversing.

"And what do you say, Hagbiah?"[28] one of the men asked the second. He was around forty years old, short and lean, and his face couldn't be seen because his cloak covered him to his mustache. Only his eyes were visible, protruding from their sockets and gleaming forth like the eyes of a viper, producing fraud and deceit. "And what do you say? Should we continue to wait for him? It's already two hours past midnight and he still hasn't come. Maybe he is laying a trap for us."

"Then they will seize only darkness," said Hagbiah. "But pray tell me, Balah,[29] how was it that you met the enemies of Adelberg."

"Didn't I tell you yesterday?"

"You told me yesterday in the wine house, but then all of my interest was on the wine and not on hearing your story."

"So what you didn't listen to yesterday, you won't know today."

"Pray tell me, please, because I really want to know."

"And will you be listening today?"

"I will listen. Just tell me."

"Listen then," said Balah, "Yesterday, when I was going to meet you, I saw two men walking and conversing, but they didn't see me.

---

28. Name means "The Hunchback" or "The Locust."
29. Name means "Swallower."

I heard the young man say to the gray hair, 'What do you think, Zevchiel? How will we find the two Frenchmen, Balah and Hagbiah, whom Napoleon sent secretly to hunt down the Baron Adelberg and bring back to France.' Dumbfounded and astounded I walked slowly after them, because I wanted to hear what they had to do with the Baron."

"'What will happen if we find them?' asked the younger. 'Then we will lend them our hand, in order that they help us stalk the maiden,' answered the elder."

"'Your advice is good,' said the younger. 'I will support them with money, and we will help one another. But I am afraid, Zevchiel,' said the other, whom the reader will have certainly recognized as that pleasant pair, Yechidiel and Zevchiel. 'I am afraid that we will not succeed now in hunting her.' 'Why?' 'Behold, I will tell you. A couple of days ago, I saw the Baron go in the evening to the house of the Minister of Justice. I hid there amongst the mulberry trees that surround the house of the Minister, and waited for him to return. About two hours later, when he came out of the house, I saw that two servants escorted him to his home. I couldn't figure out the hidden secret between the Baron and the Minister. When the servants returned, I heard one of them say to the other, 'Jonathan. Will you come with me to the wine house to drink the money that the Baron gave us?' 'I won't go,' the second answered him, 'Because I am saving my money for the holiday, and then I will buy a present for my beloved Maria that will astound her.' 'To damnation with you and your love,' said the other, 'I don't desire love. I love only Plillia ben Amzi, because he always gives me good strong wine for my money.' When I heard he was going to Plillia's place, I preceded him there and ordered Plillia to pour the wine. As I began to drink, behold, the servant of the Minister came in. I winked my eye at him that he should come over to me and I poured him cup of wine. When he emptied the first I poured him a second, and also a third. When I saw that he'd drank abundantly, I gave him a gold coin and said, 'You will receive much more from me if you answer my questions.'"

"'Ask!' he said.'"

"When I asked him what the Baron was doing just now in his master's house, he answered, 'Why do you want to know?' 'It's important to me,' I told him, and I gave him more money. Then the money spoke from his throat, 'Know,' he said, 'that Napoleon has sent secret agents to seize the Baron, because he was found to be a conspirator. When my master met him, he closed the door after them. Then I thought I would listen to what they said, and I heard the Minister say, 'Know, my friend, that the two men, Balah and Hagbia, whom Napoleon sent to snatch you, arrived today. Now don't venture out of your house until these two men leave and go back to their place.'"

"'Therefore, I fear that we won't be able to do anything to them,' said the older to the younger. 'Because the Minister protects them.' 'We shall! We shall!' I cried and made myself visible. Confused and stunned the two men turned their shoulders to see who was speaking to them. 'Don't be afraid,' I said to them. 'You and we are seeking the same man, and the more that seek him, the easier it will be to find him.' 'And who are you,' he asked me cunningly, 'Make yourself known to me.'"

"'Stay now, and I will enlighten you,' I answered him. 'You and your companion have found favor in my eyes, because you both know how to keep a secret. But did you imagine you could outdo me in cunning or keep anything hidden from me? In order that you believe me, I will give you a sign. I am Balah from Paris, sent here by his majesty Napoleon the Third.' These few words threw them into confusion. They remained in their places and said to me, 'You are truly Balah? And where is your compatriot Hagbia' 'He is also here,' I answered them, 'But he is not walking with me at the moment.' Afterwards, we talked and consulted in our secrets about how to proceed. In the end we concluded that they will snatch the Baron, because they are known to him and they will trick him. We will capture the pretty daughter, who we know because we once saw her walking with a young man who is certainly her lover. If we ambush her in the street it will be easy for us to take her, and then Yechidiel will weigh out three thousand in silver on our palms for this rare find we will deliver to him, for he is very rich."

At the sound of three thousand in silver, Hagbia jumped up from his place and said, "Will he truthfully give us three thousand silver for the maiden?"

"So he promised us, and now they are supposed to come here and give us an advance. I don't know why they are late. Perhaps they also have a job, because they aren't men to sit with folded arms. But see, who is walking there?" said Balah, "They are straying from the path."

"Here! Here! Come and we will meet you!" called Balah and Hagbia. They approached to face one another, and with the love fitting to men such as these they shook hands with each other and huddled together.

"What is new," Balah asked. "Do you have to something to report?"

"There is and there is that," said Zevchiel, and he looked at the second man as if he was afraid to speak before him.

"Don't be afraid. He is Hagbia, my friend, and he is a man like us."

"According to my estimation, we won't prevail with the Baron," said Zevchiel, "The Minister is protecting him, and he has sent his servant to their house to guard him."

"But who told the Minister that we are here?" asked Hagbia.

"How should we know?" said Zevchiel.

"I imagine that his son Ludwig Adelberg in Paris, who is now in the ruler's courtyard secretly, contacted the Minister to request him to be a shield for his father," said Balah.

"You're right," said Hagbia. "Just wait until we return to Paris and then he'll receive his full wages."

"Does he also have a son in Paris?" asked Zevchiel.

"If he didn't have a son, he would already be lost from the land of the living," said Balah. "The son always stood before the emperor and requested mercy for his father. But this time he didn't say a thing when Napoleon called him in and told him that he wanted to bring the father back and judge him, and if he had not sinned, to restore him to his place. The son answered him with a smooth tongue saying, 'Your majesty rules thirty five million subjects, and their lives and fates are in your hand. You judge them in righteousness and fairness, and you will do likewise with my father, God forbid you should pervert justice.' To this response Napoleon answered, 'Behold, I knew you were a faithful servant to your king, because you stood the test, and your love for your king is greater than your love for your father. Therefore you will be in my palace from now on, and you will live in my courtyard.' The whole city was astonished the next day that young Adelberg was taken into the emperor's palace, because no such honor had yet befallen a Jew. But he is smarter than all men because he knew how to lead Napoleon astray. He sent secretly to the Minister to be a shelter and a shield for his father. Young Adelberg can retain his honor until we return to Paris, but for the interim, we won't stand about idle. We will be here several more days and we won't be able to achieve anything with him."

"Do as I ask of you," Yechidiel said, 'And then you will have your wages."

"If we don't labor in vain," said Hagbia, "Then we will serve you faithfully and wholly."

"Ask me however much money and I will pay your price," said Yechidiel, "But why do we stand in the street in the downpour? Come, let us go to the place of Plillia ben Amzi. We'll have a cup of wine there and warm our flesh, because all of our clothing is soaked from rain. Come, let us go, and I'll give you a cash advance."

"Come, let us go," said Balah and Hagbia on hearing the words "wine" and "money."

"Did you know," said Balah, "That the daughter of the Baron is in love with Victor Schoenfeld, who currently works in the trading house of Raphia of Granavich?"

"She loves Victor?" exclaimed Yechidiel in anxiety.

"That is so," said Balah. "Why don't you believe me?"

"How do you know this? I've been living in this city for ten years and I don't know a thing. You came here a few days ago and everything is known to you," said Yechidiel in astonishment.

"A wise man, if he is in a place just a moment, will very soon know everything that goes on," Balah laughed.

"For all that, I ask that you tell me how you found this out."

"I will tell you in Plillia ben Amzi's place. I'm very cold, and I'm also afraid of the city guard, of standing here in the middle of the night with three other men when the patrol comes this way."

"We will go then," they all agreed and set off, because they had been standing the whole time leaning against a wall of a house, to be under the roof so the rain wouldn't reach them.

"But what is this?" said Balah. "It seems to me that a man rose from the foundation of the house on the other side and ran. Certainly he was lurking about us to hear our conversation. See how he has vanished from our sight in the dark street." The lightning had revealed his hiding place, but when they tried to spot him they couldn't, because the lightning passed quickly and the street returned to its former darkness.

"Behold, I will run after him and get him," said Balah.

"Do not run, lest you be swallowed up,"[30] said Hagbia.

"But I would like to know who set out to observe us."

"But who said to you that this is the case? Verily the shadow of a man seemed like a man to you. When we rose from our places, in the midst of which the lightning flashed, your own shadow or the shadow of one of us fell on the wall here, and you imagined it to be a man."

"Haven't I told you many times, Hagbia," said Balah, "Not to debate with me about the veracity of my eyes. Don't you remember last year, when we met the honorable Von Leon with ben Gila.[31] Didn't you say then that I was mistaken? But afterwards it was proved that I was right."

"You haven't drunk any wine yet, Balah, yet your whole heart pours out your lips. Are we not in a foreign land?"

"What valuable wisdom! Am I speaking in a court? Are they not men who share the same values as us? Why should I be on guard against them?"

"Here, I have a question for you," said Zevchiel to Balah. "Verily

---

30. A pun on Balah's name.
31. *[Original footnote]* – When they murdered a man and his wife from Leon and took all they had.

men like you hate the government. How can you work in a French court and yet nobody pays attention to your deeds?"

"Behold, you have grown old and gray," said Balah, "and certainly you didn't sit in idleness, but despite this, you still don't know anything. We work in the invisible court (secret police), and there they don't ask if we are murderers or thieves, because 'the robber knows well what robbery is.'"[32] And as they spoke they reached the wine house.

## ᕯ Chapter Ten – The House of Plillia ben Amzi

I will bring you now, honorable reader, to one of the streets of Milano, the dwelling place of the rabble. A street that is rarely cleaned, because those who live on the street are all dealers in rotten old rags, used clothing and patched shoes. You will pass by all the shop fronts with me, to the far end of the street. Here is the house of Plillia ben Amzi, and even though all of the houses are low and sunken, this house is lower than them all, to the point where the roof touches the dust and is covered by grass and weeds. A stranger would not be capable of believing that human beings live within. Yechidiel was the leader, and his friends went after him, and they descended the ten steps. Even though a dark light illuminated the hallway, he wasn't able to find the handle, because of the tremendous fumes and the pressing wind that went up their noses and struck them with blindness, so they didn't know where they were. Then the door was opened from within, and Yechidiel's feet slipped and he fell full length into the house, covering the entire sill. All the drinkers saw this from a distance and laughed wildly, but these gales were quickly silenced, because those who were with Yechidiel lifted him up from the ground. Then drinkers examined the guest who had come and cried,

---

32. Aramaic expression.

"Hey, the Galician is here! Come let us praise his name so he will buy wine for us."

"Sit in your places," he said to them, "I will fill your desires and your mouths. Bring wine," Yechidiel called to the servant, "and summon the master of the house." The owner came and extended his right hand to Yechidiel, and the servant quickly brought the wine and set it before the company. Yechidiel promised them three pitchers of wine, and ordered that the remainder be brought to a second room where they could be alone. He took a book from his pocket and said, "Here is your money, Plillia, my dear. Now write that I paid you for six pitchers of wine." Plillia took the money with one hand, and with the other he wrote that he'd been paid.

The other men who saw this wondered, and when they went into the second room and closed the door behind them, they asked him, "What is this, that he wrote in your book?"

"Do they call him Plillia for nothing?"[33] he answered them. "A man who doesn't know to be wary of him will be left naked and lacking everything. Here everybody pays in advance, because this house is a refuge for thieves and robbers. Plillia says, 'Maybe the police will come and you will have to flee for your lives, so you must pay in advance.' Anybody who doesn't know the procedure of requesting a receipt that he has paid will end up paying twice. If anyone tries to argue, Plillia will say, 'If you don't want to pay me, come to the court.' This he knows for sure: Those who come to visit his wine house won't find favor in the court. But I know him well, and therefore I won't pay him twice. His father was the same way, but even more so. If a man didn't want to give him a cut of his loot, he would say, 'Behold, I will show you the strength of my fist.' He was brave and strong and he always invited blows. Everybody was afraid of him because they revealed their secrets to him, as they do now to his son."

"I recognize from the look of his face that he is armed and capable," said Balah.

"You have seen well," said Yechidiel, "But how was it known to

---

33. The name Plillia is a play on a Hebrew word for criminal.

you, my friend, that the Baron's daughter Finalia loves Victor?"

"Last week, when we arrived in the city, we wandered the streets to their length and breadth in order to see what goes on in the city. There is no city in which a man won't find his counterpart, and if we could find men of our values, then it would be easier for us to finish what we started. Suddenly there were two men before us, and when we met, we stared at one another and remained stuck as if nailed to our spots. It was like looking in a polished mirror as each man gazed stared at his neighbor. Finally I said, 'Tell me my brothers. Would you like to throw your hand in with us? We can plainly see that we are brothers from birth and from the womb.' 'Brothers we are,' said one of them, extending his hand. In a few minutes we were four, like the four wheels of a wagon, that if one is lacking, the wagon will behave sluggishly."

"And what are their names?" asked Yechidiel

"The name of the first is Achbar[34] and the name of the second is Yallum,"[35] answered Balah. When we consulted over our secrets, and we mentioned the name of Baron Adelberg, they stood to attention and said, 'Do you also know the Baron? And what do you seek from him?' 'This will be made known to you later,' I told them, 'But tell me, pray. What is between you and the Baron?' 'Here I will tell you,' said Achbar to me. 'A young man, one of the Polish nobility who is here at the moment and whose parents make their home in Rome, once saw the daughter of the Baron. He swore that he wouldn't budge from Milano until she was his. When he was told that she was a Jewess and she wasn't interested in a Christian man, he made up his mind to stalk and waylay her and to bring her to Rome, the city of his birth. For this purpose he employed us, that we be his helpers. He will pay us much money if we succeed in his desire. He ordered us to dog her every step, and a couple weeks ago we saw her walking with a young man who was very handsome. By their words, they were seeing each other for the first time, because we stood concealed in the

---

34. Name means "The Rat."
35. Name means "He will disappear."

shadows of the street and overheard a little of what they were saying. They talked until nine o'clock in the evening, then from a ways off we saw them parting. She went and he stood in his place gazing after her. But, when we wanted to trail her until she reached some dark place, he ran after her until he caught her and walked with her to her father's house. When we told this to the Pole Milkovski, he told us that from then on we should stay on her trail, but first he wanted to know who was the man. Certainly he was a Jew, and woe to him who dared steal from the Pole this valuable treasure. He will pay for such impudence with his life.'

"'A thousand in silver I will pay for his head! A thousand in silver, do you hear me?'" he screamed like a madman. "You will do as you're commanded." Five days later we saw him walking in the street, first in this direction, then in that, and thus we knew he was waiting for the maiden. Every minute he looked at his watch by the streetlight, and then we saw him take a pistol from his breast, stare at it for a few moments, then put it in his pocket. Therefore we couldn't try anything with him. From a distance we saw the maiden coming towards him, and they went together to some other place. We sought to go after them, but we saw some police of the court coming towards us, so we moved off the street. Eventually they disappeared from our sight. But the next day, Yallum was walking in the street, and he spotted the young man. He asked his name from one of the passersby, who told him, "He is Victor Schoenfeld, and he works in the trading house of Raphia from Granavich." Then we both ran to the house of the Pole and told him of his identity.'

"'He will pay with his blood for this scorn and ridicule," the Pole poured out his wrath, screaming. "I will give my whole fortune for his head! My whole fortune, do you hear me?" As he spoke he gave us five hundred Italian Lira, and for this we have been numbering their steps. One day the two of them met in the street even though it was pouring rain, so great is their love. When we saw them, we went after them to see wither they were heading, and they came to a house. We stood watching the house from a distance to see if they would come out quickly, but they lingered there until evening. As we were standing watch for the time of their departure, we met you.' This is what Achbar and Yallom told us," said Balah to Yechidiel, "And now I have told you where I knew all of this from."

Yechidiel was sitting as if on glowing coals the whole story, and afterwards he said, "And what was the conclusion of all this?"

"Here, I will tell you," said Balah. "After we consulted, we concluded that we would lead the Pole on, as long as we are stalking the maiden, in order to collect more money, but the maiden will be yours. In the beginning we didn't agree, but our words prevailed over them and they consented, on the condition you give them a lot of money."

Yechidiel understood what they were after and he said, "Everything you tell me to do I will do, but you must do as you say." As he spoke he got up from his place and said, "Come to me tomorrow, all of you, and I will fill your pockets with silver. Now, let us go, because dawn is breaking. And they all rose and parted from each other, in fellowship and good spirits.

"Such is always the procedure with poisonous snakes," said Plillia as he watched them leaving his house. "So is their rule always when they want to strike a man and catch him in their net. They are unified as one man in order to do evil and get dishonest gain. The machinations of their hearts are engraved on their foreheads with the point of a diamond,[36] and woe to whoever falls into their hands."

## ∋ Chapter Eleven – The Unexpected Guest

"Finalia! Go, call your mother in here for a few minutes. I have something urgent to discuss with her," said the Baron to his daughter.

"Mother can't move from the stove right now or the three sided pastries[37] will be ruined."

---

36. Jeremiah 17:1

The Baron rose from his place and went, himself, to the kitchen, and he said, "Dina, my dear. I want to speak a few words with you."

"I don't have time on my hands right now, because I have much to prepare for the holiday tomorrow."

"Such is always the case with princesses. If the time comes that they have to bake three Challot and cook a little soup, then they will think it hard work," jested the Baron.

"I am happy and delighted," said Dina, "that you call me a king's daughter. But if you don't approve of our methods, please try and see if you can do our work, and see if you don't think it a great punishment.[38] Therefore, you shouldn't make fun of us."

"This I do know, that women are always correct in their judgement," said the Baron. "But look. I had a matter that I urgently wanted to discuss with you and you said you couldn't, but just now you had plenty to say to no purpose."

Dina looked at him reproachfully for his last words, but she didn't say a thing.

"Dina, my dear," said the Baron. "I intend to leave you at home alone this evening and to go to the prayer house."

"You're going?"

"I'm going."

"I'm afraid!"

"Why?"

"That a net will be cast over you."

"You're fears are justified, but I won't be going alone. I'll take Jonathan with me."

"Do as you wish," she said, and returned to her work, and the Baron also returned to his room.

There Finalia was cleaning all the household utensils; the candelabras, the spoons, knives, forks. She arranged the flowers and every-

---

37. 2 Samuel 13:6 – An example of going a little overboard with Biblical Hebrew rather than writing "Hamantashin."

38. *[Original footnote]* – So did the Pharaoh when he wanted to torture them and cause them to suffer. He commanded the men to do the women's work, to bake, cook and watch the children. (Talmud Bavli, Sotah. 11b)).

thing else in the proper order, and so the women did their work until evening. Then the humble dwelling was like a pleasure palace in its purity and beauty.

The Baron and the servant went out, and Dina and Finalia remained. "Woe! Woe!" Dina groaned when the Baron left with the servant. "How good were the early days. How happy I was when I saw my young man dressed in fine clothes and his face always beaming with joy. Great and respected leaders came and went from our house constantly. It seemed to everyone like God's Garden of Eden. The house was so beautiful and its splendor was known throughout the city of Paris. Now, how we have come down wonderfully. The hand of the Lord has chastised us so he can no longer leave the house without a guard, because enemies lay in wait for us on all sides." As she spoke she wiped the tears from her eyes with the corner of the white apron that she wore over her clothes.

"Why are you crying, dear mother?" the daughter said to her. "Isn't father like a king now, because a king won't go anywhere without a body guard. Why do you want to recall the past. Won't father come and find you crying and be made very unhappy?" She wanted to speak more, but the door opened and the Baron came in and gazed at Dina, and the signs of crying were apparent on her face.

"You make a jest of me today, my dear," he said. "Everyone is celebrating the fall of Haman and you are crying."

"It is not over the fall of Haman, but for the sorrows of Mordechai that I cry," answered Dina, and she blotted more of her tears on the edge of the apron.

"Don't fear, my perfect one, for the sorrows of Mordechai won't continue, and the fall of Haman will soon come," said the Baron. He went into the large room where the table had been arranged, and everyone sat to eat, including Jonathan. They had not yet concluded eating when the sound of the bell was heard.

"Who could that be who wants to come now?" asked the Baron.

"Who is this unexpected guest?" said Dina. But when Finalia rose from the table, Jonathan also got up and said, "Sit back in your place, honorable maiden, and I will open the door." A moment later he returned and said, "A young man who is unknown to me wishes to speak with the Baron, but I didn't want to let him inside before asking you."

"Many thanks to you, faithful man," said the Baron. "Go now, Finalia, and see who is there." Finalia went unwillingly and petulantly inquired, "Who is it?"

"Be so good as to open the door, because I have urgent business with the Baron," said the man on the other side of the door. Shaking and trembling seized the maiden on hearing the voice of her lover, and that he wanted to speak urgently with her father. She hurried to open the door and she said, "What are you doing here, Victor?"

"Hello, my beauty. Don't be afraid, but go and tell your father that a strange man wants to speak with him." As he spoke he put a small letter in her hand and said, "Hide this letter because it is for you." She took it, and she went to tell her father these words. Her knees were failing from anxiety and happiness as she walked, but she found her courage and gave her father the message.

"Bring him here," said the Baron, and when he came in, the Baron rose from his chair and respectfully welcomed him. And he said, "Peace to he who comes under the shelter of my roof, young sir," and extended him his hand.

"I bless the events for which I am so honored as to meet the Baron and his honorable family, and certainly I come in peace," said the young man.

"I seems to me that you are in the business of Raphia of Granavich," said the Baron, while placing before him a chair to sit. "What is your honorable name?"

"My name is Victor Schoenfeld of Rome."

"You name is Schoenfeld!" exclaimed the Baron, putting his hand to his forehead as if he was trying to raise something from his memory. "What is your relation to Reb Aaron Schoenfeld?"

"He is my father."

"You are the son of Reb Aaron?"

"That is so, my lord Baron."

"I knew your father well, because he was in Paris many times to consult with us on how to save his people, a poor and weak people, from those stout hearted Roman churchmen who place a heavy burden on them and pursue them with hot cruelty. He was a wise and hopeful man beyond compare."

"How great was our sorrow when we heard that my father had disappeared into the hands of those barbarians, and that his whereabouts were unknown."

"You haven't heard anything from him?"

"We don't know a thing, but this isn't all they did. They multiplied the evil and the destruction to my father's house, because they also kidnapped my only sister, a girl of twelve, and hid her in a convent. There is no salvation from their hands."

"They also did this?" the Baron asked in shock.

"Also this."

"A terrible thing! Very terrible!" said the Baron, but when he saw he was depressing the young man's spirits, he said, "Come here, my wife, my daughter!" because he wanted to change the subject.

Dina approached respectfully and he greeted her politely.

"Finalia," the father cried, seeing she wasn't in the room. He didn't know that Finalia wasn't able to show her face until the terrible turmoil roiling inside her had passed. But when she heard her father calling her, she gathered her courage, and appeared a moment later on the threshold of the room. She said in a weak voice, "Did you call me, dear father?"

"Yes, you. Here is an honorable guest, Victor Schoenfeld."

"I am honored to meet you, honorable maiden," said Victor, extending his hand to her. He felt that all the limbs of her body were trembling strongly and he knew that they were of one spirit, because this emotion passed through him also. In order not to not to reveal their secret, he turned to the Baron and said, "Two days ago I was sent on my master's business to the head of the railroad. When I returned, it was midnight, and pouring rain slashed earthwards. I sought a place to shelter a little from the torrent, under the roof of a house. I could hear strange men speaking from the other side, and this I overheard. Either they will ambush you or deal subtly with you until they can catch you, then they will take you to France and deliver you into the hands of Napoleon. They will assault your son with their tongues and denounce him as a rebel to his king. Therefore, I came here to tell you and warn you in order that you should know and take heed." But on the matter of Finalia, that they conspired to stalk her and deliver her to the fool Yechidiel for sin money, this he hadn't heard.

"Many thanks to you, young sir, for the goodness of your heart," said the Baron. "What did I do to find favor with you that you should worry about me."

"The heart knows its own bitterness," answered the young man. "I have suffered greatly since my father and my sister were lost from the midst of the community, and the wounds of my heart will never be healed. Therefore, when I heard these evil schemes, I hastened to come and tell you."

Finalia stood by the window the whole time, listening to the words of her lover with open ears, but she feared to look upon his face lest their eyes meet. Now that she heard the integrity of his heart and how he took his life in his hands on their behalf, standing in the middle of the night and eavesdropping on villains, she found the strength to approach him and to thank him in the presence of her father. And she said, "What a great day, sir, that in it you have made known your abilities and your courage. You didn't fear the villains in the night in order to raise the veil from their hidden trap for any injustice in their hands. Receive thanks, therefore, from the heart of a maiden who swears this day to bless you, because her father's peace is also her own peace." As she spoke she held out her right hand to him.

Victor grasped her hand and their eyes met. Finalia lowered her gaze to the ground, but Victor continued to look in her face and he thought in his heart, "Oh, but she is brave." The father looked searchingly at them and understood a little, but he didn't say anything other then to request Victor to tell him about his history. Victor was agreeable to this and he sat down, along with the Baron, Dina and Finalia, and he told them his history from start to finish.

Finalia's face glowed with happiness and joy on seeing her father bonding with her lover, and they parted in love and kisses. And the Baron requested that he come back and visit them the next evening.

"What a faithful soul and rare spirit he has," said the Baron to Dina after Victor had left them. "Believe me, Dina, one only looks at his face and feels the love of a father for his son. Believe me, if only he was in a good situation, I wouldn't withhold my only daughter from him. Verily I saw how she looked at him with love."

"Why should we speak in vain," said Dina. "Isn't he lacking a father, and is he not miserable and poor? Cease talking about such things or maybe Finalia will hear and run after him without thinking, forgetting her own standing and situation."

Finalia heard these words from the second room and laughed inside. But when they finished speaking, she went into her room to read the letter, and she opened it and read:

*My ruler amongst maidens! Be so good as to come Tuesday after midnight to the house of our friend Albert, as I have secret tidings for you. Your lover forever.*
*V.S.*

Trembling took hold of the maiden as she read these words. What could the secret news be? Maybe the Minister was not being truthful with her father, or maybe it was news concerning her. "On my life, I don't know what to think. My head is spinning like a wheel and from these few words I'm left standing on burning coals. How can I wait until Tuesday?" She got into her bed to rest but her sleep was not sweet and she had a terrible and frightening dream. She was looking about in every direction, but she was alone and abandoned, far from her parents, far from the city where she lived, and far from the love of her life. She sat crying, shut up and imprisoned in a room with no companion, only a wild and cruel leopard lurking outside the door. When she unwillingly looked upon it, all of her bones shook to the core. So she sat desolate in her room, weeping and waiting. "Oh, Victor! Victor! If you only knew the grief of your lover and the torment of her soul, then, as on the wings of an eagle you would soar to save her. An enlightened hero who doesn't fear any jump, you would leap high walls in order to rescue me. But what if instead you stood at a distance and said that you'd forgotten me?" As she spoke she raised her voice and sobbed. But afterwards she repented on her words and said, "Forgive me, my dear, that I could think such of you. Could you lie in your loyalty? You? After you swore faith by God? No! No, I won't believe it! But why haven't you come to save me? But who knows, maybe he is suffering more than I?" She approached the small window in order to breathe some fresh air and maybe revive a little. Behold! What a strange view was before her eyes, a threatening and terrible scene. Mobs and mobs of people flowed from every direction. This one screamed and so did that one, and she couldn't understand a thing. Suddenly, in the midst of the huge multitude, she saw the love of her life chained in fetters. His face was white like the face of death. His head hung to the earth and he was laid prone. Suddenly, he lifted up his eyes and saw the love of his life standing and looking at him through the lattice window, and her eyes were full of tears. He opened his mouth and he said, "Oh, Finalia. My soul and the light of my life! What will become of you? I won't complain about myself or my worldly days, which will soon be cut off and over, only about you, delight of my soul. This worry will embitter my life until the last moment." He spread his hands to the heavens, and his hands rang from the iron upon them, and he cried, 'My God! My God! Hear me! I am depositing my spirit in your hands to do with as you please. But before I go and cease to exist, promise me to watch over my soul's companion. Send your helper from your sanctuary to bolster her. Then I will be greatly comforted and die tranquilly." Frightened and terrified, she stood by the window listening to the words of her lover. She tried to break the window in order to jump to her freedom, but her strength abandoned her and she wasn't able. She held out her hands toward him from inside the window and cried, "Victor, my breath and my every happiness! I said that I would live in your shelter all of my existence. Take me with you so I can be with you in misfortune or rejoicing, in death or in life." Suddenly, the cruel, ferocious leopard fell on her and crushed her head between its great and powerful paws, like bars of metal. She screamed a great and bitter scream, and she awoke. She saw her mother standing by the bed, and she was rousing her and saying, "Finalia, why are you screaming so? It's nothing but a frightening nightmare."

"You speak rightly, mother," said the daughter, opening her eyes and passing her hand over her forehead to prove to herself it was a dream.

"Don't be afraid, dear daughter," said the mother, "Because dreams say nothing."

"May the Lord grant that it be as you say," sighed the maiden, as she hurriedly rose from her bed as if she feared to be laying down, lest she dream a second time. "My heart prophesizes bad and frightening times are being prepared for us." When she finished speaking, she dressed and put on a bright face in order not to depress her parents by their seeing her contrary and gloomy.

# ⤴ Chapter Twelve – The Anonymous

"Who could be ringing?" asked Dina, as they sat together during dinner. "Maybe it's the guest from yesterday?"

"It could be," said Finalia, and she rose from her chair thinking it was Victor. But when she asked, "Who's there?" she heard the voice of a strange man asking in Italian, "Is this the house of the Baron?"

"Who are you?" she asked him, in place of giving him an answer.

"Pray open up, noble one," said the unidentified man. "Pray, open up. Don't fear, because I'm not here to cause trouble. But don't delay, for the matter is urgent for me."

Finalia's heart was anxious, but she found strength and opened the door. She saw a tall man standing before her, but she couldn't see his face because it was wrapped in his mantle. He asked if the Baron was at home, and before she could answer him, he strode in, because he recognized the voice of the Baron.

"It is my master," said Jonathan to the Baron when he heard the voice of the unidentified man from the other room, because he knew the voice. Before the Baron could rise from his place, a man wrapped in a black coat appeared in the doorway. Jonathan rose from his place, but the Baron didn't recognize him. Dina was taken aback and didn't know what to do. Finalia stood on the sill but didn't venture to continue forward.

"Is there any stranger with you?" asked the anonymous man.

"No stranger is here," answered the Baron. "Only the family."

"Good," the unidentified man said.

"But who are you, sir?" asked the Baron.

"Is it not for the lover to recognize his beloved?" the anonymous man replied.

"Why has one strength, my mysterious sir," answered the Baron. "If not to help the weak and the feeble."

"You are correct, sir Baron," said the mystery man. "For this reason I came here." As he spoke he removed his coat, handed it to Jonathan, and sent him to the second room.

Dina and Finalia stood astonished and amazed when they saw that the unidentified man was a great and respected official, as witnessed by the ceremonial dress he was wearing and all of the shining medals on his chest. "Peace to you, my dear and honored friend," said the mystery man in greeting to the Baron and held out his right hand.

"Peace unto he who comes under the shade of my roof, honorable sir," said the Baron. "But what is this? Verily, you are wearing the uniform of a District Minister." He presented his wife and daughter before him.

The Minister greeted Dina formally in the manner of a military man, and held out his hand to Finalia.

"I am honored to meet the respected Minister in person," said Finalia.

"Is it possible that the honorable maiden has seen or met me previously?" said the Minister as he examined the girl, because her beauty, open face and pure heart had found favor in his eyes.

"How could I not recognize our merciful man, whose name we bless seven times a day for the life and kindness he has done for us?"

"Stay, first among maidens, don't praise me without cause. All I have done is to hearken the voice of the friend of my youth, your brother. But if only I had known you also, then I would have done even more, solely on behalf of your happiness. Who wouldn't desire to see the lily of the valley at the height of her beauty and glory? As her leaves unfold to receive the morning dew to drink, in order that the purple of her eyes be able to withstand the day, lest the hot wind and sun harm her."

"Who can stand against the sun?"

"But what if a man wished to shelter her, and his hands built a wall for her?"

"Wouldn't the sun forcefully breach it, to burn her and destroy her freshness, until her face grows pale and her leaves whither and she falls to earth?"

"Is it not within the power of an enlightened man to build an iron wall and surround her from all sides, to supervise guards protecting her, without commanding her?"

"And who will help in the event the wall is penetrated?"

"He that guards the guards will also guard the lily, that there be one fate for both of them."

Finalia blushed and didn't answer. The Minister interpreted the look on her face through his heart, and he hoped that the first arrow hadn't missed its mark. He sat in a chair by the Baron, Dina sat on his other side and Finalia sat in front of the Minister. Silence reigned throughout the house. Then the Minister broke the silence and said, "Two days ago I was summoned by the king to receive the post of district Minister. The Minister Julius von Piemont, who had been the district Minister in Milano until this point, was called to the city of Venice to be the district Minister there, and with his help I rose to this position."

"In that case, accept my congratulations on your new rank," said the Baron and shook his hand.

The Minister acknowledged his thanks with genuine good feelings and said, "Know that tomorrow I will have the honor of celebrating my appointment. All of the great men of the city will be invited to the feast and you will also be there. Also you, gentle one, will not hold back from being numbered amongst the beautiful maidens, because through you the banquet will be glorified."

Finalia thanked him with a nod of her head, but she didn't say a word because her heart pounded at the thought that new sorrows were being prepared for her, and with this her thoughts became confused. The Minister realized this but he interpreted it according to his own thinking and he rejoiced, because his love for her was growing by the minute. And he turned to the Baron and said, "Do you not remember, sir Baron, that you promised to tell me your history, and I yearn to hear it. Know that I have decided that after the feast I will take you to my house to live with me until those wanton men return to their place. They are conspiring against you in an energetic plot to either kill you or bring you back alive to France. I will put a guard on you in my house, and Jonathan will remain in your house to guard the women."

"Many thanks to you, honorable sir, for the growing kindness you are doing for me," said the Baron.

"With what can we repay you for your generosity?" said Finalia, "We will be your prisoners of thanks forever."

"With what?" the Minister replied. "With your words and your heart only, is it not a little thing?"

Finalia's face blanched from sudden fear, but she didn't answer.

The Minister perceived this, and in order to change the subject, he turned to the Baron and asked him to relate his history.

## ⤳ Chapter Thirteen – The History of the Baron Adelberg

The Baron began his story this way: "In the year 1665, many Jewish families fled from Spain. They were the remaining survivors of the cursed inquisition who escaped the teeth of that horrible and cruel time. They were spared from the rending teeth and not devoured because up to that year they lived under the trappings of Christianity, yet their hearts remained whole with the Lord and his holy people. That year, Phillip the Fourth of Spain died, and his father-in-law, Ludwig the Fourteenth, the King of France, knew how to purchase the loyalty of the French nation. They aspired to blood in the wars he promised them he would fight, and he decided after the death of his son-in-law to take the kingdom of Spain under his rule. Spain fell into disorder. Robbery, violence and murder occurred on every street and corner, by the priests and by the people. Then these Jewish families trembled even more, and they began to think about how they could be saved from the trap. But, to their great joy, the Spanish people had much to do to prepare everything to stand against the King of France. At this time, those few families took their wives and children and possessions and scattered one after another from that cursed land, because the path wasn't guarded against them. Amongst these families was also our family, Adelberg. Some of the families fled to Constantinople and found refuge under Turkish rule. Some fled to Britain and others to Russia, but my father's household, which included six members, along with a few other households, fled to France and settled on the island of Corsica. The name of the man was Don Phillip Adelberg and his wife's name was Finalia. The names of their three daughters were Maria, Elizabeth and Dora, and the name of their son was Meir. A few of these families intermarried with the gentiles, but the household of my father remained faithful to the Lord."

"At this time, Ludwig the Fourteenth's Minister of Interior arrived in Corsica, and his name was Calbart. This is the same Calbart who is remembered in the annals of France because he was beloved and honored by the King and his people for his heroism, and his name was known throughout the land. When he came Corsica, he saw Adelberg's oldest daughter, Maria, a maiden of eighteen years who was beautiful beyond compare. He fell in love with her and spoke to her heart, but she didn't listen to his words because he was a Christian. He turned and left her in great anger, and Maria, who saw how angry he was, feared for her life. She said, 'Haven't we come out of the fire only to enter into eternal flames. What can I do if he comes and takes me by force? Therefore I suggest that my mother and I travel to mighty Russia, where Alexi the son of the great Romanoff Czar rules. I have heard that in the land of Russia are many who are fully in the faith of Israel, because the Czars of Russia don't discriminate between nation and nation. Every man who is faithful to his czar can also be faithful to his religion without interference.'[39] So they did, and Finalia and Maria traveled to the land of Russia, and there she found a man of her own heart. Her two younger sisters also went there afterwards, and the three of them settled in the land of Russia. The son Meir married a woman of one of the rich families of France and made Paris his home. His mother returned to France and his parents remained with him for the remainder of their lives. In 1725, Meir died at the age of seventy-five, and his son Yakov inherited all of his wealth, which was approximately five million Francs. He continued in the business of his father and he made a success of it. In 1760, Yakov died, and his son, who was my grandfather, inherited his fortune, which was then around eight million Francs. He was well respected by both Jews and Christians, because if he saw somebody in hard times, he generously supported him whether Jew or Christian. He had two sons, the first was named Isaac and the second was David, my father. He educated them both in science and wisdom, and also in military skills. He was one of the happiest men in the land, but riches don't last forever, as the ancient proverb says."

"In the year 1793 began the period in which Ludwig the Sixteenth was executed by the guillotine because the French accused him of being a traitor to the land of his birth and seeking to deliver her into the hands of her enemy. There was a civil war in France at this time, because the supporters of King Ludwig sought to put his son on the throne, an eight year old boy, and they prepared to fight the Republicans. The rebels did whatever they wanted, murdering, plundering and seizing property. These bitter men also fell on the house

---

39. Note that this novel was published the year before the assassination of Tsar Nicholas the First, who was a reformer.

of my grandfather, plundering and despoiling his trading house. Even though they were only seeking gold and silver, there was no protection for the goods either, because they trampled the finery underfoot. Then my grandfather grew angry, and he cried, 'Enough, you robbers and rebels! You have taken everything. Leave me the crumbs. You have taken the gold and silver. What gain is there in trampling the goods with your feet so that they are no good to either of us.' Then one of the rebels said with a wild laugh, 'The Jew requested us to leave him something with which to support himself, but he didn't ask to escape with his life. Who will shake our hands if we leave his head on his shoulders?' The second responded, 'His money and his life!' Others cried energetically, 'His money and his life! Didn't you hear him call us rebels? He wouldn't do this unless he was a supporter of Ludwig,' and some of them approached to fall upon him and kill him. Then his two sons who had remained in the background rose up, and they stood with drawn swords and said, 'Any attacker who lifts a hand against our father, his blood is on his head, because we will fight until the last breath.' They brandished their swords here and there, and then a roar rose from the rebels, and they all yelled, 'Strike all three of them and take revenge for our honor because they shame us all,' and they drew near to accomplish their purpose. Then the two brothers were dressed in strength and heroism, and they cut to the left and the right. The end of the matter was that my grandfather and his oldest son fell slain and my father was wounded in his right arm. One of his friends took him home to recover, and to ease his sad heart, which had found no consolation for the deaths of his father and brother and the loss of his fortune. He hoped the day would come that he could revenge the blood of his father and brother, so he went to serve in the army of Napoleon Bonaparte, who was then a field marshal. He fought in his wars and he went with him to Italy and to the rest of the lands which warred with them, and he distinguished himself before Napoleon by his heroics, his sharpness and his intelligence. Napoleon loved him greatly, and once after a heavy battle he said to my father, 'Know, Adelberg, that I'm impressed with your diligence, and when we return in peace to the land of our birth,

I'll elevate you as befits you and see to your future happiness.' When they returned mighty and victorious to the city of Paris, the whole city received them with tumultuous rejoicing. Napoleon was elevated to be First Counsel for all of France. Then my father was given the rank of Colonel, and after that the title of Baron. When Napoleon rose to the royal throne of France, his love for my father increased further, and he promoted him to the rank of general. My father was then one of the happiest men in the land and many were jealous of him. My mother told me that when I was born in the year 1810, my father made a great feast, and all of Napoleon's distinguished household came to congratulate my father on the birth of his son. So my father lived in peace and tranquility until the year 1812, and then in the great and terrible war between Russia and France, my father fell slain on the field of battle. Then the storms of war became calm, and my mother who was a woman of worth, raised me in the manner that my father would have, had he lived. When I was seventeen years old I enlisted in the army, when I was in my twenties I rose to be a major, and so it went until I became a general. My honor and glory grew every day in the eyes of the French. I was also honored by Napoleon the Third in the days when he was First Counsel. But, when he ascended to the royal throne in the year 1851 and wanted me to help him do wrong, I didn't heed his voice. Then he was changed into my enemy. Even though I fled from him, he has pursued me in hot anger as you know, and this is the story of my life."

The Minister thanked him, and he turned his face to Finalia to engage her in conversation. But behold, the sound of the bell was heard and Finalia's face whitened like a sheet, because she knew who was ringing. She excused herself from the Minister and went with a stormy heart to warn the guest against entering the house at this time.

'Why" asked Victor, once the two of them were in the hallway and she told him he couldn't enter right now.

"Because the District Minister is in the house and he ordered that no stranger be in the house at the same time he is here. He also said that he would take my father into his home to be able to guard him against those who seek his life."

"If that's the case," said Victor, "I'll return home without regret, but will you come to Albert's house at the appointed time tomorrow as I requested in my letter yesterday?"

Finalia's face paled and she said in a sad voice, "I'm very sorry that I can't fulfill even this desire. The District Minister has invited us tomorrow to the banquet celebrating his new position, and all of the great men of the city will be there." Victor was seized by trembling when he heard this, his knees failed him and he couldn't stand.

Finalia understood and she said, "Why are you so frightened? If you think it's wrong, then I won't go to the banquet, but be aware that my father's life depends on it. If the Minister changes his attitude and removes his protection from my father, then he will be lost, and we will all be lost. But if you think it's wrong, tell me and I won't go."

"Not for nothing has the Minister come to your father's house. Do you imagine that he loves your father? Didn't he only come here in order to invite all of you to the banquet?"

"Please relax, my friend, the utterance of my lips is holy to me, and I won't give myself to another."

"I know your pure heart," said Victor, "But also this I know, that this banquet will prepare great pains for us."

"If so, I won't go."

"That can't be, because the lives of your parents are very dear to me. But when will we see each other again, because I have urgent matters to discuss with you."

"On Tuesday I'll go to Albert's house."

"Be well," said Victor weakly, and departed. Finalia looked after him for a few moments, sighed, then returned to the house.

"Who was here?' asked her father.

"The Goldberg's maid. She came to invite me to the party they have made for their daughter's birthday and to urge me to go."

The Minister's stormy spirits relaxed a little with her answer to her father, because the whole time she was talking to Victor he had been pacing powerfully back and forth in the room. He thought, "Who has come that Finalia is afraid to invite him in?" But when he heard her explaining to her father, he addressed her saying, "I am sorry, gentle one, that I have disrupted your pleasures, as certainly you would have gone now to your friend's party."

"And to sit in the company of a respectable Minister like yourself is lightly esteemed by me? Know that I wouldn't exchange this evening for all the pleasure in the world."

The Minister gazed at her pleasantly, and his heart was gladdened to hear such words from the mouth of the maiden he loved. He rose from his place, gave his hand to Finalia, said goodbye to everybody, and left. The Baron accompanied him to the carriage that was prepared for him and they parted in good fellowship. The wagon flew off, and in a few moments it had vanished from their eyes.

"I imagine that it wasn't Goldberg's maid who was here," said the Baron when they returned inside, "But rather Victor Schoenfeld."

"So it was."

"And why didn't you bring him inside? Doesn't he also work for our benefit and our wellbeing?"

"Could I bring a stranger into our house at the time the Minister was here?"

"Correct, my daughter," said the Baron. "I only brought it up to test you." Finalia looked at her father searchingly, but she didn't say a thing. She went to her room to recover and to consider whether or not to go to the banquet. In the end, she decided to go, but not to dress fancy. So she was thinking as drowsiness overcame her and she slept.

# ᕷ Chapter Fourteen – The Ball

The street called the Korsogrande is the largest and most splendid of all the streets in Milano. On it is found the mansion of the District Minister, which was lit up from all around. Lanterns of different colors were hung from all of the houses, and out in front of the houses were two rows of lanterns. Purple curtains and colorful embroideries fluttered about the windows. The pure breeze sometimes blew on the candles and their individual flames were wound about and mixed all together. The light fell on the purple curtains and colorful embroideries until they appeared like a pocket of flames to the passerby. The faces of the houses seemed changeable like the flames, sometimes green like the grass, sometimes red like blood and sometimes white as death. Crowds of the poorest of people streamed to look and gawk at the splendor and majesty that had been prepared for this evening. Many policemen ran about to quiet the mob and cautioned them not to break out of their places, lest they mingle in the street where the carriages and carts dashed and rattled to and fro. Even though they yelled at them loudly, lest the wheels of the wagons run them over, nobody heard them and they shouted themselves hoarse. Who can stop the course of a mob when they gather to see a happening, but they didn't reach the palace in the middle of the street where the new District Minister was to live and where the ball was being held this evening. A large number of policemen were posted around the palace and the gate and they didn't allow anyone to pass, except for the carriages with the guests.

The palace, into which we will be looking now, was not built extravagantly like most of the mansions built by rich grandees, because it was an older building. Despite this it was large and very lovely, and it was wrapped in pride and arrogance, not by its own appearance, but by the inhabitants who lived there now. But this evening it was entirely majestic. Thousands of candles of different colors were prepared on braided wicker holders and arrayed in good order on the outer wall of the palace. They were lit and burned with a moderate flame, and spread a rare light over the palace.

Curtains of purple silk rustling in the windows were held by linen cords, and gold clasps fastened the curtains on both sides. In the center of each window was displayed a wreath of flowers, a splendor to the eye, but in the main window of the palace, a rare and special presentation was before us. There stood a portrait of the King of Italy in his majesty and splendor surrounded with a garland of laurels. On each side stood a laurel tree which was higher than the portrait, and the coverage of their branches above the portrait made a sheltering canopy over which were spread green silk curtains, held by golden cords on every side and corner. On each side of the portrait stood four silver candelabras with glowing white wax candles, and they added even further to the majesty and splendor of the royal picture. This had been arranged by the new Minister to honor his king who appointed him to this high post. The lovely vision drew the eyes of all, and many of the mob surged to the front of the window. The police drove them away, but they quickly returned and all of them gathered to that spot to gaze fixedly at the window. Every minute a great cry was heard from the rabble, because one would grab another's hat and throw it away so he would have to run after it, and the other would quickly take his place. But the police couldn't do a thing because the Minister had ordered them not to injure anyone.

Behold, two young men walked in the midst of this riot looking at the splendors of the street, but by their expressions, they hadn't come to look at wonders. Their eyes weren't attracted and hearts weren't cheered like the rest of the crowd, but when they drew near the palace and saw the window with the portrait of the king, they drew up.

"Look, my friend," said the first. "Here is what the new Minister has prepared to honor our king. Look, pray, how he skillfully glorified this precious portrait."

"I am amazed at you," said the second, "Why weren't you invited to the ball?"

"I was invited," said the first, and as he spoke he took from his pocket a card inscribed with gold letters, an invitation to the ball.

"Why don't you attend?"

"Because the pleasure would turn into disaster for me."

"Why?"

"Because Emilia will be there."

"So?"

"She won't be alone. Her stepmother will be there to watch her."

"If that's the case, then the two of us will stand here together in bitterness and bad spirits."

"And what have we in common? Verily, I walk about in bad spirits every day of my existence, because her stepmother pressures her constantly and will increase her bitter provocations, until she'll be forced to give her hand to her stepbrother. Woe, how harsh and terrible is her fate. I would not have believed it had you told me such robbery and murder goes on in this century!"

"If she truly loves you she won't give her consent to scum like him," said the second.

"She loves me righteously, but oppression and compulsion are stronger than love."

"Here you aren't correct. I will answer you that love is stronger than oppression and pain, and it can destroy towers and break down fortresses, fell all enemies who raise up obstacles in its path. Love can bring two people together with a strong hand and bring them to the haven of their desire, as long as it is a righteous love."

"So according to you I can hope?"

"You can."

"On what can I base my hope?"

"On the uprightness of her soul."

"But how can I bear to watch as evil people burden my beloved with torments?"

"Relax, my friend, because a spark of hope is raised within me."

"Tell me what to do, my friend, and that which is within my strength to do, I will do also on your behalf."

"There's nothing that can be done on my behalf."

"Why is that?"

"Because he is stronger than me, and his hands hold more power and might than mine. He will tear her from my arms, and if he takes her from me by force, I can't demand justice."

"Your assessment is without value, my friend!" But suddenly he snapped to attention and said, "Quiet. There she is in the wagon passing before us."

"Who is she," asked the other, because he was also alarmed. Certainly the reader has figured out from the beginning of their conversation that these are Victor and Albert sharing the same lot. But Albert had spotted the wagon passing before them from a distance, and he recognized Emilia inside the carriage. The moment he cried out, "She is in the carriage," Victor thought that it was Finalia, but quickly he was proved mistaken. He saw Albert's face blanch when the wagon stopped by the gate and Emilia descended with her mother and brother from the coach, and in a moment were hidden within the hall. But Victor was also anxious, knowing that a similarly pleasant performance was also in store for him. However, they quickly recovered and continued their conversation.

"Tell me Victor. What is this spark of hope that I can hope for?"

"Isn't it obvious?"

"What?"

"You are in the confidence of the Minister, and if you tell him, maybe he will be your savior."

"You are correct, my friend, and from now on I can fly on the wings of hope," said Albert.

Victor laughed at his speech.

"Listen to me, Victor. Let me finish what I started to say about your estimation being worthless. He is not a despot who would take the poor man's lamb.[40] And she, what could she say if she broke her vow? Didn't you say that love can break towers and destroy fortresses if it is only a righteous love? Do you doubt the uprightness of her soul?"

"I will not be distracted. See the difference between Emilia's stepbrother and the Minister. Isn't her stepbrother a bum, while the Minister is handsome, well set up, very wise, and his wealth and honor are renewed every day? Just look at all the honor and luxury he prepared for this evening, all of it only on her behalf."

"Do you imagine that these riches which may draw her eye will also attract her heart?" asked Albert.

"It could be, for what am I compared to him?"

"Aren't you ashamed, Victor. A couple of days ago you praised her to me saying she was a daughter of the heavens, and now you scorn her and say that she lied in her pact."

---

40. 2 Samuel 12:4 – This is from the classic parable that the prophet Nathan tells to King David, to point out to him his sin in taking Bath-Sheba, the wife of Uriah.

Victor laughed with a pained heart, but when he lifted his eyes he said, "Pray look. Whose fancy carriage gilded in silver is that, with four horses in harnessed in a team and drivers upon them?"

"That is the carriage of the Minister," said Albert. "Just look at the dress of the two pages riding on either side of the box."

"Where is the Minister going while guests are arriving and assembling?" asked Victor.

"The Minister hasn't stirred from the house all day," answered Albert.

"If that's the case, let's follow and see who gets out," said Victor. The carriage began to pass before the crowd, and they all cried "Hurrah! Hurrah!" The carriage drove slowly, and Victor and Albert walked after it up to the entrance of the palace. Victor and Albert approached the carriage and stood before it. One of the pages jumped down and opened the door. The two of them stood in amazement when they saw the Baron Adelberg jump from the carriage and extend his hand to his wife, then afterwards to his daughter Finalia.

She was wearing a white dress with a trail that dragged for about a yard on the ground. Her hair was arranged in long curls that reached the snowy nape of her neck, which was almost indistinguishable from the white dress. The black curls fell at random, some on her neck and some on her garment, and added splendor and glory to the beauty of her appearance. Along side the part in her hair was fixed a small blossom of lily, and on her neck was a small golden chain. Suspended from the end of the chain was a small sapphire pendant, and she wore white gloves on her hands. This was all of the finery that the Baron's daughter Finalia wore. Certainly you can imagine, honorable reader, that at a great ball like this you will see most of the young women of the city sparkling in emeralds, sapphires and diamonds.[41] Yet we could rightfully say about her that she was the belle of the ball. She appeared at the ball without precious jewels, but are precious jewels needed for grace and beauty? Pure conduct, a dear soul, comely proportions and beauty, these are the precious jewels of every maiden.

---

41. Exodus 28:18, 39:11- The second row of gems on the High Priest's breast plate.

When she turned to walk beside her father, she saw Victor and Albert. She inclined her head to them gracefully and went on, and in another moment she was hidden from their eyes within the hall.

"But she is a maiden perfect in beauty," said Albert. "You know that I have seen her several times, but I never saw her as beautiful as today. But why are we standing here? Let us go over by the windows so we can see as they enter the house." Victor stood in his place as though fixed by nails. Finally, he went without desire after the man pulling him, and they posted themselves in front of one of the windows through which they would be able to see into the house. They saw the Minister standing in the middle of the room, and many other Ministers stood about him talking.

But let us leave them standing in their place and we will go into the interior of the house to see and comprehend the beauty and the happenings within. As the guests entered through the hallway, young men waited, dressed in black suits with white silk turbans on their shoulders and white gloves on their hands, respectfully receiving every guest and leading him to the cloakroom. There stood servants to take everyone's coat and hat, then the young men led the guests into the ballroom. There were no doors at the entrance to the ballroom, but purple silk hangings, which were held to the side by golden cords, and lined with gold and purple flowers. Suspended over the center of the room was a silver chandelier containing some five hundred lit candles. There were fifteen windows in the room, and on every window sill stood four large silver candlesticks, each holding one white candle. In order that there would be room for dancing, the room was empty, except for along the walls where chairs were set. The chairs were covered in purple silk and bound with gold cords on the edges, with flowers made from threads of gold and purple twisted together on them. There was a space between every second chair in which stood a large polished mirror, and on either side of the mirror were expensive ornamental trees. These gave off a pleasing smell, and the crowns of these trees came together and joined over each pair of chairs, so that the occupants of the chairs felt as though they were sitting in a Succah. At the ends of the hall were small tables, and on each table were two small pictures and two silver candelabras with white candles, and the walls were painted with vermilion of different colors. Such was the splendor of the ballroom.

The guests were sitting in the chairs, though a few of them were still empty because everybody hadn't yet arrived. The guests were dressed splendidly as befitted the occasion. The women wore white dresses with carnations and precious jewels on their heads. There were an abundance of expensive valuables about their heads and throats. The Ministers and the other officials wore their uniforms. The district Minister, Emanuel Maranya, was resplendent in the garb of the district Minister that had been given to him the previous week by his king, to honor and glorify him. It added even more majesty to his tall stature, and beauty to his shining face, which looked favorably upon every man. Everybody was there that evening to congratulate him, and he seemed not like a Minister but like a king. The Minister stood in the middle of the room talking with the other Ministers, but every minute he went to the window and looked out into the street. When he saw his rich carriage traveling up the street, he went to his place and sat, and all the other guests followed suit.

"Look, Victor," said Albert, lifting his head to peer into the room. "What is this? The Minister has sat in his place and all the guests are doing the same."

"We'll see what will happen," said Victor, and he also stared with wide-open eyes. Behold, the Baron with Dina and Finalia appeared on the threshold of the room.

"Look now," said Albert. The Minister rose from his place and went to greet the Baron. He shook hands with the Baron and his wife, then he gave his arm to Finalia and escorted her to the place he was sitting, seating her by him on the second chair. After presenting them to the guests, he showed the Baron and his wife a place to sit nearby, and the guests looked on and were astounded.

"Who is that maiden that the Minister has brought in on his arm and seated with him on the dais, even though her jewelry shows she isn't rich?" one maiden asked another.

"In this you aren't correct," answered the second. "Didn't you hear from the mouth of the Minister that she is the daughter of a Baron? Certainly you would find precious jewels in her house, but it's the nature of beautiful women to go without precious jewels so that everyone will look on their beauty."

"But this is an entirely beautiful maiden," said a young man to the two maidens who were speaking about Finalia as she passed before them. "I've never seen her like." The maidens grew red with anger because in their thinking he had injured their honor by praising another maiden in front of them.

"If that's the case, go to her, Adolph, if you can approach her."

"I couldn't approach her, because she is the Minister's property."

"In that case, go to the devil," said the maidens, "Because we won't be dancing with you all evening."

"Why?" asked Adolph. "What did I do to you? Because I said the maiden is beautiful you can't be beautiful also? Has the young Baronet taken a portion of your beauty?"

"The fox pleases himself with raisins when he sees he can't obtain grapes," said one of them with a laugh.

"Go away, Adolph," said the second. "Lest others hear us talking, because it's not proper."

"The others won't hear us talking," said Adolph, "They are also talking about the new guests, because the beautiful maiden has also found favor in their eyes," and he left them.

⟡

"Who is the gentle maiden that our friend the Minister has brought in on his arm and seated next to him on the throne?" the wife of the Minister of Justice asked her husband.

"I don't know myself, but this I did hear. That she is a Baronet, and her father and mother are sitting over there."

"She is very beautiful," said the wife of the Minister, "and also very wise by the look of her face. Look how the Minister speaks to her and gazes at her with love, and how all the other maidens are jealous of her."

"I believe you," laughed the Minister. "And if you were now a maiden, would you be jealous of her?"

"Listen," she said, "They're speaking French."

"I don't understand that language so well," replied the Minister of Justice.

⁂

"Emilia!" called one woman, around forty years of age. She was very handsome, and had many fine jewels like stars sparkling on her. She turned her head and neck to every passerby in order that they all see her precious ornaments, because she gloried in them. "Emilia, perhaps you know this lovely maiden the Minister has led in on his arm?"

"I'll tell you who she is," said Emilia in a low voice. "She is Finalia, the daughter of the Baron Meir Adelberg of France. We studied together in the same school for three years." Certainly the reader recognizes the speaker as Emilia, Albert's beloved, along with her stepmother.

"How is it that he isn't wealthy," said Raphia's wife to Emilia, "Yet he and his wife and daughter are at the head of the guests."

"Pray don't, mother!" said Emilia. "Pray don't speak further about them because it isn't proper."

⁂

"Death and damnation to the man who does this," cried Victor, with a face white as a sheet from rage. "Ha! What do my eyes show me. My beloved in the arms of another."

"Calm down," Albert said to him, seeing that his anger was crossing the border. "Calm down. What sin is done against you, that you become so enraged? If you were also at the ball and she was your wife, and if the mayor took her to dance, would you withhold her from him? Even now, if you can't look, let's go home."

"I won't go. Leave me here and I will see the conclusion of the matter."

"Behold, let me tell you from beginning to end," said Albert. "They arrived at the ball, and he has led them to their chairs to recover a little. Afterwards, they will refresh themselves. Then they will dance, and laugh, and celebrate and cheer their hearts. After that they will go home."

"Leave me alone, my friend, because I can't listen to your clowning now. Not while the earth on which I stand burns under my feet like coals. Here I will stand. Look, the Minister is seating her in the chair next to him to speak to her."

"So?" said Albert. "Shouldn't you be rejoicing that your beloved is showered with honor more than any of the other maidens of her age?"

"I'll take no joy from that. From now on I'll think of her as a traitor."

"Be silent," said Albert, laughing, "If not, I'll tell her everything. Let's go home," and as he spoke he grasped Victor's arm to draw him after.

"I'm not going," said Victor.

"In that case, relax. If you awaken from your jealous trance you'll be comforted."

Victor didn't say a word. He just stood looking after them until the two of them sat in the chairs and began to speak.

❦

"Tell me, honorable maiden. How do you like this evening for the beauty and order in the streets and the house?"

"It appears goodly and very nice, Sir Minister. My heart rejoices in it more than the rest of the guests."

"Why more?" asked the Minister, looking at her with an inquisitive eye.

"Because they don't know your lofty principles."

"And from where do you know them, gentle one?"

"From the goodness and kindness you have done for us."

"If a man does something, it is not for his neighbor that he does it but for himself alone, whether it is good or bad," said the Minister, and continued looking at her carefully.

Finalia's face reddened, and she said, "If a man does good or bad, he will be recompensed for his actions. But what should the one who receives the good or bad do, and how can the goat reckon with the lion. If the lion acts for good or for bad, the goat cannot raise him up for his good nor lower him down for his bad."

"Despite this, there exist men who can lower the lion from his heights to the lowest earth or to raise him higher than the stars above."

"And who are they?" asked Finalia, as she tried with all her strength to secretly conceal her threatening thoughts, realizing that Victor was standing even then before the window and seeing her sitting and conversing with the Minister.

"What are they?!" the Minister changed her question. "Do men not make nets to capture lions? And what can a lion do if its limbs are caught in a trap?"

"His wits will instruct him to beware lest he falls into it," the maiden replied.

"And if he falls?"

"Then he will labor to save himself."

"And if there are many trappers?"

"Are there not many who will help him? And if many labor on his behalf, then he will be quickly saved."

"You are right, gentle maiden, but I will ask you this. Here is a lion caught in a trap and there are many trappers. Of all of those who would be able to rescue him, only the song bird who is before him can save him. For if she lifts her voice to sing this evening, then all would be entranced by her pleasant singing, and quickly he will be saved from the trap. Even the lion would bow before her in his majesty and pride because she rescued him. Would the bird be able to reply that she doesn't wish to save him, and cast behind her back all the valuable honors[42] she will receive from him?"

Finalia's face changed, alternating from brilliant red to plaster, because she understood the target the arrow of his words was aiming for. She recovered and said, "Who could be so cruel as to do this?

---

42. Isaiah 38:17 – in original quote, "valuable honors" is "sin," quite a play on language.

Hasn't he cast his life before her solely in order that she fulfill his desire and rescue him?"

"On this the bird can be certain. She will no longer hop about the trees in the woods, causing them to rejoice, and only an echo will be heard in the forest. She will live in a pleasure palace and dwell in a golden cage to cheer the hearts of all who love song." The Minister continued looking into her face when he finished speaking, but she lowered her gaze to the ground. Then the servants came and brought confections, sweets and wine, offering them to everybody. Two servants approached before the Minister and Finalia, and the Minister took some of the confections and offered them to her. All of the maidens looked on and were jealous of her, but was she feeling happy? Did she think it an honor? Didn't she think it a disaster, knowing that Victor stood in front of the window? Hadn't his heart stormed inside him when she told him the Minister was in the house, much less now?

The Minister rose from his place and went to the second room where the orchestra sat. He commanded them to play a waltz, and took Finalia to dance with him. Finalia rose from her place, and proceeded to the center of the room on the arm of the Minister. They began to dance, and the majority of the guests went out after them, so that in a few moments, the whole room was like a boiling pot. Changing images flashed before those who didn't go out to dance and remained seated. Sometimes the Minister flew by the Baron and Dina with their daughter. She was perfectly beautiful and the Minister was boundlessly happy, and when they passed before the parents they showed off a little. The Baron and his wife glowed with hope and joy at the show that was before them.

⁌⹊⹊⹊⁌

"All of our hopes and labors were for naught," said one of the observers to another, as they stood before a window watching the Minister speaking with Finalia and taking her to dance with him. "All of our labor was worthless. None of us will get her! Not me, not Milkovski, not Victor. A cruel lion has taken the prey from us all, and he is the hero of the hunt. I hadn't counted on of this disaster."

"Relax, Yechidiel. Pray be easy. Do we not have four of the mighty of the land, Yallum, Achbar, Hagbia and Balah? Be calm and don't fear, because they will extract from his mouth what he has swallowed, despite the teeth," said Zevchiel, and they remained in their places. Victor was out there also, and he stared at Finalia as she flew by the window every few minutes. Albert also stood as if on coals and he groaned when he saw Emilia dancing with a strange man. Then the storm quieted, and the tired dancers sat down to recover. Waiters came around again with sweets to refresh them. Some people went to another room to play cards, others to play chess. The waiters brought wine, and the Minister toasted to the king's health, the guests, and everyone in the city. The guests toasted the king's health and the Minister. Finalia sat in her place and didn't mix with the other guests, and she didn't go out to dance with anybody else. So the evening passed until midnight, when the Minister called all of the guests to the meal. Then they all went to the table, the young men with the young women, the grandfathers with the grandmothers. The Minister led Finalia to the table and they all sat to eat. The musicians sang some songs from the great Meir Baer and Wagner, and for about three hours they sat at the table eating, drinking, and making merry. Afterwards they returned again to the dance. The bell in the tower sounded four o'clock in the morning, informing the guests it was time to go home. The streets were emptied, and when only a few remained whose eyes weren't yet satiated from the view, the candles began to go dark. The Minister stood in the middle of the room to receive a farewell blessing from the guests, and the wagons and the carriages returned the guests home.

Victor and Albert still stood in their places.

"When can we leave here?" asked Albert. "Are your feet held by nails?"

"I won't go," he said, but suddenly he jumped to attention. "Oh Finalia, where are you?"

"See, the carriage of the Minister is coming into the courtyard," said Albert. The Baron, his wife, the Minister and Finalia came out of the hallway went up to carriage. Dina and Finalia climbed into the coach. Victor looked at the love of his soul and she also saw him but she wouldn't look back at him while the Minister was before her. The carriage began to move and the Minister and the Baron returned to the palace. When the carriage drove before Victor and Albert, she nodded her head to them through the window of the carriage, and the two of them acknowledged her. Finalia saw the dark clouds covering the majesty of Victor's face and she sighed.

"Why do you sigh?" her mother asked.

"It's nothing, mother. I'm tired and I needed to breath the breeze," the daughter replied.

Victor and Albert left after the carriage passed.

"What is this, that they are returning alone while the Baron remains in the house of the Minister?" asked Albert.

"I don't know myself, but I'll go with you to recover a little at your house because the place I live is too crowded."

"With all my heart," answered Albert, and so they conversed until they reached his house.

❦

"And what do you have to say, Finalia?" said the mother once they were home. "Such a rare soul as the Minister defies description. You saw all of the honors he did for you and you alone."

"I know," said the daughter, and she turned to go to her room because she didn't wish to speak further about it.

❦

"Might not some evil happen to the women when they are by themselves?" the Baron asked the Minister when they returned to the palace.

"Don't fear," said the Minister, "Jonathan is with them and he will protect them. If only they had listened to my advice, then I wouldn't have let them leave my house either. But it is certain that no evil will befall them. Know, my friend Baron, that Finalia has found favor in my eyes and I love her very much. If only you will not turn me away empty."

"We?" said the Baron, "We would send you away empty? By the evidence of my eyes, Finalia will love you faithfully, because who wouldn't love a rare soul and lofty man such as yourself, my friend Minister."

"May the Lord grant it be so," said the Minister, and he bid him a tranquil rest. He commanded a servant to lead the Baron to the room he had given him, then he went himself to recover a little.

## ⤳ Chapter Fifteen – The Next Day

The next day Finalia arose in the morning, even though she was bone tired. Although she had wanted to rest for the remainder of the night she hadn't closed her eyes and sleep was stolen from her. Despite this she got up in the morning to clean her dress and to repair it, because the loops and the flowers were torn and loosened from their places. The whole day she sat as if on burning coals, but when the appointed hour approached she went to Albert's house.

"Are you well, honorable maiden?" he asked when he opened the door and saw that it was Finalia seeking permission to come in. "Are you well," he repeated his question, "after you exhausted your strength last night dancing in the ball?"

"How are you?" answered Finalia, "Haven't I already forgotten last night? And how is Victor?"

"Fine, he lodged here with me last night."

"He stayed in your house?"

"In my house."

"Were you standing in the street the whole time I was at the ball?"

"The whole time."

"Was Victor happy when he saw all of the honors I was given by the Minister?"

"Victor didn't tell me this, but the from the expression on his face he wasn't rejoicing over it."

Finalia didn't ask any more, knowing he was a man of his word.

She sat on the chair that Albert made ready for her, and Albert went to his work room. She sank so deep in thought that she didn't see Victor when he came into the house, but when Victor approached her and asked how she was, she came to, and answered, "I'm well. How are you, my dear?"

"Now I'm fine."

"Why only now?"

"Because I am seeing you."

"Didn't you also see me yesterday?"

"And who told you that I wasn't fine yesterday?"

"Your own mouth."

"How is that?"

"By your saying, 'Now I'm fine.'"

"Your logic is worthless because in your wellbeing is also mine, only I forgot that you number my words. How could I not be pleased when seeing you honored and happy and your face beaming with joy."

"I imagine that we were under the same shadow of well-being yesterday, as one light illuminates for both of us or one cloud casts shade for both of us," said the maiden and blushed.

"Verily, when the clouds cast shade for me and darken the evening stars, at the same time there was bright light for you, luxurious light," said Victor.

"And where do you get this from?" the maiden asked him, and her entire face became white as if were covered by snow.

"My eyes showed me."

"Weren't my earliest words to you that a man's eyes will always mislead him? That sometimes a man will walk in the dark and the black of night, but the darkness won't obscure his way. And sometimes a man will walk under the blue skies on a bright day, with the sun standing like a clear body in the heavens, and he will grope along the wall like a blind man because a dark black cloud will fog him all around." Thus the maiden answered, and two teardrops like pearls rolled down her lily cheeks. She tried to hide them from Victor and she turned her face away from him. From him? She would hide them from a faithful lover like Victor? He saw them and he understood, but he remained silent in order to hear how she would finish. She continued, saying, "Today you began speaking to me in riddles, so I answered you the same way. But we have already spoken too much in riddles, and I know where hints can lead. Now, you will judge which of us is right. What else could I do? The Minister invited us to the ball. Could I have contradicted his will after the life and kindness he did for us and will do for us? Believe me, being in the Minister's palace yesterday was like being in prison for me. All of the honors and majesty are nothing to me. I would chose to live with you in a poor tent rather than to be the lady of his palace. Is this nothing to you? Now you judge who is guilty, and who is destroying our happiness over mists. If my life is dear to you, please stop saying hurtful things like these because they go to my soul."

Victor stood for a few moments gazing at her. The energetic words that came from the depths of her being struck his heart, because he had made her miserable. Then he said, "Forgive me my beauty, that I was foolish and sinned against you. Verily the purity of your heart and the uprightness of your soul are known to me, and I never thought that you would break your word. If only you could feel the hot jealousy of a man when he see his soul's beloved in the arms of another when he cannot approach her, then you wouldn't jump all over me. Therefore, forgive me and don't cry. Your tears are melting my heart."

"I forgive you," said the maiden and gave him her hand. "Now if you would only tell me why you called me here, in saying I would hear some secret news."

"Behold, I will tell you, and ask your advice according to your clear intellect, because it concerns our happiness and our future. Know that in a couple days I must leave Milano."

"In a couple of days! Why?"

"Evil men who are jealous of my happiness are conspiring to kill me, so I must stay ahead and flee from them."

"Where did you learn this?"

"Four days ago, a man whom I didn't know came to my dwelling. He appeared to be one of the rabble, and he kept looking about my room until I feared to be in one house with him. 'Don't be afraid,' he said to me, 'Because I'm not here as your adversary.' 'Thank you,' I replied, 'But do I have adversaries and enemies?' 'A youth like you doesn't yet know the ways of the world and its deceits. Do you think that only evildoers have enemies? Know that an upright man has many more enemies than an evildoer, because the criminals don't do evil to those of their own kind. Unless, that is, they don't find enough to satisfy them in the houses of the upright, in which case they will harvest the vineyards of the wicked. But you are a decent man, so they will divide you up first. You must know that wicked men have decided to kill you when they find you, and you must watch your every step. If you don't distance yourself from this city, then your blood is on your head, and I will be very distressed for your earthly existence.' 'And who are you, worthy one? Tell me your name so I can thank you for the goodness of your heart.' 'My name is hidden from you,' he said, 'But you will soon know it. In order that you believe my words I will give you a sign. Know that the men who came from France, in pursuit of the father of your beloved, are similarly conspiring against you to kill you. Therefore I warn you again. Question me no further even though I know much more than this. In addition, tell Finalia to beware of them.' When he finished speaking he left me, but today in the street I met him and he said, 'You're still here? Know that it is your life.' He said just that and went. What do you think?"

"What do I think? Flee for your life, quickly and expeditiously. Even though it is hard for me to be parted from you, your life is very dear to me."

"Thank you, my beauty, on your generous words. But how will we proceed with exchanging letters?"

"Send them to Albert's house. So where are you going?"

"To the city of my father. Let me ask that when I send you a letter, you reply very quickly. That way my heart will comforted from afar, and I will be satisfied when I awake with your image."

"I will do as you say."

"Thank you. Now tell me what you think about the man who came to warn me. I think he was sent by my enemies in order to distance me from you."

"I think that there is no fraud in this, but describe the man's appearance to me."

"He was short with a sad, handsome face."

"He is Azariya,[43] Yechidiel's servant. He is a man of faith and upright in his way, and he hates his master with a consuming hatred. Surely there was a treacherous assembly in his house planning evil against us. Because of his anger he will be a protector for me always, and he came out of the goodness of his heart to warn you."

"Where do you know him from?"

"I saw him in Goldberg's house when he came seeking his master, and when he didn't find him, Henrietta and I held him up in order to learn about the nature of the Galician."

"You could be right," Victor said, "But the time has come for us to part because tomorrow morning I will leave the city with all that I love. But why are you crying? Will you be the first they will fall on?"

"You are right, my dear," said the maiden, "But how many are the wounds that love inflicts, and how countless are the victims. I am afraid that I will be the first sacrifice to be completely consumed on the altar."

Victor laughed lightly at her simple heart and said, "Don't be afraid, my precious, because you will live in joy and happiness and you will be brought to a pleasure palace. Now live well and don't be sad."

"May the Lord bring success in your journey and protect you from all evil," said the maiden in a sad voice as she rose from her place. Victor also stood and they said goodbye to Albert and left. Victor walked with Finalia until her father's house, and then they parted. Finalia stood in the doorway of her father's house watching after Victor until he disappeared from her eyes.

---

43. Name means "Helper of God."

# ⁀ Chapter Sixteen – The Letter

Days passed and week replaced week from the time the lovers parted. Finalia worried about her beloved because all word from him ceased. Her previous happiness turned to grief, and her cheeks and face were reddened from crying. But who was there to see now if she was crying or sad? Dina also sat in the corner of the house crying, because it was six weeks since she had seen the face of her husband Meir. The Minister had instructed them not to come until the danger had passed, because the villains laid in wait around his house. One time, a servant came from the Minister and said, "The Minister and the Baron request that the two of you come." Dina wanted to go, but Finalia told to the servant to bring proof he had been sent by the Minister. Dina laughed at her words, but Finalia said that she wouldn't go. The servant left and in a few minutes he returned with a note written by the Baron and the two of them went.

"What is this, that you are so frightened?" the Baron asked his wife and daughter when he saw them.

"It is Finalia's intuition," said Dina, "She is always frightened by the sounds of rustling leaves."

"Why?" asked her father.

"Because I know more about the danger that hovers over our heads than mother."

"And from where do you know about this?"

"My heart forewarns me."

"And why has your face fallen so?" asked the father examining her closely, "The color has entirely fled from you."

"It's nothing," the daughter replied. "Only that I was worried about you, dear father."

"Don't you worry, everything is fine with me," said the father. "When the Minister returns from his work we pass the time together, and he entertains me with his evening conversation. He is wise, enlightened, and understanding like no other, and also a very dear soul."

The Minister came in and greeted Dina and Finalia, spoke a few words with her and left.

"Hope in the Lord, my darling," said the Baron, "that soon I'll be back on my feet, because the Minister tells me that soon the wicked will return to their tents. But you Finalia, my only daughter, will be happy and joyful because the Lord will spread pure new skies over your head. Once I am standing on my own I will make your happiness permanent. Even if I were back in Paris in my former glory, I couldn't have hoped for such happiness as this." Finalia didn't say a word, and the Baron grew very angry because he understood what was in her heart. But he hid his wrath in his bosom, and he said, "Tell me, my daughter, has Victor Schoenfeld visited our house?"

"No."

"Why?"

"I have heard that he left Milano."

"Why?"

"I don't know."

"And where did he journey?"

"To his father's city, Rome."

"I am very sorry for that dear man, for all of the appalling and horrible things that those savage men have done to his father's house. It is a very terrible thing, for if they stretch out their hand over a man, they will pursue him to his destruction."

"It distresses me, my dear father, but my depressed heart compels me to tell you that men like them are also found amongst our own people. They pluck the fatherless from the breast,[44] and they spread a net for the innocent just to do evil."

"If this is what you are looking for, my daughter, then you will find much of it. But don't accuse your brethren, because they aren't guilty in this matter. Their neighbors mingle amongst them and teach them their ways.[45] Furthermore, a Jew in these scattered lands without money is like a soldier without a weapon."

---

44. Job 24:9.
45. Psalms 106:35.

"If only it were like you say, dear father, but another time I will show you that I am also in the right." She kissed her father, and the two women left. When they arrived home, Jonathan told Finalia that a man named Albert had asked for her, and said that she should come tomorrow morning. "Good," the maiden said. "Will you come with me tomorrow, Jonathan?" Then she turned and went to her room. "I'm very unhappy," she said to herself. "The day is closing so I can't go now even though a letter has certainly come from Victor." She got into bed, but she didn't close her eyes and the night seemed like an eternity. When dawn broke, she rose and dressed and called to Jonathan, and the two of them left to go to Albert's house.

"How are you, Albert?" the maiden said as she stepped over the threshold of his house. "I thought that you'd still be sleeping."

"I got up early this morning," said Albert, "because I knew that you wouldn't sleep all night, and you would come with the first light. So here I am to deliver to you the letter from Victor that has waited for you since yesterday." As he spoke he gave the letter into her trembling hand, and she opened it and read these words:

*Here I am in Rome, the great city of the Gods that rose to the pinnacle of power in ancient times. The remains of her destruction and her ancient monuments are still found within her. These were put in place in the days of Vespian and Titus, of whom memories of their power yet remain, and these wonders give witness to splendor and majesty of days gone by. Even now she is the glory of all lands and full of everything good, such as first pressings of oil and balsam, and even the skies drop dew. She is a city entirely splendid, and on every street and corner my eyes see precious things that broaden the perspective of those who see them and cheer every heart that feels. Wealth and might have ruled here since ancient times. She is the city that imposes boycotts on the gentile kingdoms, and mighty men humble themselves before her and go in fear of her majesty and the deceit and fraud in her.[46] The tears of the*

---

46. *[Original footnote]* – (Every reader of history knows about the boycotts imposed by the rulers of Rome over all the kings of the world, and especially about what Gregory the Third did to Heinrich the Fourth until he abandoned the Calvinist faith and embraced Catholicism. Only then did Gregory remove the ban from him and he succeeded to the throne of France in 1593).

*oppressed water her soil until she is exceedingly fat, because the leaders of the Jesuit brotherhood rule over her. The ruler of the city is also the Holy Father who stands between God and the people, and he is one of them. The children of our covenant wail and groan under the hard yoke and heavy burden that is laid on them until their heads hang in the dust. Come here, my soul's companion, to the houses of our brothers, and you will see only tears and hear only moaning, because the hands of the Jesuits abuse them. Here they steal a father from his children, and rip boys and girls from their mother's bosom. They bring them inside their walls and they entice them and force them to abandon the teachings of their fathers. On all of our brothers they levy a tax that must be paid every year on behalf of those who become Christians.*[47] *Oh! Be still my pen, in order not to melt the soft heart of the gentle maiden, whom it is my responsibility to comfort. But every time I speak about this city, my anger burns like fire at she who has spilled blood since the moment of her inception. Thousands of our faith found their graves in her eighteen hundred years ago. Many of our brothers sank like lead in the waters of the river Tiber, and our holy mementos, which were our pride and glory, sank in them and descended to the deeps. And who threw down our glory for us if not these fierce and impetuous people, these Romans. Despite this, they haven't repented at all, and their hands are stretched out over us. Why should I speak about ancient history, so distant from us. I will speak about the robbery and murder that touch my bones and flesh. About my father and sister who are taken prisoner, my mother who was the pride of women, and now all that remains is the breath within her. And who is to blame if not that savage people, who pervert everything decent, and to whom everything bad is good? "Woe," I thought as I walked in those great wide streets with pleasant views raised up before me on the pinnacles of power. "What good are all these to me? Will they pleasure my eyes or cheer my heart? The more I look at the riches of Rome, the more a burning fire is kindled within me. All the pleasant views add to the bonfire,*

---

47. See Ha-Melitz, No. 19, 1878. It reports that the Jews of Rome are forced to pay a special tax to the monasteries to finance Jewish children who are kidnapped and brought into Catholicism. This evil decree was given over ten years ago.

*like the burning of many trees that can never be extinguished. Under each stone is heard only groans, and under every wall mourning and wailing. You were entirely correct, Finalia, when you said that sometimes a man walks under the bright light of the sun, and it is dark all around for him, and sometimes a man walks in the dark, and despite that he has bright light. Now I see how well your words fit. How happy I was when I walked about the streets of Milano, even when the light was absent from them. But you were there, my soul's companion, and with your sweet words you lit the way for me and brightened my heart, and I soared on the wings of hope. But how my heart languishes now when I walk the streets and see all of the riches of the world, because what is there for me here? Who is there for me here? My father is gone and my sister, Woe! May the Lord grant that I find her so I can give my life for her. But what use is my life to these barbarians? They only have eyes for gold and silver. This is the bloodsucker that says, "Give, give."[48] When will this exactress of gold cease! Forgive me if I have depressed your spirits, but I decided I would speak and be relieved, and who can I talk to if not you? Therefore I have poured my complaint of the bitterness in my soul in the bosom of a letter, and in my mind it was like talking to you face to face. You will gather the words and hide them in your heart, and will I not then be relieved? Forgive me that my letter is so late, but the guilt is not mine. I found my mother in a terrible condition, and this week I obtained work in the trading house of Hiedelberg. Now that I've had a little respite from my sadness, I took up my pen to write you, my dear. I ask you that you will quickly write back and tell me how you and your honorable parents are doing. Answer in order that you may revive the spirit of your beloved forever.*

*Victor Schoenfeld*

With a broken heart and eyes full of tears, she placed the letter in her pocket after reading it a second and a third time, then she said goodbye to Albert and she left. This same day we see her walking with a letter to the express house to send to Rome.

---

48. Proverbs 30.15.

# ✑ Chapter Seventeen – Henrietta and Finalia

"What has been going on with you, Finalia, my dear friend?" The speaker was an eighteen year old maiden, pretty and delicate, whose expensive clothes bore witness to the fact she was a daughter of the wealthy class. She sat on the bench with Finalia. "What's been going on that your feet have been absent so long from our house, to the point that I came to see you? It must be that your happiness, flying on the wings of hope, has taught you forget your beloved friend who you always called sister. But what is this? Why has your face fallen so? Have you become ill?"

Finalia looked into the face of the maiden whom the reader has certainly recognized as Henrietta Goldberg and she said, "My life and soul, my dear, you riddle with me today."

"Riddles?" asked the maiden, and amusement fleeted over her face. "Riddles, you say! Do my lips not speak clearly? The happiness that flies on the wings of hope, you will be dressed in pride and arrogance and distanced from your friend."

"Pray explain your words to me. I don't understand what happiness you are talking about."

"Isn't everybody saying that the Minister Emanuel Maranya is in love with you? I saw this myself on the evening of the ball, that he honored you more than any of the other maidens who were invited."

"Were you at the ball?"

"No! But I stood in the street in front of the window, and I could watch as if I was in the house. Therefore, don't hide from me, but cheer the soul of your friend. I see you, my dear friend, as the happiest in the world, because it will happen for you."

"Believe me, my dear Henrietta, your assumption is flawed."

"If I believe you, then I will have to say that you treat him with contempt. I ask you, could you find in the whole world a man more honorable and lofty than he?"

"I have found one," Finalia said forcefully, in order to put an end to the conversation she thought burdensome, and she blushed a little.

"If that's the case, my dear, forgive me that I have distressed you. Now tell me everything, and why your countenance has fallen so."

"Believe me, my dear, that this isn't what steals the joy from my face. Rather it's the events that have occurred and will come to pass on my father's house."

"And what is this?" Henrietta asked.

"You don't know about it?"

"No."

So she told her all that had befallen them, of the kindness of the Minister to them, how if it hadn't been for the Minister, her father would already be cut off from the land of the living.

"If so, isn't it your obligation to repay him for all of the favors he has done for you?"

"This will never happen," said Finalia. "But tell me, my dear. Why are you also so downcast?"

"Have you not heard of my tragedy?"

"I didn't hear a thing. What is it?'

"My father has bound me with chains to the scum of the earth. Imagine for yourself my depression when I recall that this man will be the guide of my youth. Now I regret that when Yechidiel wanted me, I scorned him. The man my father has designated for me is inferior to Yechidiel, ten steps backwards."[49]

"Pray don't, my dear. Don't say this," said Finalia. "That man Yechidiel gathers his fists full of the wicked of the land. If he opened his hand and tossed out just a smidgen of them on a city or family, then everyone there would be struck with terrible boils from the soles of their feet to their heads, and they wouldn't be quickly healed."

"How do you know this?"

"How do I know? The disaster that your father has prepared for you comes from him, from the hands of Yechidiel."

The maiden screamed and jumped up from her place. "God in

49. Isaiah 38:8.

heaven, from Yechidiel? Tell me, how do you know this?"

"Verily he told your father that he saw you walking with a youth, one of the young men of Milano. Your father was very frightened and he decided to put an end to your straying."

"My God! My God!" screamed the maiden, "How great is the evil of man."

"He has done even more," said Finalia. "He has made friends with the wicked, and they gather together about the house of my father. What do you say about that?"

"What do I say? I will call all of the Galicians robbers and murders. It is a terrible thing, very awful. Listen now, my dear Finalia, to the thoughts of my heart. The Lord has sorely chastised me that I am tied to a fool. For now I will do as my father commands, and I will go like a tame sheep to the slaughter. I will not be held for long by these insubstantial bonds. I will be free! I will be free forever! Heaven will be my witness that I am guiltless in the matter, and I won't be made to stand before the throne of judgement because my soul is deserving and pure. But those who lay affliction on their children, they will be forced to go in the shadows. They will serve strange new gods and draw near to them. They will rebel against the true God, and their children will also rebel after them. Therefore they will be forced to seek the wandering, to gather the scattered." So spoke Henrietta, and her face reddened like scarlet, to the point where Finalia became frightened.

"What is happening to you, my dear," she said. "Think about your meditation. Why does your anger burn like fire? Speak to the Lord about what evil you have found in him. Did He withhold from you favor, a handsome and rare soul with a pure heart, even riches and happiness? But marriage has almost overtaken you. You are frightened, and you thought to give a prayer to God in heaven. I will not believe that you have spoken these words."

"Will you speak thusly, Finalia? Will your mouth say such words to me as, 'Pray think it over'? They will steal my freedom from me. How hard will a man fight for independence and freedom? How many lives are lost in the cause of freedom, and how many suffer uncountable evils just for freedom? How can you say that it has almost overtaken me and I am frightened? But we won't speak further about this. Prepare yourself for my wedding day, which will be in another two weeks. Don't refuse me. You will come to be happy with me or to console me for my tragedy, and that kindness will never be forgotten." In love, but not in gladness, each woman took leave of her friend. Henrietta returned sad hearted to her father's house, and Finalia remained in her room, depressed.

## ⇜ Chapter Eighteen – Mother and Daughter

"I don't know what is with you, my daughter. If I look at your face, so full of sadness and worry, it adds anguish to my pains, and the spark of hope that time has hidden in the corner of my heart will be quickly extinguished."

"I don't understand your words, my beloved mother. Why is it a wonder to you? Will I see the natural order overturned that we make treaties with our sworn enemies? The skies that have been clean and pure these ten years we have lived in Milano, are darkening now, and blackness covers the sun. Even the bright lights of the night are covered so that their glow is entirely absorbed. Black clouds rise from everywhere to seal the way against every spark of hope and ray of light that begins to cast a little illumination before us. And you ask me what is with me? Father isn't here and there's been no contact with my brother who is our last hope. My heart predicts that more sorrows than these are waiting for us, and you will also go into your room to cry. How could I be happy? One more thing I will tell you. When I went to the Goldberg's house for the wedding of their daughter, Yediya asked of me that I and Henrietta's other friends help him receive the guests, and bring for everybody whatever he was lacking. We didn't sit for a moment, just served the guests all day and all night. We didn't eat, we didn't drink, we didn't sit to recover. We just

ran from place to place to bring whatever was needed. This one wanted meat and fat, that one wine. This one ate so much that it became
loathsome for him. He yelled that he be brought something to revive
him, because his heart was hurting, and when I gave him liquor and
seltzer, he made fun of me. He said, 'You haven't tasted a thing yet,
while I, after I drink this and feel better, I will go back to eat some
more.' What do you say about the feelings of a man like this, dear
mother?"

"What can I say? He is not a sensitive man."

"Believe me, dear mother, most men feel that way. So we labored
throughout the feast until the guests departed. Then Yediya called us
all to sit around the table, and he and his family sat with us to eat and
drink and enjoy ourselves. He ordered the musicians to play for us to
cheer our tired hearts, but if only you could see, mother, what it was
like there. Were we not all tired and weary, not to mention hungry
and thirsty? Within a half an hour almost everybody sitting there
drowsed off and fell asleep. They only brought the food to their
mouths and tasted a little of the wine prepared for them, then their
heads began to spin like wheels and they were drunk. Some drank
their cup down to the bottom, some didn't empty it halfway, some
fell asleep as they began to drink. The servants and the maids took
everything from the table and enjoyed themselves with portions that
weren't theirs. What do you say about this now, dear mother?"

"Who can ascertain the breadth of your understanding, that is
what I say. But don't forget this either, that there was a feast in that
house . . . I hope in the near future to show you that you are mistak-
en." Thus the mother spoke and she went to her room. Finalia
remained alone in her room and plumbed the depths of her thoughts.
"I don't know what is happening," she thought. "It's been a half a year
now since I received the second letter from him, and I replied to him
quickly. Since then there has been no word from him. It must be that
the letters have fallen captive into the hands of our enemies. I'll read
the second letter another time, and maybe I'll find the root of the
matter that prevents him from writing." She got the letter and
opened it, and read in it these words:

*My Soul's Companion*

*Your letter is dearer to me than all the riches of the world. I read it with great joy, and your voice is the sweet voice I heard walking in the garden. The letter refreshed the day, but the words melted my heart like water, when I heard that you walk around pining from worry and sadness and that you constantly worry and are distressed over me. As to your words of complaint about my not writing for so long, I cannot justify myself before you. But first let me say that your letter was sweet like the drippings from honeycombs, but also dipped in confusion on both sides. For all of that, I drank your reeling cup and wrung out the dregs,*[50] *and in my mouth it was like the sweetest honey, because the right is with you. You are my beloved, and there is nobody like you. The wounds that your letter inflicted on me are real, and I welcomed them with open arms. I opened before them my closed and injured heart in order to squeeze the life from my breast. Your pleasant words profited me greatly, but the embers that you poured on my head were a little exaggerated in measure, as my eyes informed me. This I know truly, that a precious sacrifice you have offered up on the altar of our love, and this I know to value and recognize. But it's no wonder to me, because there is only one Finalia to be found in the whole world. Believe me, my dear, I don't know what to write. Should I write a friendly letter? Behold, to be reassuring is very bitter for me. I hoped for good and here is horror. I didn't want to depress your spirits, and as I wrote you these lines, my eyes dripped tears as I recalled that you, my perfect one, would melt in tears. You! Was I not a happy planet and you the sun? You comforted me and guided me on my path, and you opened before me the gates of spirituality and hope for a refuge, until the spirit came upon me and gave me wings to fly high into the heavens. Once you said that shining planets distribute their glow to guide us to the proper place. If the Lord stretches out his hand to the wheel of our lives, palm branches will shelter us and create shade to supply our mutual joy, and then I will know that it is you who prepared my happiness. If a weeping oak bends its roots and its chief branches bow in mourning,*

---

50. Isaiah 51:17.

*then I will be frightened and I will know that this is also by your hand. But I will hope that your memory and your thoughts will dress me in heroism and might, and cause me to be as solid as an iron pillar. But what has happened to you! In the words of your letter, I see your spirit flagging and enveloped in shadow, and you turn away. Where is your courage and your wonderful loyalty to me? You continue to smile even with the terrible pains complaining within you and with the dark spirit hovering over your face. The worm comes into the heart of the flower and it droops downwards, and its lovely flower-cup withers like the heads of grain. But even in a time when the world is languishing, how desirable she is, there is no end to her heart-stopping beauty. Be easy now, my soul's companion. Verily, for a little while, the lily will wither under the strong hand of the sun, but eventually she will bloom again because I will make a shelter for her and hide her so that the wind and the sun don't strike her. This is what I am always thinking, my soul's companion. I will sleep in your love, when dreaming or awake. But immediately I remember that you are afraid of the accomplishments of the wicked that are always before your eyes. My anger burns hot and I say, "May the Lord grant that in that evil time I will be near to you, and with my life I will pave a path for you. I will slash to the right and the left and I will pour out my blood on the altar of your happiness. I will not be still nor rest until I put you back on your feet. But how can I be of use to you now, when my hands are tied and my feet are in fetters? I have been expelled from God's Garden of Eden, and I can't return now because the flaming sword which turns every way.*[51] *Here I have only empty consolations. My sister is still within the walls of the Jesuits and I won't be able to quickly extract what they have swallowed from their mouths. One spark of hope is fanned at the base of my heart, and hope and fear will make it a terrible flame. Despite this, some consolations have come from above. I came to know an initiate in a miraculous manner, and he told me that my father lives. He made me swear to stop up my mouth until the proper time, and said that my father is also in the hands of the Jesuits. All the things that they*

---

51. Genesis 3:24.

*say to him to entice him are in vain. At first I didn't believe his words, but afterwards he proved that the truth was with him, because the next day he came a second time to this place and, behold! A letter written by my father in pencil. I held it with trembling hands and read:*

My son! My son! How my heart languishes as I write you to tell you that I, your father, sit in prison. Not only in prison, but in a place remote from God and man. But I am greatly strengthened by the hope brought to me that I will hear you are doing well and be able to write you. I ask you, my son, to tell me how everybody fares, and how is my only daughter Shoshana, and that you all be consoled. Hope in the Lord for good expectations in life. If the Lord will begin to open the gates of life before us and begin to show us His kindness, He will not withdraw his hand until He returns us to our dwelling. And He will bring us consolation and our inheritance. Now, my beloved son, pour out on paper the expressions of your spirit. This man is not like all the other initiates, but a rare soul, and he has promised me to be a messenger between us. Go now, my son, and quickly inform your mother and your sister Shoshana that their spirits be restored. May all of you live in prosperity and may the Lord remove the iron wall that separates us, and then tranquility will be restored to you and to your father.

Aaron Schoenfeld

*These are the things that have occurred and came to pass. Pray imagine the pain in my heart on knowing that my father lives, but I cannot get to him. Now, my soul's companion, support me with your pen and your unsullied intelligence. Write me a letter full of the spirit of your understanding, and I will quickly write my thanks for this. Your lover for eternity,*

*Victor Schoenfeld*

"God in heavens!" cried the maiden from the disquiet in her heart. He said that he would quickly send me a reply. It could be nothing other than the letter fell captive in their hands. Therefore, I will write him a second letter." So she spoke and she put the letter in her garment pocket, and she lay on her bed to think of what to write him.

Just as she was solidifying her ideas, a terrible and threatening dream ran before her like lightening, and her face whitened like plaster. But she awoke when she heard the voice of a strange man, and she saw that he was the servant of the Minister who came to summon Dina to the Baron.

Dina left, and Finalia remained with Jonathan. She sat in a chair in the second room plunged into deep thought, when suddenly her ears heard a tortured cry, weak and stricken. Before she found the strength to rise from her place, two strange men appeared before her. Men, who just seeing them would cause a hero's heart to die, not to mention the heart of a soft and gentle maiden like Finalia. Her knees collapsed, her eyes grew dark and her teeth rattled in her mouth. She opened her mouth to scream and call for help, but her voice failed her. Only her eyes looked here and there, and she saw that Jonathan was no longer. She remained paralyzed and meek with her eyes wide-open, and one of them approached her said, "Forgive us, my beauty, for dragging you from your rest. But do not fear, no evil will come to you." As he spoke he took from his pocket ink, a pen and three letters, and he said, "Come over here, my beauty! Sign your name on each one of these, and we will desire no more."

Finalia's face reddened from fear and anger and she said, "What have I to do with villains? What if I don't want to?"

"You will want to, and you will sign," he said, "And you'll do so in a few moments." As he spoke he seized her arm in his savage hands and dragged her to the table. He put the pen in her hand and in a commanding voice said, "Write!"

"I won't sign until I read everything written within "

"Write!" he said in a strong and powerful voice, "or in a moment you'll be no more." He showed her the place to sign, and with the last efforts of her strength she wrote her name. 'Your family name also," shouted the villain. "Sign the second and the third sheets also!"

When she signed the third letter, her strength abandoned her and she fainted, because with a glance of her eyes she saw a few words, and they terrified her heart. This worked out well for the villains, because they wrapped her face and her body in her mantle, put her on their shoulders and left.

## ⤝ Chapter Nineteen – New Sorrows

"What is this! What's happened!" cried Dina as she stepped over the threshold of the house. "Oh, what has happened. Finalia! Where are you?" she shrieked, and clapped her hands. "Here is a new sorrow come upon our house. Would Finalia go out with Jonathan and leave the house empty and wide open? Finalia!" she cried, and moved on, looking in all of the rooms, but Finalia wasn't there. Suddenly, the servant noticed a letter on the table, and he said, "Look here, ma'am. I found this on the table." Trembling with anxiety, Dina took the letter and opened it. But she wasn't able to read it because her eyes went dark after she saw the first few words:

*My Dearly Beloved Parents,*
*Forgive me . . .*

She wasn't able to read any further, and the letter dropped from her hands. She fell to the earth, powerless and fainting. The servant called some people who lived in the house next door to lift her up, and he ran to tell his master.

"Why are you so dismayed, Edward?" asked the Minister, looking at his frightened servant.

"Sir. A terrible wrong has occurred in the Baron's house just now."

'What is it?"

"When we got there, we found the house wide open and the young Baroness and Jonathan were gone."

"The young Baroness and Jonathan weren't there? So why all the confusion!" said the Minister. "Surely they went to her friend's house, and Jonathan went along as is always his habit."

"No, my lord. The wife of the Baron said that she wouldn't do this, that a great tragedy must have occurred, a tragedy you cannot charm away. Suddenly she fainted and all of the neighbors hurried to lift her up, and I ran to tell my lord and the Baron."

"Behold, this is a characteristic of women, that they faint over every trivial thing," said the Minister.

"No, my lord. That isn't it. She didn't faint right away, but after I found a letter spread on the table and she began to read it. Then the letter fell from her hands and she fainted."

"She fainted because of the letter?" The Minister asked perplexed.

"Because of the letter."

"Go to the coachman and order him to harness the carriage. Then you will go to the house of the Minister to find out the state of his wife and to tell her that in a little while the Baron and I will be there." The servant bowed and went out.

"I don't know what to do," the Minister said to himself. "How can I tell this to the Baron?" The Minister walked weakly about his room, a step this way, a step that way, without order, like a man lost in thought. Then there was a knock at the door.

"Pray enter," called the Minister, and he turned his face towards the doorway. The door opened slowly and the Baron appeared on the threshold. In a polite voice he said, "Forgive me, sir, that I interrupt your meditations."

"It's nothing," said the Minister hurriedly, because he wanted to hide his perplexity from the Baron lest he be suddenly startled.

"I've been waiting the whole time for my daughter," said the Baron, "But when Edward returned and my daughter wasn't with him, and since he came running in confusion and fright, I thought it might be something."

"I don't know myself," said the Minister, "But when we get to your house we will know everything." The Baron was very frightened and he wished to speak, but the servant came in and said, "The carriage is ready and at the gate."

"Be so good, my friend Baron, as to put on your cloak, and the two of us will travel to your house." The Baron didn't know what was going on, but his heart informed him that a new sorrow was in store for him. Without speaking, he donned his coat and hat, and he sat next to the Minister to travel to his house.

"Woe," said the Baron. "Who will tell me what has happened in my house . . . But why does the carriage move so heavily."

"The carriage isn't performing poorly," said the Minister, "It's just that the time is dragging out. If you won't be frightened, I will give you some news."

"I won't be afraid, because I have already prepared myself for this."

"And if I tell you that Finalia . . . " said the Minister.

"If Finalia what? What are you asking?" cried the Baron as one insane, and he tried to leap from the carriage which was running along like lightening. The Minister grabbed him by the sleeve of his coat and said, "Pray be calm, it's nothing. Edward told me that Finalia and Jonathan aren't there. It's quite possible that all of our fears are for naught and they are just wandering about. But there was the matter of a letter Dina found on the table."

"Woe," cried the Baron. "My only daughter is missing." The carriage quickly came to a stop and the Minister leapt out, and he pulled the Baron along with him into the house. Terrible and threatening was the scene that awaited the Baron within his own home. When he had left his house everything was in a proper eye pleasing arrangement, but now all was desolation and destruction. The flowers were wilted, the window curtains were blackened, the whole house was disordered. Here and there were a couple chairs grouped together, while another area was entirely empty. The table was not in its place, and neither were the remainder of the household furnishings. The Baron's bookcase was covered with dust on every side, but who paid attention to this? From the time the Baron had gone to the Minister's house and Victor had wandered far away, every spark of happiness had left the house with them. Who noticed the wilted flowers or furniture, and these recent events had added to the mess. The Baron went forward with the Minister after him. Edward came to meet them, and said, "The Baroness is lying powerless on her bed." The Baron and the Minister approached Dina, and she was lying with her eyes wide open, waiting for them to arrive. Her face was white like plaster, but also reddened from crying. When she saw them she wiped away her tears and lifted her head a little.

"What do you have to say about this, Meir?" Dina said. "Were our previous troubles so few that we will have new ones? Our last hope is lost, Finalia is gone, and Jonathan is also missing."

"Pray relax," said the Baron, "We won't despair yet. But where is the letter?"

"Woe!" said Dina, "The letter bows us to the dust." As she spoke she gave it into Meir's hands. He beckoned the Minister to the other room to read the letter, but the Minister said to his servant, "Go and fetch Doctor Pirot and tell him that I await him." The servant left, and the Minister and the Baron went into the other room, and with trembling hands the Baron opened the letter. The Minister also stood with him peering at the letter, and he read:

*My Dearly Beloved Parents,*

*Forgive me. Forgive your only daughter. Forgive an ungrateful maiden like me. Certainly I will be seen as a rebellious daughter in your eyes, because at the very time you sought to arrange for my happiness and success, and at the time your gentle souls wished to elevate me higher than the skies, I rejected your goodness. I trampled on the kindness of my parents, because my heart followed after my eyes. Therefore I was brought down from the heavens to the earth and my honor will abide as the dust underfoot. If you should ask me why I chose this? Is it not in man's hands to choose good or bad, happiness or tragedy? If you ask me this, I will reply to you, my dear parents, that this is not the way of mankind. A man can fight everything, he is made without dread.[52] No weapon formed against him shall succeed,[53] and he laughs at every mishap and injury. He fights against the roaring, pounding waves of the sea, and battles with wild beasts. But nobody can stand against cruel love, which steals the treasures of every man. His wisdom will vanish, his strength will be removed from him, he will be left powerless like an ox or an ass laying down under a load. And if love does this to heroes and men of name, how much more so to a seventeen year old*

---

52. Job 41:25.
53. Isaiah 54:17.

*maiden. A maiden such as myself who was raised on her parents knees,
upright, with an untouched heart, in the presence of righteousness. But
suddenly love stood up against me in the crossroads, and blocked the
path of righteousness before me, so I could find no where to turn. I
joined forces with her because I could find no other advice to make use
of. I knew that the Minister loved me, and I could not contradict his
will, because he is so honored and did so much for you. For this reason
I left your home and I abandoned my dear parents. Jonathan allowed
himself to be persuaded by my request, and he will go with me until I
reach the place that destiny will provide for me. I am thinking about
sending a letter to the honest and honorable Minister to request that he
not be angry with you on my account. Do not cry or be sad, because I
am alive, and my soul is clean and pure. My only guilt is that I saw
Victor Schoenfeld, and from that time my soul and my heart are his. I
hope you will not be angry with your only daughter, and maybe I will
again see your beautiful faces and hear from the generosity of your
mouths that you have forgiven the sin of your only daughter.*

    *Fin a l ia  Ad e l b er g*[54]

    Like a scarecrow in a cucumber field,[55] the Minister stood in his
place. His black eyes stared forth in anger and compassion, sometimes at the letter and sometimes at the Baron, who was white as
death. "Verily, nobody can imagine your terrible pain," he said. "But
you should still be comforted that she is alive, and that she hasn't fall-
en into the hands of villains. Victor is an honorable man from a exalted family, so why should you be afraid? Believe me, my friend Baron.
If I had known about this earlier, when Victor was here, then I would
have guaranteed their happiness and success. But they didn't know
me, and they thought I would pursue them in hot anger. Therefore
they hastened to escape, both to their distress and to my own, because
I know that it was through me this tragedy came to them."

    "What are you saying, honorable sir," said the Baron, because
these refined feelings touched his heart. "The feelings you express are

---

54. Spaces in name from original Hebrew.
55. Jeremiah 10:5.

not those of a man but of the children of God. I thank you and bless you for your beneficence to us, but from now on I can no longer accept your kindness. I will remain in my house, and whatever the Lord has in store for me, I will suffer and bear it. I can no longer accept benefits and kindness from your hand, since . . . "

"Hush! Hush!" the Minister checked the Baron's speech. "I don't want to hear words like these. As I was faithful with you until now, I will be from now on. Maybe even more so, because now I will be acting out of the love of a man for his brother. Therefore I advise you to leave this house where you will not quickly forget all the things that occurred in it. I will prepare a place for you in my palace, and there you will live until the Lord expands your borders. But now let me ask you, my friend Baron, verily the letter is no twin of the signature. Maybe there is some evil hand of treachery in this, and she is innocent and pure. Maybe she is in great trouble."

"That's not it," said the Baron energetically. 'The fact that the letter and the signature aren't uniform is because she had already prepared the letter, and she added her signature when she fled. Therefore she was trembling and rushing when she signed, because she is not accustomed to doing things like these."

"But maybe the agents who came from France did this to take out their vengeance on her. I am afraid that they killed Jonathan and they carried off your daughter."

"No! That can't be it."

"Do you trust villains more than your daughter?"

"More, because she has done things like them."

"Maybe she is innocent and untainted in all this?"

"I am uncertain."

"Have you proof in the matter?"

"I have proof."

"In what?"

"In the letter."

"Did you find things in the letter that were already known to you?"

"I found things."

"Did she know Victor?"

"She knew him."

"Did she already love him?"

"This I don't properly know."

"What will be will be, but I forgive her, and I ask that you also forgive her. Now let us go to your wife to comfort her and see if the doctor has arrived yet. When they went into Dina's room, they found the doctor sitting next to the bed. When he saw the Minister, he rose from his place.

"How is the patient doing?" the Minister asked.

"The danger has passed, but a weakness of the heart has seized her and she requires rest now."

"Can we bring her in the carriage to my palace?" The Minister asked the doctor.

The doctor stared dumbfounded at the Minister and said, "We may."

The Baron approached Dina and said, "Dina, my innocent one. Are you able to travel in the Minister's carriage to his palace? He wishes us to live there from now on."

"And what will be with Finalia?"

"We will speak about this when your strength returns."

"In the few days that you weren't at home, did you forget your daughter Finalia? Your only daughter!"

"Did you read the letter that she left?" asked the Baron.

"I read it. So?"

"Therefore we can be of no use to her."

"Because of this we will despair of her request?"

"Didn't I tell you that we will speak of this when your strength returns. Now we can't contradict the will of the Minister. Come and I will guide you to the carriage."

"Take your daughter Finalia's things and they'll be keepsakes for us," said Dina in a tearful voice.

"I'll take them," said the Baron, "But come." The Baron and the doctor brought her to the carriage, and they traveled with her to the Minister's residence. There they laid her on a bed, and an old woman remained with her. The doctor also remained there. The Baron returned to the Minister, and found him pulling on his moustache, but when he saw the Baron, he awoke from his trance and said, "Behold, I have ordered my servants to take all of the items in the house and to bring them to my home. Now let us travel to our places." The Minister and the Baron returned home, and the house was emptied of valuables and furnishings. It remained barren, barren and empty.

## ⇗ Chapter Twenty – Victor

In the attic room of a house on the edge of the city of Rome, a young man sat by a small table, supporting his head in both his hands. A dim candle burns, but it doesn't illuminate the occupant, and he continually gave voice to heavy groans from his torn heart. Suddenly he jumped up and said, "I won't believe that it can happen. Angels from on high will descend to earth and forget the stone they were hewn from. The entire natural order will be overturned. Every land will stagger about like a drunk. The stars in the sky will withhold their light because they will alter their role, but she will never go back on her word, and she will never break her covenant until the last day." So spoke the young man and his face reddened like fire. "Alas, what am I saying! Didn't I read the letter that she sent me? Words that I cannot charm away. They were so clear that a little boy could understand. But no! It's a lie! I will read it another time, because maybe I was mistaken." Fearfully and hurriedly he opened the letter again and read:

*My Heart and Soul's Companion,*
*With a sad heart and bent knees, I approach with this letter to plead before you. Forgive me for the rebellion that I'm forced to make against my desires, against the Lord and against you. The terrible mischance that my father's house is enmeshed in is known to you, as is my love for my father, which I didn't hide from you. If somebody were to say to me*

*that I could ransom the life of my father with my own, wouldn't I hap-*
*pily say 'I will die in place of my dear father.' This is the message of the*
*letter.*[56] *My father is in great trouble, and his enemies are in place all*
*around him. The district Minister is a wicked and worthless fellow,*
*and he loves me mightily. Therefore, he said if I will yield to his request,*
*then he will do everything for my father and mother. If he withdraws*
*his hand from them, then we will surely be destroyed, because they lay*
*in wait like robbers, and they won't be satisfied with his blood. Even*
*though I see my tragedy before me, I'm compelled to give my hand to*
*him in order to save my father. Please don't be wroth, and the Lord will*
*send you a heart as faithful your own, one who won't lie in her pledges.*
*You will see happiness and life with the woman the Lord arranges for*
*you. Never come to Milano if my life is dear in your eyes, because if I*
*see you another time I will put an end to my life and my sorrows togeth-*
*er. I loved you with a love I will never forget, but we will always be*
*remote, because I am parting from you forever.*

*Fin a l iaA d e l b er g*

"Oh Lord," cried Victor, spreading his hands to the heavens.
"Why do you give light to the suffering and life to the bitter in spirit?[57] I don't know where I stand. Should I put an end to my life and
add sin to iniquity? But why should I live! I will live no longer! Ha!
The matter is true! True! She betrayed me! Traitoress! The treacherous
have acted very treacherously.[58] I thought Finalia was a daughter of
the gods. Finalia betrayed me! She! She will give her hand to another! I won't believe it. I will get the first letter that she sent me and with
my candle shining above my head, I will see the difference between
them." He took the first letter from the chest and read:

*Greetings to you, my shining star, my star of happiness in days of sor-*
*row. I walk in the light of your illumination, and without you both my*

---

56. Esther 3:14.

57. Job 3:20.

58. Is. 24:16 – This is the quote from which Foner takes the title of her novella, "The Treachery of
Traitors."

*peace and my rest vanish. I walked in blackness all the time that you withheld the fruits of your pen from me, and I cried all the time. I said that you stole my heart and forgot me, but now that I have received your letter, my soul comes alive. I repeated it and repeated it, until all of your words were captured in my mouth. Let me respond to the expressions of your soul. You aren't right to pass crooked judgement on Rome, the crowning city, even though your words were true, that from all the cries of the suffering, her splendor is turned into destruction. Despite that, I will think of her like the Garden of Eden. I value her earth over fine gold, her dust I will praise over gold. Why? Because the cradle of my soul's beloved is there. He grew at her breast and played on her knees, until he was a man, beautiful in his greatness. His heart is full of wisdom and understanding and a rare spirit abides within him. Where is the place of his birth if not Rome? From whose womb did the man emerge with such refined characteristics if not Rome? Therefore, the renowned city of Rome is very dear to me, because I will honor the place where your feet have tread. You must swear in the name of our true love that you won't worry or be sad, only hope in the Lord who has it in His hands to change destiny. Can we recognize light without darkness, or can we know good without evil? Therefore I command you not to be sad, but to be strong and brave. Hope will comfort us and guide us and transport us across the angry sea until we reach the port. Do not weaken, my friend, because the teachings of sorrow are a medicine to a man in days of misfortune, as a wise man said. Do not ever refrain from informing me how you are doing, and walk in wholeness and righteousness. Your lover forever,*

*Finalia Adelberg*

"Ha! Ha! Ha!" he laughed from the pain in his heart like a madman as he gazed at the two letters. "Sometimes this, sometimes that, I won't believe this is happening. She couldn't write this one time and that the other time. It can be nothing other than the hands of our enemies at work here. They desire to separate us and to tear apart our union. But who could have written the counterfeit letter? The purity of her language informs me that the hand of Finalia composed this cruel letter. But even if it is true, then I will forgive her, because her love for her father is stronger than her love for her beloved. You are justified, dear soul, justified. You show that you know the obligation of children to their parents. You are a standard for the children of your people. She will not be thought of with scorn or disdain in the eyes of those who honor their parents when they know of her refined feelings. All those whom the Lord favors with a rare soul would do as you, but you are at their head. Now, forgive me for all of the angry words I spoke, for profaning your honorable name and calling you a traitoress. I forgive! I forgive you, dear soul, for everything you have done to me. May the Lord grant that you find solace in the house of the man you are entering. But no! Cursed is the man who has done this. I've made up my mind to race to Milano and fight him. I will say to him that he is low, that the Lord has given him honor and fortune, but he went and stole a meek lamb, because the Lord will not revenge those who do so." As he spoke, he took his jacket and his hat and he ran outside, but there he stood a few minutes and thought things over. "No!" he said suddenly to himself. "No!, I won't journey to Milano. Didn't she say that she would put an end to her life the moment she saw me? Therefore I will desist, and I will go about with a bitter spirit under the Lord's heaven until my final day. From now on my only concern will be for my parents and my sister, until I bring them out to freedom." When he finished speaking, his fury was exhausted, and he returned to his room and his work.

## ᔰ Chapter Twenty One – The Captive

"Where am I! Tell me where I am!" cried the maiden when she returned to consciousness and sensed that she was in a moving carriage. The carriage moved along slowly. "Tell me where I am! Am I a captive of the sword taken by robbers? Who gave you permission to do this abominable thing!"

"A little longer, and you'll know," the driver replied. He turned his head back to the horses to strike them with his staff of wrath, and to watch their forms closely. Only their neighing and galloping gave him pleasure, this and nothing else. They were his life and his days, he was obsessed with them dreaming and waking. He didn't answer the beautiful maiden, except for a few short, sparse words, in order not to withhold this pleasure from himself for even a moment. He kept his watch as he had been verbally commanded, in every detail and specific. He struck the horses and cursed, reproached and scorned every one of them. He dressed himself in haughty pride before whoever he saw, because every time that he struck the horses, they began to exert themselves and run in fear. He cursed them and abused them as much as he desired, and even then they didn't open their mouths to reproach him a word, so he knew that he was truly king of the beasts. Therefore this mission suited him, because he didn't set his heart or lend his ears to hear the cries of the captive, which tore the heart of heaven.

"My God! My God!" cried the maiden when she saw that the carriage was moving on and distancing itself from her father's house. "You have put an end to the remnants of my father's house! What will be their fate? Can they bear the heavy suffering that You have loaded on their shoulders? Won't they buckle under the load? Who will stand them up? . . . Verily, I am a daughter of death. I cannot watch the way the driver hits the horses for no fault of their own, because they don't want to be counted amongst these evildoers. Because they don't want to go in the way of robbery and murder, they are beaten and tortured! You whose eyes are too pure to look upon evil,[59] why do You think of me as a beast that You deliver me into the hands of evil, like these horses into the hands of this driver? Why doesn't he beat the horses in the city? Is he not afraid to, because the threats of the officers terrify him, and if he is seen he will be beaten according to his wickedness. How can You look on silently while the wicked devour the righteous?"[60] Yechidiel sat on the other side of the partition in the car-

---

59. Habakkuk 1:13 – first half.

riage in order that she not see him. He heard, but didn't understand her words. Yet he knew that they were something very lofty and unattainable to him. Thus the maiden spoke bitterly, then she fell back helpless on the cushions of the carriage and slept.

When she awoke from her sleep, she saw placed before her in the carriage, grapes, figs and some baked items. She didn't put out her hand to touch any of these, just cried without cease. So the carriage journeyed for several days.

"In a little while we will arrive at our destination," said the driver to Finalia, opening the hatch of the carriage, and the horses began to slow down. Finalia looked out the window and saw that it was the middle of the night, but she could tell that she was in a strange city. The carriage stopped by a large house, and Finalia descended from box. The driver led her up the stairs, and when he opened the door he said, "Behold, the daughter of the Baron Adelberg." A woman of about fifty years was sitting at the table and eating, but on hearing the name she rose and came to greet her.

"Blessed is she who comes in the name of the Lord, honorable maiden," said the woman, and extended her hand.

"The name of the Lord be blessed," Finalia responded, and her eyes filled with tears. The woman examined her, but didn't say anything, just showed her to a room.

"This room was prepared for you by the master of the house," she said. Stunned and amazed, the maiden stopped on the threshold of the room when she saw the splendor and majesty within. She couldn't solve the puzzle of what was going on and what the master of the house wanted from her.

She turned to the woman and asked, "Tell me, what is the name of this city?"

"Brody is the city's name," the woman answered.

"Brody! I'm in Galicia!" cried the maiden. "God in heaven, what do my ears hear? I'm in Galicia! Now my eyes are opened to see where I stand. Now I know who's hand is in this kidnapping." As she spoke

---

60. Habakkuk 1:13 – second half.

she fell on her bed powerless, and she wailed with bitter tears. When the woman left, she closed the door behind her, and Finalia lay on the bed but didn't close her eyes. At midnight she heard the voice of a man speaking, and he said, "Tell me, mother. Where is the maiden now, and what did she say when she entered the house?"

"She didn't say a thing. But when I greeted her in the name of the Lord, she replied like a man responding to some great misfortune. Afterwards she asked me the name of the city, and when I told her that the name of the city is Brody, she began to scream and say, 'Ah, I'm in Galicia! Now I know everything.'"

"I will go to see her," he said. Finalia quickly recognized the voice of Yechidiel, and a great terror fell upon her on hearing he was coming to her room. But when he reached the door and saw that it was closed, he returned to his place and said, "I don't want to disrupt her rest."

"Tell me, my son. What will be with her? Don't you know that she won't speak with you, whether you are kind or harsh? She will only cry, and she is so very delicate that in a few days she'll become ill, and then you'll be forced to set her free."

"No! That won't come about!" he cried in anger. "She will live here until she either yields to me or dies. She will not see again that Victor, who I hate in my soul. But don't fear, mother, for she won't cry forever. When she sees that there is no help for her then she will yield to me. If not, I will compel her by force." Thus he spoke in a very terrible rage.

Violent trembling took hold of the maiden and her bones shook with terror when she saw that all hope was lost. All night she thought of ideas to save herself, that maybe she could find an escape and a refuge, but she despaired. "Alas! Alas," sighed the maiden. "The dream I dreamt came to show me what would be with me . . . He. He is the cruel leopard that lies by the door . . . when I looked out the window and saw my soul's beloved bound in fetters and I wanted to jump out the window . . . He fell on me in anger and rage and sought . . . to maul and to tear open . . . the casing of my heart!" She couldn't speak any further for her strength abandoned her and she fell powerless onto the cushions and slept. When she rose in the morning and the woman came in and asked how she was, she didn't answer her. When the woman left, she tasted a little of the delicacies that had been put before her, and so five days passed. She still hadn't seen Yechidiel because he said, "I will wait until she gets over the first shock," but on the sixth day, he got up in the morning and dressed in his finest clothes. He went into her room, where Finalia was sitting at the table, supporting her head in her hands because it was spinning like a wheel from all of her crying. When she saw Yechidiel, she didn't get up or raise her eyes. Yechidiel stood in his place for a few minutes, but afterwards he approached her and said, "Forgive me, honorable maiden, that I have ignored you for so long, but I was afraid to appear before you until your anger passed."

Finalia rose and stared at him scornfully, and with heartfelt contempt said, "You seek pardon from me? You will get the other! If you don't reach the seventy years of a man[61] then I will forgive you. But now you will never know the passing of my anger."

"A beautiful maiden like yourself will not remain angry forever."

"I am no gentle maiden anymore! Now I stand against you, against he whom my soul hates. Like a skilled champion fighting in his youth, I will fight to the end for my honor and the honor of my father's house against robbers and kidnappers whose blood is cursed. I will fight Amalek forever. I will die in this war, but I'll relinquish my honor to nobody."

Yechidiel's face turned white from anger and rage, but he hid his temper and he said, "God Forbid that I should fight with a maiden as lovely and enlightened as you, or with a skilled champion such as yourself who fights only to kill or be killed. Slowly, slowly, I will weave my net around you until you are held firmly in the trap. Then you will be acquainted with me and at peace with me. You will come to know and understand that one doesn't steal a maiden unless he loves her. I may be called kidnapper, but I don't seek evil for you, rather your happiness. You will walk on lilies and possess gold and sil-

---

61. Traditional life span.

ver, but independence and freedom you cannot hope for."

"If I see that I have lost all hope because the Lord has delivered me into the hands of a fool, I will put an end to my life. With joy in my heart I will enthusiastically deliver myself to the King, because he will only take my life, and my honor and the honor of my father's house will be saved."

"The words of maidens are like a joke to me because they never fulfill what they promise."

"If that's the case, I will be the first that fulfills her promise. I will not change the pronouncements of my lips."

"I don't believe you, because you desire to fulfill your promise to Victor if you can . . . ."

Finalia's face paled when she heard the ungodly man raise the name of her lover on his lips, and she became aroused and said, "This you can believe. I will fulfill it if your hand as much as touches me." As she spoke, she lifted her right hand to swear.

Quick as lightening Yechidiel grabbed her hand and said, "Silence! Silence! What did I do to you?" He turned and left the room, and Finalia breathed deeply when she saw she was alone. She went and closed the door and lay on her bed. She cried and poured out her heart like water until she fell into a trance and slept.

# ⤳ Chapter Twenty Two – Raphia and his Wife

"Woe to a father who raises a daughter like yours," said the woman of around forty to her husband as he entered her room.

"Didn't I tell you, Vannah my dear, that there is nothing I can do to help the matter."

"So you always say. A father who can't cure the backsliding of his daughter!"

"Tell me, pray, what it is, and I, with all my effort and strength, I will . . . ."

"I don't wish to talk about this further. My throat is hoarse and you always toss my good words behind your back, thinking I am seeking what is best for my son. According to the way you know your daughter, you should understand that it won't increase a man's honor or happiness to take her. And, unless he does everything I command him, he won't even get a look at her."

Raphia heard the honor of his beautiful and gentle daughter profaned in the mouth of her step-mother, who had never learned in her youth whether to eat or drink so that her flesh had increased upon her like the cows of Bashan.[62] But he didn't want to quarrel with her and was silent, and when his anger had passed a little he said to her in a quiet voice, "Believe me. If only your son's looks and intelligence were like my daughter's, then with all my heart I would give her to him. But . . . ."

"Silence! Silence!" cried the woman leaping up from her place with her face flushed with anger. "My son! You insult my son, who has the greatest lineage. This is the teaching of Emilia, your daughter, who is always calling him the scum of the earth. Whatever will be will be for you, but I hope that in a few days everybody will be talking about you and your daughter the way they talk about the Baron Adelberg and his daughter, because the Baron's daughter has fled the city and gone to Victor. Your daughter is going flee to Albert."

"What's all this?" Raphia asked perplexed. "Explain your words to me because I don't understand them."

"The daughter of the Baron fled with Victor from the city."

"How can a thing like that be possible?" asked Raphia. "Didn't Victor leave here last year, while she fled just a few days ago? How could this be? Besides, Victor is a poor man, so how could she desire him?"

"Oh, you heartless fool! I imagine that old age has robbed you of your wisdom and understanding to the point where you are no longer a man. A young maiden can deceive her old father so that all of her corrupt and shameful doings are good in his eyes. You are like Baron

---

62. Amos 4:1.

Adelberg whose daughter deceived him right up to the moment she fled him. Now husband, prepare yourself to hear the fate of the honorable maiden who was the first to do this shameful deed, and your daughter will be the second. The daughter of the Baron fled with the servant of the Minister. She left a letter on the table in which she asked forgiveness from her parents for fleeing without their permission. She gave her hand to Victor because she couldn't remain here any longer. They are scorned and ridiculed in everyone's mouths and they are the taunt of drunkards. I know that your daughter loves Albert, so it is my obligation to warn you not to be idle but to do something."

"You are right, my dear. You are right," said Raphia, who followed after his wife. "But what can I do? She hates your son, and her end will be like the fate of Goldberg's daughter . . . ."

"What happened to her?"

"She tried jumping into the river a month after she was married, but Yechidiel and some other men saved her. Therefore I am also afraid, for she is my only daughter."

"Shame on you. You are to be ridiculed for returning to your vomit.[63] Wouldn't it have been better for Goldberg to lose his daughter from this earth and hide this suffering from his eyes? From now on she will be a sorrow to her father and her righteous and pious bridegroom. But now things may change for them, because he will send her to his land, to Galicia, and there she will as one of them. Either she'll forget the backsliding youth of Milano or she'll find her grave there, but she'll be guiltless before the Lord and before man. And now you are afraid! But I don't want to talk about it any more because you stop your eyes from seeing." When she finished speaking she rose, and said, "This time I am blameless before the Lord and before you," and she turned her face to the door.

"I pray, my dear! Don't abandon me in this evil time," Raphia said to her. The apparent integrity of his wife blinded him, and he didn't know about the sevenfold abominations in her heart. She wanted to

---

63. Psalms 28:11 – "As a dog returns to his vomit, a dullard returns to his folly."

put an end to the life of his daughter who had become an obstacle and stumbling block to her. The whole time since the two of them had gone to the ball, and the young men scarcely looked at her or approached to greet her because they all gathered around her stepdaughter, and her fury had increased until there was no cure for it. Therefore she wanted to put an end to her stepdaughter's everlasting life. Once this shamefully acting woman found that the last spark of pity and compassion hidden in her heart had been extinguished by her energetic speech, she reminded her husband that his honor would be sullied through his daughter. He, in his feeble spirit, believed all her words, and she turned her shoulder to go and to leave him suffering just as his sickness came upon him.

"Pray, my dear!" said Raphia getting up from his place and grasping her hand. "Pray don't leave me in this evil time, when my only daughter wishes to strip my honor from me. I will trust in only you, dear soul. Counsel me with advice and I won't deviate from your words."

"Don't you know me, my dear?" said Vannah with the sycophant's mouth that had bought her his old heart forever. "Don't you know that I don't like speaking if my words aren't heard? I'll speak to you in this matter and you won't listen."

"Haven't I always done what you wanted? Didn't you ask that the house I bought last year be called by your name, and didn't I do it!"

Vannah colored with anger, but she hid her rage and said, "With whose money did you buy it? Wasn't it money from my fortune?"

He didn't want to quarrel with her, and he said, "It is proper and definite that I won't deviate from your words."

"If that's the case," said Vannah, she returned and sat with him on the couch and sighed. "If that's the case, I have no advice but that your daughter be a wife for Shlomiel,[64] my son. He has ten thousand Liras as an inheritance from his righteous father, and you will give a dowry to your daughter, and after the wedding he will apply himself to business. So what will your daughter lack?"

---

64. Word play on the Yiddish for a great fool.

"It will be as you say," he said. "You prepare everything for our children's celebration, which will be in a few days. If she doesn't want this, my hand will be heavy upon her."

"Now I know that you really love me," said Vannah and went out. Raphia got up and went to deliver these pleasant tidings to his daughter.

"Where is Emilia?" asked Raphia, as he stepped over the threshold of her room. He didn't find her, but her maid Ada was sitting there. "Do you know, Ada, that I'm putting an end to the backsliding of Emilia, who is always running around outside."

"Your are mistaken, master Raphia. You are very mistaken, for she doesn't run about," said Ada. "Just now she has gone out for a few minutes."

"Be aware, Ada, that in a few days my daughter will be betrothed to Shlomiel."

"Are you not her father?" said Ada. "Certainly you seek what is good for her." But her heart was torn to pieces because she knew the good heart and the honest soul of the maiden, because she had been her nurse from the day of her birth. Now she saw her bitter fate, because her father had sold himself into the hands of his wife, who wanted to bring her to destruction.

Raphia saw this and he understood, but he didn't say a thing and he went out. "Woe," said Ada when he left. "Is this the father of an only daughter, and a rare soul like her! Verily I remember when Esther, the mother of Emilia, was yet alive. Then he said that all of his labor and all of his work was done on the behalf of his only daughter. It's been eight years now since that cursed woman came into this house, and she has turned the whole household upside down and distorted a father's heart to hate his only daughter. Woe. Your day will also come, subtle hearted woman, and your end will be groaning. And to you, cruel father, the cup will also pass, because you gave your daughter into the hands of this shameful woman. But I won't hide my hands in my pockets, I will advise her what to do to save herself. I will go to find Emilia in order that she may know what will be. She will seek advice from Albert to halt this evil," and as she spoke she went to seek her.

"Where are you going, my dear Ada?" said the maiden on meeting her in the street.

"I came seeking you."

"Seeking me? What news do you have?" the maiden asked, and fixed her lovely eyes on the woman.

"Why do you stare at me so, my dear? Do you imagine that I would conceal something from you?"

"And what is it? Pray tell me!" said the maiden, and her heart pounded.

"Do you know that your father and mother decided . . . "

"What did they decide?" asked the maiden impatiently.

"That in a few days you will be betrothed to Shlomiel."

"Do they think to force me? It won't be so, for I'm no longer a five year old girl. But give me your advice what to do."

"Come with me to Albert and we will take counsel together," said Ada, and they went.

Albert was sitting in his house and thinking. "Verily, I don't know what will be. The day I was hoping for has come and I will serve in a higher office, because starting tomorrow I will be the secretary of the District Minister. Will Raphia say even then that I am a poor man? But what is he to me! She isn't a little girl that her father can tie her with rope to some fool. But where can I find her now, in order to give her the news about my new office?" Suddenly he heard the sound of a knock at the door, and he quickly opened it. "Ha, what is this my eyes show me. How are you my dear?"

"I'm well, but pray know that I came to your house on an urgent matter."

"What is that?"

"Father wishes to betroth me to that fool Shlomiel, and he has said that he'll do it by force."

"Pray, be easy my dear! You will be happy and joyful if you just follow my advice."

"Isn't that why I came here?"

"My advice is, for now, you should do what your father commands."

"What are you saying!" said the maiden. "This I won't do."

"Pray be calm. Didn't you promise you would hearken my advice? It is right and certain that this will turn out well for you. Don't be afraid and do as he tells you. This is just in order to gain time, and I will know what to do next. Faithful Ada will be appointed to carry our letters, and I hope that this day will be to our benefit. As a wise man once said, 'Put light in the place of shadows.' Behold, the Minister has chosen me to be the secretary in his house. Now promise me that you will do as I advised."

"I will do it," said the maiden, and she said "Shalom" and left, with Ada after her. Three days later, the beautiful Emilia was betrothed to the beast Shlomiel. Vannah danced on one foot when she saw that her husband did as she advised, and that she could twist his heart to whatever she wished, just like she had with her first husband. This is always the way with Galician women, for whom the name "cows of Bashan" is fitting. The say to their men, "Bring something and we'll drink," and they don't search after or investigate whether it came into their possession by stealing or pilfering, or by cunning and scheming. Just as long as their stomachs aren't lacking, and a sapphire is displayed over their corrupt hearts to cover every blemish. Their broad necks are draped with pearls so they can stroll about Rome, grind the faces of the poor and laugh at those who walk in integrity. Vannah was one of these, and therefore she was happy and joyous now. Vannah, the wife of Raphia from Granavich was the daughter of a Galician Hassid, and she had been very beautiful. Her parents loved her and brought her up according to their love. If you ask me, dear reader, 'Why are you telling us that parents love their children? Is it news!' I will answer you, 'Am I not also a daughter with parents, and my parents also love me very much.' But for all that, they always showed me my faults and punished me severely for minor things. But that wasn't the love of Vannah's parents for their daughter. Their love was like the love of all the Galician Hassidim for their children. They didn't lick her into shape or withhold from her anything her heart desired. Everything she did they thought was brilliant, and every shameful and abominable thing their daughter did was concealed by their love. One time she came and showed them that she had stolen a toy from another girl, and they didn't scold her or say, 'Keep yourself from such sins as coveting and stealing a thing that isn't yours.' Instead they were happy about it, and when the girl saw that she could please her parents through these actions, she went even further in the path of hard-heartedness, and her backsliding increased from day to day. She always ran around with rebellious boys and girls of her age, and when her parents sought to teach her languages and books, she didn't want it, and they didn't force her. Therefore, she remained empty of all learning, and her backsliding grew until she reached the age of fourteen. Her two parents dressed her in jewels and long dresses that dragged for a yard on the ground, in order that she be thought a great maiden. Then the matchmakers began to knock on the door, and the parents showed all of them their valuable merchandise, for in truth she was very beautiful, as no burden had ever been placed on her. In the fifteenth year of her life, Vannah was married to the ben Gila,[65] who was also a Galician Hassid. He hadn't learned any wisdom or trade, but he went three times a year on a pilgrimage to the Tzaddik. He continued doing so after his marriage to Vannah, to the joy of her parents, because they were devotees of the Tzaddik like her husband. Then the time came that he lost all his fortune in some bad deal, and their daughter was left empty of everything. But Vannah didn't adjust to this, because there was always something to drink in her father's house, and as long as her parents were rich, she wouldn't lack a thing because their table was always set for her. But even a well can be drawn dry, as the folk saying goes, and so it was with the riches of the Galician Hassidim. Their Tzaddik was imprisoned in fetters and he had to pay a huge ransom for his life with hard cash. So the Hassidim were stripped of their money, their wives of their jewelry, and so the end came to her parents wealth. But what one kind of locust left over, another consumed, because the son-in-law went to the parents house and took the little that remained to

---

65. Second use of the name ben Gila, first was a murderous comrade of the French agents.

bring as a gift to the holy man. When he returned home from there, his wife Vannah said to him, "Do you imagine that you can sit with your arms folded while I starve, become thirsty and go naked? Do whatever you want, but don't leave me lacking anything because I'm not accustomed to it."

"And what can I do," he said. "I never learned any trade."

"Neither did Chaim Pasalas learn any trade. Where do his wife's fine, expensive clothes and many fancy jewels come from? When she comes to the prayer house, all the women look at her and are jealous of her."

"Do you know what Chaim Pasalas does? He trades in counterfeit notes and base silver."

"It's all the same to me what you trade in, but don't leave me lacking anything. If you don't do this, I will make myself horrible, understand?"

Dispirited and sullen, her husband, Hamuel, left the house. She ran after him and said, "Don't think that you can come and go from time to time and I will open the door of my house to you. It is right and sure that you'll spend the night on the other side of the door and the mezuzah if you come here empty handed. Go to the devil, you and whoever gave birth to you and brought these sorrows on me."

Dispirited and sullen,[66] Hamuel went on his way. For a whole year she didn't hear anything from him. She and Shlomiel her son, who was then a boy of six, supported themselves by selling the household furnishings one after another. A year passed and Hamuel returned home with money in his hand. He gave the money to his wife and told her that he happened on a man who traded in the merchandise of Chaim Pasalas and joined with him, and in a short time, accumulated all of the money.

"Oh, my husband, my happiness and my joy," said Vannah wholeheartedly and hugged him in her arms. "How happy I am. I'd wondered about your fate. I would give my life and soul in place of yours. Just wait here a moment and I will bring you something to restore

66. Literal repetition.

you, because I know what you like." As she spoke she ran and brought very strong vodka and sweets, and put them before him. "Drink and eat, my dear, in order to strengthen yourself, and afterwards we will talk." Hamuel drank and also gave the same to his son in order to educate him according to his ways. Vannah didn't look at anything but the money, and it made her happy. "Pray know, my dear," she said, "That if you work in this trade for a long time then we will be the richest people in the land, and we will buy houses and possessions, silver, gold and dresses. Pray tell me, my darling. Will you continue to trade in this business, or will you be satisfied with a little?"

"A little!" said Hamuel. "Didn't I bring home five thousand Florins? I am thinking of entering some other trade so we can sustain ourselves honestly."

"Do you think this a sin?" she asked him.

"Certainly it is a sin to mix with others, and the wisest of all men ordered us, 'Fear God, my children, and the king.' Therefore I'm afraid, because this is against our religion and against the kingdom. If they catch a man in this trade, they send him to the land of exile and confiscate all of his household."

"God forbid, Hamuel my dear. Don't do that. What can we do with this little money and a house empty of everything. Verily, I suggested this trade to you. Don't leave off until we gather great riches, and then we will do a great business and our names will be known throughout the land."

"I'm afraid," said Hamuel, "Because they lay in wait for us on all sides. Our wise men of blessed memory said, 'The earthly kingdom is like the heavenly kingdom,'[67] and I have sinned against the Lord and the king."

"Don't be afraid, my dear. You won't get in trouble over this, because you are a husband with a wife and children. Would it be better if you were to follow the laws of the Lord and of man while your wife and son expired from hunger?" With words like these and many

---

67. Talmud Bavli – Tractate Brachot, 58a.

others, she seduced her husband and prevailed over him, until he promised to do as she wished. And so he did. For six years he worked that trade and accumulated a mighty fortune. She bought valuable gems and many expensive clothes of the sort worn by the daughters of kings and Ministers.

But who is the man who can raise his hand against the anointed of the Lord! Therefore, also to him the cup passed, and even though there was no guilt in him, only that he had been incited by his wife, Vannah, he bore the burden of her sin. He was caught red-handed and put in prison. He was there for a whole year. Finally the verdict was decreed and he was sentenced to ten years of hard labor, but he didn't live very long in this work. After another year passed, he died from oppression, affliction and sorrow. He was also angry and heart-broken because his wife, on who's behalf he lost his earthly life and honor forever, never once came to comfort him and lighten a little his hard burden. She was afraid that if she went there and saw his bitter condition, then her heart would pain her, and this isn't desirable to a cow of Bashan. Once he sent her a letter, full of tears and groaning that she have pity on his life, and he said, "I know that the police didn't take everything because you beat them to it. Therefore, have pity on my miserable soul, and remember that it is my money that I accumulated with the blood of my heart, in terror of death, because my heart prophesized this bad ending to me. Therefore, have pity and come to me with three thousand in silver, and you'll be able to lighten the heavy work that I do. Then I will be able to bear the punishment that I was sentenced to. After nine terrible years I will be given my freedom if I live, and I am yet a young man. Have pity on my unfortunate soul, for I didn't obey the voice of the Lord or the king."

But she laughed at his words and she said, "I should spend all that money on you and be left naked and lacking everything? No! I won't do this." Therefore he died from anger and disappointment, because these terrible times taught him understanding, and he saw for whom he had labored and lost his earthly existence. She remained with great wealth that exceeded fifty thousand florins. Seven years ago, after the death of her husband, she went to the spa in Italy. Raphia and his daughter were also there, because his daughter sickened with a serious illness after the death of her mother. So they got to know one another, because her money and her beauty drew Raphia's heart, and he fell in love with her and married her. Thus she became the mistress of his household, and therefore her advice was now being carried out. The beautiful Emilia was betrothed to her wild son who had grown up like his mother. So she was happy while Emilia wept and groaned. But "Let not he who girds on his sword boast like he who takes it off,"[68] as the early proverb says.

## ⤝ Chapter Twenty Three – The Prisoner

"Where are you from? What brings you here?" the Minister asked the man standing before him, as his eyes measured him from the soles of his feet to the crown of his head. The Minister recognized him as a bad and worthless fellow, one who wasn't accustomed to somebody penetrating into his heart. The man stared at the ground, but occasionally lifted his sparkling eyes, which glinted robbery and murder, to look all around him.

"Your servant has just returned from Venice, sir Minister. I lived there in a hotel for five days with a young man, and on the sixth day a beautiful and refined young maiden came to him. It seemed that he was waiting for her, because he was happy when she arrived. The name of the man was Victor Schoenfeld."

The Minister stared at him with loathing and said, "What was the name of the maiden?"

"This I don't know. But the servants in the house told me that she came from Milano and also that they were traveling to Germany. When I arrived here, I heard everybody talking about the daughter of the Baron Adelberg and who fled from her parent's house, and how

---

68. 1 Kings 20:11.

you were protecting the Baron from his pursuers and had gathered him into your house. She gave me a letter to you, and that's why I came here."

"Do you have the letter with you?" asked the Minister.

'I have it," and as he spoke he took the letter from his pocket and gave it to the Minister. But, before the Minister opened the letter, he went for a moment into the next room, then quickly returned.

"What is your name, so that I know?" the Minister asked him.

"My name! My name!" he said as he thought.

The Minister laughed inside, then said in a commanding voice, "Didn't I ask you your name? Have you forgotten it?"

"You asked me my name, sir? I didn't hear you. My name is Lotan ben Shoval."[69]

The Minister was about to continue, but four armed men appeared at the doorstep of the house, and they stood in their places. Lotan looked anxiously at these men.

"Come close here," said the Minister, and they did as their lord commanded. The servants approached the man and before his wits returned to him, he was bound in fetters from head to foot. He roared like a lion over his prey and gnashed his teeth. "That won't help you," said the servants.

"But what is my crime and sin that you have put my feet in stocks?"

"Take him to his place," yelled the Minister in a rage.

"Who made you Minister and judge over me?" cried the prisoner.

"Silence, ungodly man," yelled the Minister. "Take him away. What are you waiting for?" In a couple moments the clinking of his iron chains were heard throughout the courtyard as they took him to the cell assigned to him. The Minister remained alone in his room, held by a multitude of thoughts. "I am afraid," the Minister said to himself, "that we accused the maiden without cause. Maybe these worthless and reckless men have risen up to practice wicked deeds against her. I won't quickly be setting this ungodly man free, because

---

69. Genesis 36:20 – two names picked from a single Biblical passage, an obvious fabrication.

maybe I'll get some truth out of him. By the look of his face, he's the head of the villains. Woe, if she is innocent of all this and fell into these criminals hands. But don't I have a letter here? I'll see what's in it." He took the letter from his pocket and spread it out before him, but behold, there was a knock at the door.

"Who's there?" the Minister quickly thundered, because he couldn't control his agitation.

"Adelberg seeking permission to enter, sir Minister," was the answer. "If it's not a good time, I'll go and come back."

"Are you here, my friend the Baron? Come in, pray, come in," said the Minister, and he quickly hid the letter in his pocket.

"Pray forgive me, my friend," said the Minister when he saw the Baron in his room, and he extended his right hand in brotherhood. "Certainly I didn't know that it was you. Pray sit," said the Minister, trying to hide his confusion. But the Baron saw his embarrassment and said, "I was in the courtyard just now, and I heard the prisoner that your servants were bringing to his prison cell. He spoke words in French that I don't know how to charm away, and they frighten my heart. 'What is this!' he roared, 'I just mentioned the maiden, and he got excited and enraged. Isn't he like one of us dealing treacherously."

"You heard this my friend?"

"I heard this."

"This man came like a messenger and told me that in Venice he saw Victor and Finalia, because he lived with them for a few days the same hotel. Then they went to Germany, and before they traveled off she gave him a letter to me. But I recognized him as a worthless fellow, and he only wants to seek and inquire of me about your hiding place. He is from the gang of thieves, therefore I ordered him arrested here until I get some truth out of him."

The Baron's face whitened like plaster and he said, "Didn't you say, sir, that the man gave you a letter? Let's look inside."

"You're right," he said, took the letter from his pocket, and he read:

*Honored and Exalted Sir,*

*My spirit is stormy and I feel many emotions in my heart as I grasp my pen in hand to write these lines. I will leave it to your refined sensibilities to judge and decide, because only your broad intelligence can purify and refine the words coming out from the depth of the heart of a depressed and afflicted soul. Verily, I rejected riches and fled to poverty. I distanced myself from joy and embraced tragedy. I fled from the lap of upright parents, and lightly esteemed my pursuers every step of the way. But there is no going back, and before I die, don't hide this consolation from me. I have a request of you, exalted sir, and I depend on your refined sensibilities that you won't turn me away empty. I ask that you don't withdraw your generous protection from my dear, upright parents until the anger of their enemies passes. Then I will be able to calm a little the storms in my spirit and my heart, which witnesses all of the injuries of time. I will continue on a sea of worry forever, never reaching port, because I am endlessly pursued by the noise of the waves. In time they will crush me to death, and with eyes wide open, I hope for that happy moment that I am dragged down to the deep. Then my tired and cast away soul will find tranquility. These words are written in the stillness of my heart.*

*F in a l ia A d e l b e r g*

"Alas and woe!" cried the Baron from the groans of his heart, and the letter fell from his hand.

"Pray be calm," said the Minister. "Isn't it urgent now that we be firm and stand upright? Now consult with me what to do, and tell me what you think about this."

"Pray know, sir," said the Baron, "That I don't understand how to interpret the words of the letter. I think that Victor deceived her, and she is ashamed to return home now. Therefor she complains about her hard days, and says that she goes on a sea of worries, and the waves of time will pursue her until she is plunged into the deep. Alas! Alas! What has happened to my only daughter?"

The Minister nodded his head and said, "Do you know that I think otherwise, that robbers have stolen your daughter and taken her some place far away. The two letters we have are counterfeits, the work of the kidnappers. They were never in Venice. I'd already sent there to seek them."

"I'm have my doubts about this," said the Baron.

"We will know tomorrow," said the Minister, "because I hope to get some truth out of the prisoner." When he finished speaking he gave his hand to the Baron, and the Baron returned to his quarters. The Minister remained in his room and didn't appear to the Baron until the next day, when he went to the courthouse.

The judges in the courthouse sat around a large table covered with a red tablecloth. The court recorders sat to one side, and policemen came in and out every minute to get orders from the judges. One empty chair was placed higher than those of the judges, but the man who sat there hadn't yet arrived. Above the chair, on the wall, was a portrait of the King, in all his majesty. His eyes seemed alive and they stared forth full of anger and vengeance to frighten and warn them not to pervert justice. The Minister strode into the room, and walked with measured steps to his place and sat. The judges grew silent to await his words, and quiet reigned throughout the court.

The Minister looked around the room to all sides, after which he broke the silence and said, "Bring in the prisoner from the third cell whose name is Lotan ben Shoval." Two policemen who stood before him went out and in a few moments returned with the prisoner and stood him before the Minister. The judges examined this new guest and wondered but were silent.

"Pray listen, sirs," said the Minister to the judges. "This man came to me yesterday and said that he saw the daughter of the Baron in Venice. According to his words, he saw her three days after she disappeared."

"He speaks lies," cried one of the judges. "Didn't we spend two weeks sending people on every railroad to seek in all of the cities in Italy her without finding her?"

"Did you know, sirs," the Minister continued to speak, "That the daughter of the Baron who disappeared didn't flee to Victor, but robbers carried her away from her father's house and put an end to my servant Jonathan. This man is one of the robbers, but I hope to extract what he has swallowed from his mouth, because he knows many mysteries."

The judges looked first at the Minister and then at each other. Afterwards they examined the prisoner, and they saw that his face was as white as plaster from fear and confusion. But he gathered the remnants of his strength, and he answered bravely, "No, sir. You are mistaken in your judgement. I never cast my lot with the lot of criminals. I am innocent of all sin, and I don't have the slightest idea as to what you are talking about. I swear by the Lord that I saw the daughter of the Baron in Venice with her lover, Victor."

"Silence, godless man," shouted the Minister in the heat of his rage. "It's not for you to mention the name of the Lord." Even though they examined and investigated him for two hours, they couldn't get a word of truth out of him. They decided to contact the city of Rome and have the judges there seek after Victor, to find whether he was in that city or whether he had journeyed from there, and thus find out if the prisoner's words agreed with theirs. The prisoner was taken back to his cell. After the Minister completed his duties at the court, he rose and went home, where he found the Baron waiting for him. He told him what had happened in court, "But I hope," he said, "that time will make him talk. If not today, then tomorrow." The two men parted from one another with faint hope.

# ∽ Chapter Twenty Four – A Brother in Sorrow

"Who is knocking on the door?" asked Finalia in anxiety.

"Don't fear, gentle one. I'm not hear to harm you. Pray open up quickly."

Finalia heard the voice, which was not strange to her, and she opened the door. "Ha!" cried the maiden with wholehearted joy, "It is you, Azariya! Certainly you are like your name. You saved Victor from the hands of the wicked who sought to swallow him, and you were born for me like a brother in sorrow."

"Pray be quiet, gentle one," he said to her. "I didn't come here in order to save you. I only came in order to give you some news. Listen, pray, to what the villains are doing. After they captured you from your father's house, they left a letter behind on the table. Written in your name, it said that you requested pardon from your parents, and that you traveled to Victor because you were afraid that the Minister might take you by force."

"My God! My God!" cried the maiden and clapped her hands in despair. "That letter will put an end to my dear parent's lives. Cursed is love, cursed forever, for it has destroyed me and removed the protection of the Minister from my dear parents."

"Not so, gentle one," said Azariya. "When the Minister saw the letter he was very angry with you, but he had mercy on your parents and took them into his palace. But listen to what else they did. They sent a letter to Victor in your name, and wrote that you gave your hand to the Minister because you were forced to do so on behalf of your parents, and commanded him not to dare to come to Milano."

"God in Heavens," cried the maiden and fell to the earth in a faint.

"Pray get up," said Azariya, and he lifted her from the floor. "Wake up now. This isn't the time now for fainting, when you walk between happiness and damnation."

She opened her eyes and she asked him, "Did they truly send a letter to Victor?"

"The matter is true."

"Ha! My last hope in the world is lost. If I am saved from this trap, where can I flee? Who can I escape to for help? Can I flee to Milano? Won't I be a joke to all who see me, and won't the Minister despise my name in thinking that Victor drove me away? Can I flee to Victor in Rome in whom I placed all of my trust? Will he even look at me? Will he not scorn and despise me, turning my honor into shame. Now I remember the few words that I saw in the letter I was forced to sign before I fainted. How can I lift my eyes before him? No! No, I won't go there, but can I stay here in the hands the evil and unrighteous? Won't he then revel because he hunted me with a high hand and caught me in his net? Pray tell me, Azariya my dear, are you speaking the truth in these things, or did Yechidiel order you to tell me this in order that I see there is no salvation for me and cooperate with him! Believe that I have sworn by the Lord to choose all the wounds of time that the future may bring over him."

"On my life and soul, gentle one, I spoke the truth. When I was in Milano, he made everything known to me, and to my joy he brought me with him now in order that I speak with you to incline your heart to him."

"Has Yechidiel also returned here?" the maiden asked in fear.

"The two of us arrived this morning. He is presently wrapping up everything he started, and therefore the villains who helped him in evil are asking to be paid their reward. He said that he won't pay them a cent until you are his wife. Now you must think and decide what you will do."

"I implore you, my dear Azariya. Save me from the hands of this animal and I will never forget you."

"With all my heart I am here to save you if only the Lord will be my helper, but how can I smuggle you out before him? You know that it means my life!"

"Why do you remain here? Look, I'm just a maiden, and despite that I won't be afraid as long as the Lord sets me free. Can't you earn your bread any place you go, especially a man skilled in his work as yourself? My advice is that the two of us flee together to another city, and there we'll take counsel on where to turn, and I'll put my trust in you."

"And where will we flee to? You can't go to Milano or Rome, so where?"

"Where you ask me? Is not the land broad?"

"Good," said Azariya. "It is right and certain that from today on I will think only about your rescue."

"Thank you, good man," said the maiden, and she extended her hand to him.

"Let me advise you that if Yechidiel comes today you don't quarrel with him too much," said Azariya. "I hope that you will be able to compose your words sensibly. You have a wise heart beyond compare, as the kidnappers also say."

Finalia laughed bitterly and said, "So I have also found favor in the eyes of the kidnappers?"

"You find favor in the eyes of all who see you."

"But not in the eyes of the Lord," said the maiden and sighed.

"Hope in the Lord, gentle one, and you will yet stand again on your own," said Azariya.

"Like a standing sheep that has to ask every day of a different shepherd," said the maiden and sighed. "But if the Lord will set me free I will be happy."

Azariya looked out the window and said, "Yechidiel is coming." Finalia started, but she quickly regained her strength and found her courage.

Azariya went on his way and met Yechidiel who said, "How is the maiden?"

"Fine. She is in her room," Azariya replied to him.

The joy was apparent n Yechidiel's face because the hope was strengthened within him that slowly, slowly, she was becoming accustomed to him. He fixed his hair and his mustache in the big mirror that was before him, and he looked at his back to reassure himself that he was perfect in his splendor. He went to her room and slowly, slowly, opened the door and stood on the threshold. Finalia remained in her place, and he stepped in.

"How are you, my beauty?" he said. "Does your heart still rage against me?" Finalia didn't answer him a word. Yechidiel approached her and said, "Lift up your beautiful eyes to me, honorable maiden. You will see a man pleading before you, and if you only hearken his voice, he will be your slave forever. Now I don't request anything from you, but that you take from my hand a small present that I brought you."

Finalia lifted up her eyes against her will and saw a star of purest gold encrusted in expensive stones that shined like the stars in the sky, but she remained motionless in her place. The heart of the Galician, who had thought that she would certainly throw it on the floor to burst into fragments, was filled with joy and happiness. The calmness of her spirit was like a door of hope to him because he didn't know the thoughts of her heart. He thought that the time was favorable, and he took the ornament and fastened it over her snowy white breast, which was exposed a little by the black dress. "Ha!" he said, "How beautiful and delightful, lovely Finalia. There is no limit to your beauty, and these jewels add further to you until you seem like a star in the heavens on a bright night." He seized her hand and tried to bring it to his lips.

Finalia sat the whole time without moving, but when he grabbed her hand she jumped up and cried, "Let me alone, Yechidiel, and get out! Did you bring me here to abuse me? I know that you are stronger than I, and that a maiden like myself can't stand up against a strong, courageous and powerful man like yourself. But pray know that a man doesn't prevail with strength. Verily, you came to me like a wolf to a lamb, which has strayed a little from the flock and is without a shepherd. Will it flee and be saved? I am in your hands for you are stronger than I. Tear me to pieces, tear the arm with the crown of the head.[70] But before you fall on your prey, behold I will surely expire and die before you," and as she spoke, she covered her face with both hands and wept bitterly.

For a long while Yechidiel stood, seeing her in tears, and finally he said, "Why are you crying? What did I do to you? God forbid I should tear you to pieces. I want you to live and I only seek your well-being."

"If you want me to live, Yechidiel, then I ask you to have mercy. Leave me now, because my spirit storms inside me. It rages to injure me and will quickly steal my life."

"Behold, I will hearken your voice this time," said Yechidiel. "But not for long, because you will be mine. Even if I lose all of my fortune and even my soul, such is the great strength of my love for you."

"Pray tell me, Yechidiel. How can the natural order change? A

---

70. Deuteronomy 33:20.

Galician man, from the day he can say 'Father' and 'Mother,' knows no other love aside from love for the Tzaddik alone. You know that if you love me then you will be forced to hate the Tzaddik. I ask you, have you utterly rejected the Tzaddik and do Hassidim disgust you? Pray tell me, Yechidiel."

"Believe me, gentle one," he said. "Everything you tell me I will do, even this contemning. From the moment I recognized your high value, I changed into another man. I have despised the Tzaddik and I have hated the community of Hassidim. What are they to me with all their delusions and foolishness? Surely the Tzaddik himself knows that all of his deeds are empty. But my portion with them is a fat one, therefore I make common cause with them. If I'm successful in my suit, then I will make my place of dwelling wherever you chose, even if you say to distance myself from them to the ends of the earth. But don't think that you will evade me forever. Do you imagine that a beautiful maiden like yourself will live in my house like a pretty picture hung on the wall, just to look at? But now I will leave you as I promised you."

"Pray sit now," said the maiden, "Because I want to talk to you." With joy in his heart, he took a chair and sat. "One more thing I will ask you and you answer me, Yechidiel," and she turned to him. Over her heart was displayed the star of sapphires, as she carried it upon her breast. Yechidiel's heart expanded with happiness and he thought, "She is in my hand, now. Certainly the jewels I brought her did all this work. Tomorrow I'll bring more, bigger than this one. Behold, she was right in saying that a man triumphs not through strength but through wise counsel." He regarded her to hear her question.

"Tell me, pray, Yechidiel. When were you in Milano?" Yechidiel's face paled from anger and rage but he stopped it up in his bosom and said, "What is Milano to you?"

"Didn't you promise me to fulfill whatever I asked? Why do you repent?"

"You are right, gentle one," he said "Let me answer you. It's been three days since I returned from there."

"Was there news?"

"I don't know. I only heard that Emilia, the daughter of Raphia, was betrothed to Shlomiel her step-brother."

"Emilia and Shlomiel? Was her father's hand that strong upon her?"

"This I don't know."

"How is Henrietta?"

"Now she is fine."

"Now? What about before?"

"She jumped in the river because she wanted to put an end to her life, but Zevchiel and I saved her from death. Now her parents are sending her with her husband to Hamia."

"I'm very sorry for my dear friend. Do you know, Yechidiel, that she won't last long in a small town, in a mountainous place. There she will become an permanent offering on the altar of her father's stupidity."

"Don't worry, she won't die."

"If only it will be as you say, but let's speak no further about this. Have you heard anything about my parents?"

"I heard that the Minister took them into his palace, and that they are alive and well."

"Thank you, Yechidiel. Please leave me now because I wish to rest a little." Yechidiel said goodbye to her and left.

"Woe, what a fool and imbecile!" the maiden said with a bitter laugh after he left her. "He thinks that he has caught me in his net, but wait a bit and he will know who I am. And you, Victor, forgive me for speaking with him peacefully, because we can't hunt a fox without grapes. Truly I will draw him very near with my words, but I do this in order to distance myself from him forever. You will see my heroism and the strength of my spirit. How I fought with all the injuries of time and chance, and how I fought with wild animals and overcame them. Then you will see and be enlightened. But what am I saying? Didn't he receive a letter from me that I utterly despised him and chose the Minister. Ha! My strength abandons me instantly when I recall this."

"How was she today," Azariya asked Yechidiel. "Was she raging like before? I spoke with her a long time today, and I hope in a few days to bend her whole heart to you."

"Thank you, Azariya," Yechidiel said in great joy, taking a bag of money from his pocket and giving it to the servant. Yechidiel went on to the city to buy some excellent jewels for her, more expensive than the earlier ones, and he hoped to give them to her the next day. But who can boast about tomorrow if he doesn't know what the day will bring? When Yechidiel was gone, Azariya opened the door of her room and put a short note in her hand, in which the following was written:

*Be prepared, for if the Lord will help us, you will be free this night. The skies are darkening with clouds and surely it will be a dark night, and if so, it will be tonight. Will not the darkness be light for us?*

Finalia's heart was filled with joy and happiness when she read the letter, and also with a new hope. So she passed the day and also most of the night.

Midnight arrived and there was black darkness. Thick dark clouds covered the splendor of the heavens and applied a dark wrapping over all the lights in the heavens, absorbing their glow. Pouring rain also sliced earthwards, and thunder and lightening were heard and seen on all sides. The stormy night cast a trance on every man. Yechidiel returned from his business tired and weary, fell upon his bed and slept. A few minutes later, the sound of his snoring was heard throughout the house. His mother slept in her room, and only Azariya was awake. He said to himself, "Now the time has arrived that I can save the gentle and upright maiden, lest she sink in the mud, because she won't be able to retain her honor for much longer." He approached the door and opened it slowly, but Finalia wasn't sleeping because her heart was greatly anxious, and she waited for him in hope and fear.

"Are you dressed?"

"I'm dressed."

"Then get up quickly and come, because everyone lays dreaming." He held her trembling hand and guided her from the house and down the steps, and in a few moments, they stood in the street. The servant covered his face with his mantle, and Finalia covered her head and face with a thick kerchief to shelter herself from the heavy rain, and they walked to the train station.

"How can I thank you, my kind man and angel of salvation?" said the maiden to Azariya as they sat in the carriage. Thick clouds of smoke from the engine wound upwards to the heavens. Quick as lightening, with a tortured cry, the engine ran from its place dragging the carriages after it. In a few minutes, the city and everything in it had disappeared from their eyes. "How can I thank you for saving me from that shameful man? Now I can breathe the air of freedom and independence and I can go wherever I want."

"Don't thank me, but the Lord who emboldened my heart to save you," replied Azariya.

"Where are we going now?" asked the maiden. "In all my joy I forgot to ask you."

"To Vienna, the capital. There we can consult with one another on what to do."

"Oh, that it will be as you say," said the maiden, and she took the kerchief from her head. Then she put it on the bench under her head as she lay down to rest a little, because her heart was pounding from fear and happiness, and she slept.

*End of Part I*